FIELD GUIDE TO THE

BIRDS
of Britain
and Europe

Produced by AA Publishing

© Automobile Association Developments Limited
1998
Reprinted 2002
Reprinted Sep and Nov 2004
Reprinted Apr and Oct 2006

Published by AA Publishing (a trading name of
Automobile Association Developments Limited,
whose registered office is Fanum House, Basing
View, Basingstoke, Hampshire RG21 4EA.
Registered number 1878835).

Find out more about AA Publishing and the wide
range of services the AA provides by visiting our
Website at www.theAA.com/travel

ISBN-10: 0-7495-3669-1 (softback)
ISBN-13: 978-07495-3669-5

A CIP catalogue record for this book is available
from the British Library.

Contributing authors: Paul Sterry (consultant
editor), Andrew Cleave, Andy Clements,
Peter Goodfellow
Designer: Stuart Perry Associates
Artists: Richard Allen, Norman Arlott,
Trevor Boyer, Hilary Burn, John Cox, Dave Daly,
John Gale, Robert Gillmor, Peter Hayman,
Ian Lewington, David Quinn, Darren Rees,
Chris Rose, Christopher Schmidt
Maps: Advanced Illustration, Congleton
© Automobile Association Developments Limited
1998
Colour origination by L C Repro & Sons Ltd,
Basingstoke, England
Printed and bound in Dubai by Oriental Press

A03216

CONTENTS

THE BIRDS

INTRODUCTION

This is a practical guide to Europe's rich
and diverse bird life, from the borders of
the Persian Gulf to Iceland, and from the
Urals to northern Africa. Superbly
illustrated, this book will allow anyone
interested in birds to identify the species
they encounter with greater certainty.

STATUS CATEGORIES Each bird is given a status
category consisting of two elements: the first
part clarifies when the bird is present in the
region (Europe); the second element
indicates how common the species is. Taken
together with the distribution map, this is an
important aid to accurate identification. The
definitions of the terms used for status are:

How to Use This Book

FACTFILE A clearly laid-out
fact panel contains all the
practical background
information that the
reader might need for
reference for each species
and for direct comparison
between species. All the
essential basic
information concerning
the physical attributes of
the species is included
here, together with details
on status and habitat.

SPECIES DESCRIPTION This
paragraph contains a full
but concise description of
the bird, highlighting key
features and the main
differences between
similar species. All
plumages are described,
even those seldom
encountered in the field.

6   WILDFOWL

Mallard
Anas platyrhynchos

Status: Resident/summer visitor; common; **Voice:** Female
gives familiar quack; male a weak nasal note; **Length:**
50–65cm; **Wingspan:** 80–100cm; **Habitat:** Almost anywhere
with water; **Behaviour:** Very tame on urban lakes

 Common and familiar duck. Male has yellow bill,
green head showing sheen in good light, chestnut
breast and otherwise mostly grey-brown plumage;
shows black stern and white tail. Female has orange-yellow
bill and rather uniform brown plumage. Eclipse male similar
to female but more reddish on breast. In flight both sexes
show white-bordered blue speculum.

Pintail
Anas acuta

Status: Resident/winter visitor; common in winter; **Voice:**
Male utters quiet whistle; female gives short quacks; **Length:**
51–66cm; **Wingspan:** 80–95cm; **Habitat:** Open areas with
shallow water; **Behaviour:** Often seen in pairs or small groups
in winter; rather shy

Male is an elegant duck with chocolate-brown head
and white on underparts and on front of neck,
forming narrow stripe up side of face. Flanks grey
and black with elongated feathers. Stern buff and black, with
long tail often characteristically cocked upwards. Female has
dark-grey bill and largely brown plumage; has long-bodied
appearance. In flight both sexes look particularly long-
bodied.

Shoveler
Anas clypeata

Status: Resident/winter visitor; common; **Voice:** Quiet 'tuc'
uttered by male; female quacks; **Length:** 44–52cm; **Wingspan:**
70–85cm; **Habitat:** Shallow water; **Behaviour:** Easiest to see
in winter, when small groups often gather to feed in the
shallows, moving slowly forward sieving food from the mud
with their bills

Unusual duck, the most distinctive feature of both
sexes being the broad, flattened bill. Male has green
head with sheen visible in good light. Bright orange
belly provides striking contrast with otherwise white breast
and flanks. Back and stern dark; bill black. Female mottled
brown. Bill dark but with lower edges orange. In flight
both sexes show blue forewing separated by white band
from green speculum.

RESIDENT: Present all year, but may migrate within Europe
SUMMER VISITOR: Present in summer only
WINTER VISITOR: Present in winter only
PASSAGE MIGRANT: Passes through Europe on migration only

VAGRANT: Only appears in Europe as a vagrant (time of year of most sightings usually given)
(VERY) RARE: Numbers low, any distribution
SCARCE: Numbers between Rare and Local
LOCAL: Numbers between Rare and Locally Common, concentrated in specific area(s)

WIDESPREAD: Widely distributed but not necessarily common
LOCALLY COMMON: High in numbers in specific area(s)
COMMON: High in numbers, widely distributed

WILDFOWL 7

Mallard

Pintail

PINTAIL ECLIPSE ♂

SHOVELER ECLIPSE ♂

Shoveler

ILLUSTRATIONS Specially commissioned from some of Europe's finest bird artists, the full-colour illustrations accurately and strikingly identify each species. All plumages and poses that the observer is likely to encounter are shown. Unless stated otherwise, birds are shown in adult male plumage. Feature pages throughout the book compare easily confused species.

MAPS Clear, colour-coded maps show the range of each bird throughout the year.

Green – present all year
Yellow – present in summer
Blue – present in winter

Maps for birds with complex migration habits are also marked with directional arrows. Vagrant and very local species do not have a map.

The changing plumage of the dunlin from juvenile to winter adult

JUVENILE, SUMMER

JUVENILE, AUTUMN

JUVENILE, EARLY WINTER

ADULT, SUMMER

ADULT, WINTER

for the secondary wing feathers, while the primary feathers are attached to the modified 'hand'.

A wing must provide propulsion to drive the bird forward, and lift to keep it aloft. On the downbeat the primaries are held tightly together and the wing is swept downwards and backwards. It is then twisted and the primaries separated for the upstroke. The wingtip describes a figure of eight as the wing makes a rowing-like action through the air. The aerofoil shape of the wing also aids lift.

Different types of flight demand different wing shapes. Many passerines have medium-length, general-purpose wings. Gliding birds like albatrosses need long, thin, pointed wings to give lift at speed. Soaring birds, such as buzzards, obtain lift from rising thermals of hot air and need long, broad wings. Short, rounded wings are good for speedy take-offs and manoeuvrability, and are characteristic of gamebirds, while the pointed wings of ducks are adapted to fast, sustained flight.

each other. However, usually with their first moult in the autumn, the sexes of some species take on very different plumages, with the male usually displaying the brighter colours. Females tend to be duller since they benefit when nesting from the extra protection afforded by excellent camouflage.

Wings

Wings are the supreme evolutionary achievement of birds. The elongated humerus, usually covered by the body feathers, is joined to the body with a ball-and-socket joint, giving great mobility. Between it and the keel is the powerful pectoralis muscle, used to pull the wing down, and the smaller supracoracoideus used to pull it up again. The lengthened radius and ulna are the point of attachment

Bills

A bird's bill (sometimes referred to as its beak) is an extension of its jaw. It has two parts, the upper and lower mandibles, both covered in a horny, protective layer of skin. The lower jaw can move, but the upper is fixed to the skull, although some birds have flexibility in the upper mandible. Bills come in a variety of shapes and sizes, each one adapted for a specific feeding task.

The long bills of waders like the whimbrel are sensitive probes used for detecting worms in mud. The unusual bill of the avocet sifts small animals from mud and water as it is waved from side to side.

Birds of prey and owls have hooked bills for tearing skin and flesh. Falcons have a notch near the bill tip, which is used to kill prey by biting into the neck.

Puffin *Whimbrel* *Green woodpecker* *Kestrel*

The brightly coloured bill of the puffin is used to attract a mate, and its razor-sharp edge is good for gripping fish.

The green woodpecker and its relatives use their bills to chisel into wood. They also use them to 'drum' instead of singing, hitting the beak tip hard and very fast against a dead branch to produce a resonant, penetrating drumming. Spongy bone at the beak's base cushions the head against vibrations.

Some birds, like swifts, have very small bills but very large mouths, which, with the aid of bristles, enable them to 'trawl' through the air for insects.

Legs and Feet

The legs and feet of birds are little more than skin-covered bones with a few tendons. Most of the muscles are hidden away at the top of the leg. Legs are usually scaly or leathery, but some are feathered: to give protection in birds of prey, to act as insulation in some birds, such as ptarmigan, or to reduce noise in owls. As with bills, a bird's leg and foot design is largely determined by how much, and in what, it walks.

Wading in water and walking on dry land require long legs but unspecialised feet, as demonstrated by the whimbrel. The rear toe is often absent or reduced.

The feet of the merlin and other birds of prey have long toes, widely spread, with rough soles and sharp claws to catch and hold live prey.

Passerines have a tendon along the back of the leg that automatically curls the toes as the leg is bent, keeping the bird on its perch with little effort. The claws are often long to give extra grip.

Waterbirds, like the eider, have webs between their toes, creating effective paddles. The puffin also has sharp claws to help in digging its burrow.

As well as having two toes pointing forwards, most woodpeckers have two backward-pointing toes to increase their grip and stability when climbing a trunk.

Aerial birds have very poorly developed legs and can often barely walk. The swift's four toes point forward so that it can cling to rough surfaces.

Tails

The bird's tail has evolved to become a bony stump, the pygostyle. From it protrude the large tail feathers called rectrices, of which there are usually an even number. These are overlaid with feathers: greater and lesser uppertail coverts above, and a few undertail ones below.

Whimbrel *Eider* *Serin* *Kestrel*

A kestrel bearing down on its prey

The rectrices are more mobile than most other feathers and are of great assistance in flying. Acting like the tail of a plane, a bird's tail aids manoeuvrability; a forked tail, like that of kites, may improve this further. The tail is also vital when landing, as it spreads to act as an air brake. During flight, the rectrices are brought together to give a neat, tapered end to the bird.

A strong tail is a good prop. Woodpeckers and treecreepers rest their unusually stiff tails against a tree trunk as they probe beneath the bark. Even ground birds use their tails as props when they pull worms and other food items from the soil.

Eyes and Senses

Birds are very visually biased, and many have largely dispensed with the senses of taste, smell and touch. Their eyesight, however, is often superb, and their hearing, too, can be far better than a human's.

Birds' eyes are big. The bigger the eye the more light-sensitive cells it can contain, which results in vision that is not telescopic compared to the human eye's, but is up to eight times clearer. This is important for all birds, but particularly so for hunters like buzzards, which can spot prey a kilometre below them. Birds' eyes are usually sited on the sides of the head, giving good all-round vision. Predatory birds, however, have the eyes pointing forwards to increase binocular vision, vital for accurately judging distances.

All birds have good hearing, but it is especially well developed in those that are active at night. The 'face' of the owl directs sound to the ears, which are often at different levels in the skull. Each ear will therefore hear a sound at a slightly different time, making it easier to detect from which direction it has come.

Behaviour

Courtship

To enable successful breeding, there must be some degree of courtship behaviour between the male and female. Generally it is the male that courts the female before she will allow him to mate with her, but exceptionally the roles are reversed, as occurs in phalaropes.

The purpose of courtship is to establish a bond between the two participants. It may lead to a pairing that lasts for life, for just one season, or only until copulation has taken place. Because courtship behaviour is very specific to each species, it also serves to ensure that each individual mates with a member of the same species. A complicated courtship display, which may be energy-sapping, may also enable the female to assess the strength, and hence the suitability, of the male to be the father of her offspring.

Nest-building Behaviour

The nest is where a bird lays its eggs. For some birds, it is a remarkable achievement, but for others it is simply a depression in the ground, or a rock ledge.

The simplest nest construction consists of dead vegetation, which lifts the eggs off the ground, protecting them from damp. The most familiar type of nest, built by many passerines, is lodged in a bush or hole in a wall. Twigs or pieces of straw are used to bind the structure in place, and then softer materials are interwoven to form the cup shape that will protect the eggs or young. It is often lined with hair or feathers for greater insulation. For further protection a roof may be added, while long-tailed tits build a completely enclosed nest.

Birds from diverse groups build their nests in holes, either natural ones or ones they have excavated themselves. Sand martins will tunnel into sandy banks, and woodpeckers chisel themselves a hole in dead or even living trees.

Territorial Behaviour

All birds defend a territory while breeding, even if it is only the square metre or so around the nest in a dense breeding colony, in which case both male and female will usually keep their neighbours at a distance with ritualised postures, specific calls, or a jab of the bill. At the other extreme, the territories of large birds of prey cover several square kilometres.

If a large area is defended, it is usually the male's main responsibility. He will defend the territory from other males and use it to attract a female. The nest will be built here and it will be a place in which to collect food and rear the young.

At the start of the breeding season there is much fighting, although the fights are rarely serious, as both participants have too much to lose by risking serious injury. Instead, many disputes are resolved by ritual signals. Robins are a vicious exception: territorial disputes are not infrequently fought to the death.

Song is part of territorial behaviour and is both a proclamation of ownership and an

A formal exchange of greetings accompanies a grey heron's arrival at the nest

attraction to females. All songs are specific to each species, and with practice it is possible to identify every bird by its song.

Communication

Birds communicate through sound and visual means as hearing and sight are their most developed senses. Sound is the most important, since many birds live concealed from one another by dense vegetation.

A moorhen keeps a close eye on her chicks

The simplest type of vocalisation is the call. It is usually short, and given throughout the year by both sexes. Typically, calls are used to maintain contact within a flock, give an alarm or attract the attention of another family member.

Songs are generally more complex than calls and are produced mainly by the male during the breeding season. Their purpose is to warn other males off as well as to attract a mate, and they may also help to bring a pair into sexual readiness at the same time. Songs are usually delivered from a prominent perch, but species in open countryside often sing in the air, on a so-called 'song flight'.

Social Behaviour

Many birds are solitary for much of their lives, but when they do come together the spectacle and numbers can be phenomenal: flocks of thousands are not uncommon.

Birds congregate as a defence against predators, there being safety in numbers, or because of the need to exploit a patchily distributed resource. Many birds feed in flocks, especially outside the breeding season. This may be because food is localised, as is the carcass upon which a flock of vultures comes to feed, or because the birds may derive a benefit from having many eyes to see potential predators.

Seabirds in particular also breed in colonies. As they wander over huge areas outside the breeding season, coming together at particular places to breed makes it easier to find a mate. Also, being ground nesters, islands and cliffs are safer places to breed, and such places are in short supply.

Some species, for example swallows and starlings, come together at night-time to roost. It is possible that by roosting together birds that have had a poor feeding day can the next morning follow other birds that know of better feeding grounds.

Dunnocks gather in flocks at rich winter feeding sites

Migration

Birds go to incredible lengths to avoid harsh winter weather: Arctic terns migrate 17,000km between their Arctic nesting areas and their winter grounds in the Antarctic; whooper swans have been seen migrating at an altitude of over 8km; and birds as small as finches may travel up to 600km in a day on migration.

Good navigation is essential to any long-distance traveller, and birds are excellent navigators. Their internal 24-hour clock ensures that they can migrate in the right direction during the day by monitoring the sun's position. At night, which is when most smaller birds migrate, they have been shown to use the stars for navigation. There is also evidence to suggest that some species at least can detect and respond to the Earth's magnetic field, using this to determine north and south.

Keeping Clean and Warm

Feathers are essential to a bird's survival and must be carefully maintained. Therefore birds spend much time preening, which involves passing the bill through the feathers to 'zip' together the feather barbs, and remove dirt and skin parasites.

Most birds have an oil gland at the base of their backs. When preening, they rub their bills against it to extract some oil, which is then smeared through the feathers. The gland seems to have various functions, but it is particularly well developed in waterbirds and its secretion certainly helps to waterproof feathers.

Most birds bathe. It helps to keep the feathers clean and may help to dislodge parasites. Land birds can be seen ducking and wriggling in puddles or the edges of ponds with their feathers all ruffled. Waterbirds bathe while afloat. Bathing is followed by vigorous shaking and further preening. Curiously, some birds appear to bathe in dust, probably to help dislodge and discourage skin parasites.

Another behaviour that probably helps to remove skin parasites is anting. Apparently confined to passerines, it involves allowing species of non-biting ant to crawl over the plumage. The formic acid produced by the ants when irritated may help feather maintenance.

Birds are warm-blooded and must maintain a body temperature of about 41°C. To increase the insulation afforded by their feathers, they fluff them up to trap an insulating layer of air. In very cold weather they may also stand on one leg to minimise heat loss from that source.

Avoiding Predators

A bird's first line of defence against predators is to avoid being seen. Many birds therefore have a camouflaged plumage to help them blend into their surroundings. Females are often better camouflaged than males as they must sit undetected while guarding their nests or young. A few birds, such as the ptarmigan, make seasonal changes to their plumage, becoming white in winter to 'disappear' in the snow. Camouflage is of little use if the bird does not 'freeze' in position when a predator is sighted, and the best-camouflaged birds do just this. A jack snipe may almost be trodden on before it takes to the air as a last resort.

Birds may warn one another of a predator's presence by giving alarm calls. Many species' alarm calls sound much the same and they can be viewed as an international 'language' of all birds. Alarms are usually high-pitched, short notes, which are difficult to locate, thus concealing the whereabouts of the caller.

When a predator is spotted birds may mob it *en masse*. This is especially noticeable at a seabird colony, where the adults will repeatedly dive-bomb and sometimes hit a predator on the ground in an attempt to drive it away.

Fieldcraft

When and Where to Watch Birds

The weather has a serious influence on bird behaviour, which is something to be aware of when planning a birdwatching trip. For example, do not to expect good raptor watching on overcast days, since large birds of prey need sun-generated thermals to take to the air. These same dull conditions, however, often encourage swallows, martins and swifts to feed low over water and sometimes induce migrating black terns to pause at gravel pits and lakes.

Wind speed and direction have particularly profound effects on migrating birds. Northerly winds across Europe in spring will prevent most

Ptarmigan in summer (right) and in winter (below)

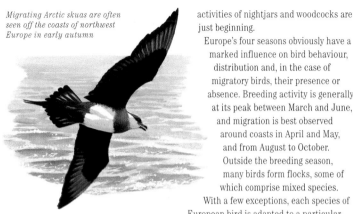

Migrating Arctic skuas are often seen off the coasts of northwest Europe in early autumn

activities of nightjars and woodcocks are just beginning.

Europe's four seasons obviously have a marked influence on bird behaviour, distribution and, in the case of migratory birds, their presence or absence. Breeding activity is generally at its peak between March and June, and migration is best observed around coasts in April and May, and from August to October. Outside the breeding season, many birds form flocks, some of which comprise mixed species.

With a few exceptions, each species of European bird is adapted to a particular habitat and to specific niches within this environment. Dippers, for example, are found almost exclusively on fast-flowing rivers while woodpeckers are always associated with woodland. Being aware of these limitations can help the birdwatcher in a number of ways. When trying to identify a mystery bird, for example, taking note of the habitat can help exclude many species on the grounds of location.

Interestingly, birds on migration and out of their normal range also favour habitats similar to those chosen on their breeding or winter grounds. You would be unlikely, for example, to find a migrating spotted crake

migrants from heading northwards from their winter grounds in Africa, but as soon as the wind changes direction, a flood of migrants will sweep northwards until they reach their breeding territories or are grounded by other changes in the weather. In autumn, easterly winds over northern Europe are likely to bring migrants and rarities from Siberia to western Europe, while westerly gales bring vagrants from North America as well as the chance to observe storm-driven migrating seabirds off the western coasts of Europe.

Use the time of day to get the most from your birdwatching. The best time to listen for woodland songbirds is invariably the two-hour period following dawn. For watching soaring birds of prey, particularly vultures, the period between 10am and noon is usually the most rewarding time, since they are then just taking to the air and will not yet have achieved any great height. At the other end of the day, roosts of starlings are best observed at dusk, and this is when the nocturnal

The nightingale is extremely difficult to see in dense foliage

*Lapwings may move to feed on coastal
marshes in severe winter weather*

or little stint anywhere other than beside a
freshwater pool, or a migrating shearwater
anywhere other than over the sea.

The coast acts like a magnet for many
species of bird, and estuaries have a
particular lure. At low tide, vast expanses
of mudflats are exposed, revealing rich
feeding grounds for waders and wildfowl,
but invariably distant observation
opportunities for birdwatchers. Since the
birds themselves often follow the rising tide
to feed, birdwatchers can strategically site
themselves, with their outline obscured,
just above the high-tide line. This way the
tide will push the birds close to them.

Identification of species new to the
observer is not always easy, even if the bird
is seen really well. One way to improve
your chances of identification is to learn
which characteristics to look for. These
naturally vary from species to species, but
groups of birds do tend to have features in
common that are of particular significance.
For example, among wheatears the shape
of the black and white markings on the
rump and tail are the key features, while
with ducks, the shape and length of the bill

and the colour of the speculum are of
greater importance.

Binoculars and Telescopes

Buy a young ornithologist a bad pair
of binoculars and he or she
may be put off birdwatching
for life. Some of the
cheapest models even seem to create the
illusion, if not the reality, of making the
image appear smaller than that seen with
the naked eye, and flimsy models soon get
broken or misaligned.

Binoculars come in all shapes, sizes,
and prices. The first step is to avoid over-
small models since they are often flimsy
and have low magnification; at the other
extreme, steer clear of huge, bulky pairs
as you will soon tire of carrying them
around your neck. It is important to look
at the set of numbers stamped on each pair
of binoculars: typical examples might be
7×30, 8×40 or 10×40. The first number in
the set denotes the magnification, and the
second the diameter of the objective lens.
This latter figure gives an indication of the
light-gathering capacity and hence
brightness of the binoculars in question. An
optimal pair for most people would be 8×40,
but tastes vary.

As your interest in birdwatching grows,
so will the number of occasions when
binoculars are just not powerful enough to
give you the view you want, and a telescope
becomes a requirement. Before you buy
one, talk to as many telescope owners
as you can and visit a specialist shop
to try models out side by side. If you

A male shelduck chases off an intruder

choose a fixed magnification model then 30× is about the best option; zoom telescopes should include this magnification in their range.

Photography

These days, the only sensible choice of camera is a single lens reflex (SLR) model. Make sure the camera has automatic light metering and is robust enough to cope with rough treatment, and that a wide range of lenses is available to fit it. Many models come with auto-focusing as standard; although excellent in many circumstances, this facility does have drawbacks and you should be able to turn it off if desired.

The next task is to choose a lens. Although on occasions, such as at seabird colonies, a standard lens (50mm) will suffice, you need at least a 300mm telephoto lens for most bird photography. Using a tripod to avoid camera shake is a wise precaution with medium focal length telephoto lenses but essential with those with focal lengths of 500 or 600mm.

The simplest way of taking a bird photograph is just to stalk the subject. Although natural cover will sometimes allow this approach unseen, it is often the best policy to remain in view but keep your movements slow and deliberate. Some species are more approachable than others, and juveniles are often more trusting than adults. Try enticing birds into the open by providing a tempting food supply.

Bird Classification

The smallest unit of classification is the species. We all instinctively know what a species is – a magpie or a kingfisher, for example – but it is difficult to define one precisely. A commonly accepted definition is that it is a group of birds that can

A kingfisher makes a splendid photograph but can be hard to spot when perched motionless among vegetation

actually or potentially breed with one another but not with other such groups. The word 'potentially' is important, as starlings in North America, for example, do not actually breed with starlings in Europe, but if brought together they could.

Each species is given a different scientific name, the binomial, consisting of two parts. The chaffinch, for example, has the name *Fringilla coelebs*. *Fringilla* defines the genus, or closely related group of birds, to which the chaffinch belongs, and this is called the generic name. The second part, *coelebs*, is unique to the chaffinch within the genus *Fringilla*, and this is called the specific name. Sometimes a species is divided into several races or subspecies, in which case a third name is added to the binomial.

GLOSSARY

Abrasion Wear and tear on feathers, which can change a bird's appearance dramatically. Pale parts wear more easily than dark; for example, white spots on gulls' wingtips wear off to leave a uniform dark colour

Barring Narrow bands or stripes on a bird's plumage

Basal knob Swelling seen at the base of the bill in some species of wildfowl

Boreal Northern

Brood Set of offspring

Calls Sounds uttered by bird other than song, generally concerned with contact and alarm functions

Carpal Area of feathers at wrist joint of wings, contrastingly marked in some birds of prey

Carr Type of woodland; occurs in damp situations and normally comprises alder

Cere Naked wax-like membrane at base of bill in some species

Courtship In order to mate and rear young successfully, pairs of most species must first break down their natural instinct to keep their distance, must reduce aggression and maintain a firm relationship, or pair bond, which is created and reinforced by courtship behaviour

Coverts The name given to a group of feathers covering a particular part of a bird's body. Thus ear coverts cover the ear, undertail coverts are found on the undertail area and underwing coverts are found lining the inner part of the underwing. Those feathers on the upperwing not concerned with flight are also referred to as coverts; they are arranged in zones which are, from the leading edge backwards, referred to as greater, median and lesser coverts; those covering the bases of the primary feathers are called primary coverts

Culmen Upper ridge of the bill

Display Behaviour designed to demonstrate a bird's presence

Diurnal Active during the day

Eclipse A dull plumage, notable of male duck, acquired after breeding to reduce conspicuousness (ducks moult all their flight feathers and lose the power of flight for a short period while 'in eclipse')

Extralimital Outside the normal range

Feral A species or individuals once domesticated or captive but since released or escaped and living wild

Flank Side of breast and belly

Gape The opening or the corners of the mouth; 'to gape' is to hold the bill wide open

Garigue Sparsely vegetated habitat characteristic of arid, stony terrain in the Mediterranean region

Gliding Effortless and usually level flight without wingbeats

Hirundines Swallows and martins, members of the family Hirundinidae

Immature Not old enough to breed. With birds this usually refers to a certain stage of plumage, so some birds, such as eagles, are confusingly said to 'breed in immature plumage'. Others, like the fulmar, may not breed for several years even though visually indistinguishable from an adult

Irruption Sudden large-scale movement of birds out of one area and their arrival into another

Jizz Field characteristics that are unique to a species

Juvenile A bird in its first set of feathers, or juvenile plumage

Lek Communal display ground

Lores Region of feathers between the eye and the bill

Malar stripe A marking originating at the base of the lower mandible of the bill

Mandible One half of the bill

Maquis Shrub-dominated vegetation typical of many parts of the Mediterranean region

Migration Regular, seasonal movements of species; more or less predictable, with a return trip. Irregular movements caused by, for example, hard weather or food shortage also occur. Young birds invariably spread away from breeding areas in autumn – this type of movement is termed dispersal

Mimicry Copying other sounds, natural or man-made

Mobbing Small birds that discover a roosting owl or bird of prey, or sometimes a mammalian predator or snake, will flutter around or dive at it with loud calls, attracting mixed species to join in. The purpose is uncertain

Moult Shedding and replacement of feathers or plumage in a regular sequence, which may or may not affect the appearance of the bird. Many species have feathers with dull tips that crumble away in spring to reveal brighter colours beneath. This is sometimes referred to as moulting by abrasion

Nest Where a bird lays its eggs

Nocturnal Active at night

Partial migrant A species where only some individuals migrate

Passage Refers to migrants and migration – a bird 'on passage' is en route to its winter or summer grounds. A 'passage migrant' is a species that appears in the spring and/or autumn but does not necessarily breed or spend the winter; the curlew sandpiper is an example in Europe

Passerine One of a large order of birds called the Passiformes, all members of which can perch (although many other birds can perch as well)

Pelagic Found in the open sea

Plumage The whole set of feathers covering a bird. Also used to describe different combinations of colour and pattern according to sex, season or age (for example, summer plumage, adult plumage etc)

Predator An animal that eats other animals. Among birdwatchers the term is often

used to describe an avian predator of other birds

Preening Using the bill to clean and adjust the feathers

Puszta East European grassy plain

Raptor Bird of prey

Resident A species that remains in a given area all year round

Roost Rest or 'sleep', or the place where a bird or birds do this

Scapulars Region of feathers between the mantle and the wing coverts

Scrape Nest site of some wader species, where small stones form a small depression

Secondaries Inner flight feathers

Sedentary Non-migratory and non-dispersive

Soaring Effortless flight by broad-winged birds rising on heat thermals and updraughts

Song Voice of a bird in a recognisable pattern for its species, be it an irregular flow or a repetitive phrase; intended to identify the individual and its species, to proclaim ownership of territory and/or attract a mate.

Species A 'kind' of organism, basically isolated from others by its inability to cross-breed and produce fertile young. A subspecies is a recognisably different group (because of size or colour) within a species in a defined area. Apart from subspecies the remarkable

feature of a bird species is the lack of variation within it, in terms of size, colour, pattern, voice, behaviour, food, nest and many other factors, which remain surprisingly constant

Speculum Coloured patch on a duck's wing, often used in display

Steppe Treeless, grassy habitat associated mainly with Russia and eastern Europe

Supercilium Stripe above the eye

Taiga Forest type found at northerly latitudes, just before the tree-line is reached; often comprises spruce and birch

Territory An area (or 'home range') occupied by a bird (or a pair), and which is defended against other individuals of the same species

Thermalling Method of flight employed by broad-winged birds, including raptors and storks, where lift is provided by currents of hot air

Tundra Northern, treeless habitat; normally characterised by the presence of permafrost

Vagrant Usually a migrant that appears outside its normal range. During spring migration, southerly winds often induce migrants to overshoot. On autumn migration inexperienced juveniles are sometimes blown off course by strong winds or engage in 'reverse migration' (flying in the wrong direction)

Vermiculation Feather pattern where numerous worm-like lines create a close-packed pattern

Red-throated Diver
Gavia stellata

Status: Resident; widespread; **Voice:** Only heard during breeding season: evocative, goose-like calls; deep, rhythmic quacking in flight; song rapidly repeated: 'kwuk-uk-uk'; **Length:** 53–69cm; **Wingspan:** 110cm; **Habitat:** Breeds on northern coastal pools; overwinters around coasts; **Behaviour:** Shy and easily disturbed at nest; when swimming dives regularly for extended periods

Swims low in water with superficially shag-like appearance but head and bill have characteristic upward tilt. Bill dagger-like and eyes red. In breeding season both sexes have red throat, black and white striping on nape and otherwise grey head and neck. Back dark brown and underparts white. In winter, upperparts grey-brown with white speckling on back, and underparts white. Face and throat very white when seen in good light. Juvenile similar to winter adult but with grubbier appearance to underparts. Looks goose-like in flight with neck outstretched; in winter looks very pale in flight.

Black-throated Diver
Gavia arctica

Status: Resident; widespread; **Voice:** Only heard during breeding season: raven-like croaks and wailing calls; **Length:** 58–73cm; **Wingspan:** 120cm; **Habitat:** Breeds on large lakes; overwinters around coasts; **Behaviour:** Swims buoyantly and dives smoothly

In breeding season, bill dark and dagger-like and eyes red. Sexes similar: grey head and neck with black throat and black and white stripes on sides of neck and under chin. Sides of breast have black and white stripes, which grade into black on back and upperparts; distinctive white chequerboard pattern on back. In winter, bill grey with black tip; plumage dark on upperparts and pale on underparts. Throat and cheeks often look conspicuously white; white patch on flanks at waterline. Juvenile similar to winter adult, although upperparts not clean white.

Red-throated diver

SUMMER

WINTER

Black-throated diver

SUMMER

WINTER

Great Northern Diver
Gavia immer

Status: Local breeding species; widespread in winter; **Voice:** Only heard during breeding season: loud, eerie wailing calls; **Length:** 69–91cm; **Wingspan:** 135cm; **Habitat:** Breeds on large lakes; overwinters in sandy bays and around rocky coasts; **Behaviour:** At home on rough seas, diving constantly

Size and markings make breeding-plumage bird distinctive; sexes similar. Bill, head and neck black except for band of narrow white stripes on sides of neck and under chin. Eyes red. Underparts white. Upperparts black except for tiny white spots and white chequerboard pattern on back; black and white stripes on sides of breast. Winter birds have mainly dark upperparts and white underparts. Bill grey with black tip, and neck often shows dark band on sides. Juvenile similar to winter adult but with dirtier white underparts and pale fringes to feathers on upperparts.

White-billed Diver
Gavia adamsii

Status: Winter visitor; rare; **Voice:** Wailing calls on breeding ground; otherwise silent; **Length:** 75–91cm; **Wingspan:** 150cm; **Habitat:** Breeds on Arctic coastal lakes; overwinters at sea; **Behaviour:** More pelagic than other divers in winter

Superficially similar to great northern diver except for bill, which is large, dagger-like and pale yellow. Head and bill characteristically held with upward tilt. In breeding plumage head and neck are black except for band of narrow white stripes on sides of neck and under chin. Eyes red. Upperparts mostly black except for white chequerboard effect on back and scattering of small white spots. Underparts white except for black and white stripes on sides of breast. In winter upperparts mostly dark brown and underparts white. Head and neck grubby brown with dark smudge on sides of neck and behind eye. Whitish face. Juvenile similar to winter adult.

Little Grebe
Tachybaptus ruficollis

Status: Resident; common; **Voice:** High-pitched, whinnying trill; **Length:** 25–29cm; **Wingspan:** 40–44cm; **Habitat:** Shallow-edged lakes, ponds, slow-flowing rivers and canals; **Behaviour:** Swims buoyantly and dives frequently

Small, dumpy bird with powder-puff appearance to body feathers. Feathers at rear end are often fluffed up. Yellow-green legs and lobed feet sometimes visible in clear water. In summer looks mainly dark brown except for bright chestnut on neck and face. Shows lime-green patch at base of bill, which is dark with pale tip. In winter appears paler brown but darker on cap, nape and back. Tail end is whitish; white patch at base of bill. Young birds are striped.

Great northern diver

SUMMER

WINTER

White-billed diver

WINTER

Little grebe

SUMMER

JUVENILE

SUMMER

Great Crested Grebe
Podiceps cristatus

Status: Resident; common; **Voice:** Barking 'rah-rah-rah' and a clicking 'kek'; most vocal in spring; **Length:** 46–51cm; **Wingspan:** 85–89cm; **Habitat:** Breeds on lakes, gravel pits and slow-flowing rivers; occasionally on the sea in winter; **Behaviour:** Display features head-shaking, penguin dances with bills full of water plants, and noisy outbursts

Elegant waterbird with slender neck. At a distance can look black and white. Sexes similar. In breeding season has pink bill, white face, black cap and large, showy, orange-chestnut and brown ear tufts. Nape and back brown but underparts white. In winter loses ear tufts and has mainly brownish upperparts and white underparts; black cap appears above level of eye and contrasts with white face. Bill pink. Juvenile in early autumn is striped but resembles winter adult by late autumn. In flight shows white wedges on leading and trailing edges of innerwing in all plumages.

Pied-billed Grebe
Podilymbus podiceps

Status: Late autumn and winter vagrant from North America; **Voice:** Vagrants to Europe generally silent; **Length:** 32–35cm; **Wingspan:** 58–62cm; **Habitat:** Freshwater wetlands with emergent vegetation; **Behaviour:** Generally retiring, keeping close to cover and partially submerging when alarmed

Small, dumpy grebe with proportionately longer neck and larger head than superficially similar little grebe. Bill noticeably bulky for size of head. Sexes similar. Tail short with powder-puff of white undertail feathers. Adult in breeding plumage (seldom seen in region) has largely grey-brown plumage; upperparts darker than underparts. Bill pale pinkish-grey except for striking, vertical black band midway along length. Throat and chin black. In winter loses black on throat and chin; bill colour pale buffish-yellow without black markings. Plumage otherwise similar to breeding adult. In flight, adult shows uniformly grey-brown upperwings at all times.

Great crested grebe

WINTER

SUMMER

WINTER

SUMMER

Pied-billed grebe

WINTER

Red-necked Grebe
Podiceps grisegena

Status: Resident/winter visitor; common; **Voice:** During breeding season utters cackling and ticking sounds and loud wails; otherwise silent; **Length:** 40–50cm; **Wingspan:** 80–85cm; **Habitat:** Breeds on shallow lakes with abundant water plants; overwinters mainly on coastal waters; **Behaviour:** Distant winter bird looks diver-like, but distinguished by habit of jumping at the surface when diving

Most easily confused with great crested grebe, but smaller and more compact. Sexes similar. During breeding season very distinctive with black-tipped yellow bill, white face, black cap and brick-red neck. In winter loses red neck, although a hint may remain in autumn birds. Black cap extends down to level of eye. White cheeks look conspicuous in most birds and black-tipped yellow bill still a good feature. Juveniles have stripy heads but soon resemble winter adults. In flight shows white wedges on leading and trailing edges of innerwing; less extensive than in great crested grebe.

Slavonian Grebe
Podiceps auritus

Status: Resident; local breeding species; widespread in winter; **Voice:** Various screams and cries heard at nest; **Length:** 31–38cm; **Wingspan:** 60–65cm; **Habitat:** Breeds on well-vegetated lakes and pools; overwinters on coastal waters; **Behaviour:** Nests in loose colonies; displaying pairs race upright across the water

In breeding plumage neck, underparts and flanks brick red, and head black except for striking orange-yellow feathering from eye to ear tufts. Bill black with white tip; eyes red. Back black with small white tuft of feathers at rear end. In winter appears mainly black and white and easily confused with black-necked grebe. Cap black, leading to narrow black line on nape that widens on back of neck. Back black and underparts white. In flight shows white patches on leading and trailing edges of innerwing; leading-edge patch is small.

Black-necked Grebe
Podiceps nigricollis

Status: Resident; local; **Voice:** Chittering trill; **Length:** 28–34cm; **Wingspan:** 55–60cm; **Habitat:** Breeds on shallow, well-vegetated ponds; overwinters on coastal waters; **Behaviour:** Gathers in small flocks outside breeding season

Superficially similar to Slavonian grebe but with steep forecrown, upturned bill and upward-tilted head and bill. Sexes similar. In summer plumage head, neck and back are black. Underparts brick red. Eyes red, and have orange-yellow feather tufts behind them. In winter has mostly dark upperparts and white underparts. Black cap more complete than Slavonian grebe's, while neck appears greyer. In flight shows white wedge on trailing edge of innerwing only.

WINTER

Red-necked grebe

SUMMER

SUMMER

WINTER

WINTER

Slavonian grebe

WINTER

WINTER

SUMMER

Black-necked grebe

Black-browed Albatross
Diomedea melanophris

Status: Vagrant; most birds seen in northwest Europe; **Voice:** Generally silent at sea; **Length:** 90cm; **Wingspan:** 220–240cm; **Habitat:** Open oceans; **Behaviour:** Gliding, effortless flight on stiffly held wings

Immense seabird. Unmistakable when seen well but, at a distance, plumage pattern superficially similar to that of adult great black-backed gull or immature gannet. Sexes similar. Seen in flight, wings look disproportionately long. Upperwings and mantle appear all dark. Underwings dark but with strking white band along their length. Body pure white except for black 'eyebrow' line above eye and darkish tail feathers. Legs dull pink; seldom seen in flying birds. Bill long, large and yellowish-orange. Juvenile similar to adult but with dull-pink bill; sub-adult birds have dark-tipped yellow bill but otherwise identical to adult.

Fulmar
Fulmarus glacialis

Status: Resident; common; **Voice:** Loud cackling and crooning at nest, grunts and cackles in feeding flocks; otherwise silent; **Length:** 45–50cm; **Wingspan:** 102–112cm; **Habitat:** Coastal waters, especially near cliffs; **Behaviour:** Rides updraughts on stiffly held wings; pairs mate for life and greet each other with head-bowing and loud cackling

Superficially gull-like but distinguished by stiff-winged flight and large tube-nostrils. Sexes similar. Adults have white head with dark smudge through eye. Bill comprises horny plates and has hooked tip and tube-nostrils. Wings relatively narrow and pointed; upperwing blue-grey and underwing white. Underparts white, and back and rump grey. Rarely seen northern birds look all grey. Chick is large, white and fluffy.

Cory's Shearwater
Calonectris diomedea

Status: Resident; common in Mediterranean; rare visitor further north; **Voice:** Wails and coughing screams on breeding ground; otherwise silent; **Length:** 45–55cm; **Wingspan:** 100–125cm; **Habitat:** Breeds on islands; otherwise at sea; **Behaviour:** Acrobatic flier, often rising to considerable heights on gusts and eddies

Large shearwater; similar to great shearwater but lacks that species' black cap and white nape band. Sexes similar. Bill proportionately large and yellow with black tip; colour seen only at close range. Upperparts brownish except for darker wingtips and black tail; scaly effect caused by pale feather edges. At close range shows faint pale base to tail. Underparts white although leading and trailing edges to wings dark, and face brown.

Black-browed albatross

Cory's shearwater

Fulmar

Great Shearwater
Puffinus gravis

Status: Passage migrant; seen in northwest Europe Jul–Sep;
Voice: Silent within its European range; **Length:** 45–50cm;
Wingspan: 100–115cm; **Habitat:** Mostly far out to sea;
occasionally close to land; **Behaviour:** Powerful flier, showing
masterful control in strong winds

Noticeably larger than Manx shearwater. Invariably
seen in flight on stiffly held wings. Sexes similar. Seen
from above, dark cap is clearly separated from grey-brown
mantle by white nape band. Upperwings and back dark, but
pale feather edging to mantle and wing coverts visible in good
light. White-tipped uppertail coverts produce white-rumped
effect. Underparts white except for dark bands on underwing
and dark undertail feathering.

Little Shearwater
Puffinus assimilis

Status: Resident; best seen off Madeira and Canary Islands
Apr–Oct; **Voice:** Screaming churrs heard at nesting colonies;
silent at sea; **Length:** 27–28cm; **Wingspan:** 60–65cm;
Habitat: Nests on island sea cliffs; otherwise always at sea;
Behaviour: Flight direct and low with fast, fluttering
wingbeats giving passing resemblance to puffin

Small sea bird, nearly always seen in flight.
Superficially similar to, but appreciably smaller than,
Manx shearwater. Sexes similar. Adult has white underparts,
including underwing; undertail coverts white in race *baroli*
from Madeira and Canary Islands but dark in race *boydi* from
Cape Verde Islands. Upperparts, including upperwing,
blackish-brown, appearing very dark in most conditions.
At close range white on face is seen to surround dark eye
(eye of Manx shearwater is surrounded by black). Wings
proportionately shorter than those of Manx shearwater,
resulting in more whirring flight action. Juvenile post-
fledging indistinguishable from adult at sea.

Sooty Shearwater
Puffinus griseus

Status: Passage migrant; seen in Europe Jul–Oct; **Voice:**
Silent within its European range; **Length:** 40–51cm;
Wingspan: 94–109cm; **Habitat:** Open oceans; close to land
only during onshore gales; **Behaviour:** Typical stiff-winged
flight pattern

Invariably seen in flight; appears all dark except at
close range or in very good light. Sexes similar. Larger
and longer-winged than Manx shearwater. Body is cigar-
shaped and bill looks long and thin compared to other
shearwater species. Body and upperwing dark sooty brown.
Underwings are mostly dark but show a pale, silvery stripe
along their length that can be conspicuous in good light.

Great shearwater

Little shearwater

Sooty shearwater

Manx Shearwater
Puffinus puffinus

Status: Resident; common; **Voice:** Excited cackling noises at breeding colonies; otherwise silent; **Length:** 30–38cm; **Wingspan:** 76–89cm; **Habitat:** Breeds on offshore islands; otherwise seen at sea; **Behaviour:** Gathers in sizeable groups when feeding is good; hardly able to walk on land

Usually seen flying low over water. Sexes similar. At a distance appears all black above and all white below. Body cigar-shaped and wings comparatively narrow and pointed. Tube-nostrils only visible at very close range. Upperparts almost black. Underparts, including undertail feathering, white. Underwing white except for dark margin. Flies on stiffly held wings except in very calm conditions, when employs rapid wingbeats interspersed with long glides.

Mediterranean Shearwater
Puffinus yelkouan

Status: Resident; widespread; **Voice:** Raucous cackles at breeding colonies; otherwise silent; **Length:** 33–38cm; **Wingspan:** 80–89cm; **Habitat:** Breeds on inaccessible islands and cliffs; otherwise seen at sea; **Behaviour:** Large numbers gather to feed in late summer, favouring inshore waters; sometimes makes shallow plunge-dives to feed

Usually seen flying in long lines, low over water. Shows short, cigar-shaped body and narrow, stiffly held wings. Upperparts sooty brown. Underparts and underwing whitish in race *yelkouan* but buffish or dusky in race *mauretanicus*. Both races have dark undertail feathering distinguishing them from similar Manx shearwater. At close range legs can be seen projecting beyond tail.

European Storm-petrel
Hydrobates pelagicus

Status: Summer visitor; locally common; **Voice:** Churring and hiccuping from burrow; otherwise silent; **Length:** 14–18cm; **Wingspan:** 36–39cm; **Habitat:** Nests on sea cliffs and islands; otherwise at sea; **Behaviour:** Patters feet on water when feeding; birds congregate round fishing vessels to feed on offal

A tiny seabird, superficially recalling house martin; readily distinguished from this species by flight pattern and habitat. Plumage usually appears all black except for conspicuous white rump. At close range brownish edges to wing covert feathers may be revealed as pale bands, and white band on underwing sometimes visible. Legs black and trailing and bill black and slender, bearing delicate tube-nostrils.

Manx shearwater

Mediterranean shearwater

RACE *YELKOUAN*

RACE *MAURETANICUS*

European storm-petrel

Wilson's Storm-petrel
Oceanites oceanicus

Status: Summer visitor; rare; **Voice:** Silent in region; **Length:** 16–18cm; **Wingspan:** 40–42cm; **Habitat:** Always seen at sea in region; **Behaviour:** Tends to patter feet on water; sometimes appears to stand still when facing into the wind

Tiny seabird, usually appearing all dark except for white rump. Sexes similar. Adult at all times has mainly sooty-black plumage except for broad white rump. Dark upperwings show broad sandy-brown panel on secondary coverts. In direct flight legs are clearly seen to project beyond tip of tail. Tail square-ended. When pattering on water to feed, yellow webs sometimes visible at close range.

Leach's Storm-petrel
Oceanodroma leucorhoa

Status: Summer visitor; rare; **Voice:** Agitated churrs and hiccups at nest; otherwise silent; **Length:** 19–22cm; **Wingspan:** 45–48cm; **Habitat:** Breeds on remote islands; otherwise at sea; **Behaviour:** Flight pattern erratic

Slightly larger than European storm-petrel, with distinctly forked tail visible at close range. Wings relatively long and pointed. Plumage can appear all black. In good light, however, head, back and wing coverts look smoky-grey; trailing edge of coverts shows pale feathering, producing a transverse wingbar. Rump conspicuously white; at close range, narrow grey bar revealed down centre. Varied flight pattern distinctive. Sometimes glides like shearwater then engages in darting, fluttering or hovering flight. Direct flight confident and powerful.

Madeiran Storm-Petrel
Oceanodroma castro

Status: Resident; rare; **Voice:** Purring calls heard at nest; silent at sea; **Length:** 20cm; **Wingspan:** 45cm; **Habitat:** Breeds on remote islands; otherwise at sea; **Behaviour:** Breeding colonies very inaccessible and only visited after dark; does not patter feet on water at sea

Tiny seabird; often appears all black except for white rump. Very similar to Wilson's and European storm-petrels and only separable with extreme care. Sexes similar. Adult has mainly blackish-brown plumage at all times. Seen in flight, dark upperwings show faint pale band across secondary coverts (much less conspicuous than on Leach's and Wilson's storm-petrels). Tail slightly forked but often looks square-ended; all-dark legs do not obviously project beyond tail in flight as do Wilson's storm-petrel's. White rump appears smaller and more rectangular than on other storm-petrels. Juvenile similar to adult.

Wilson's storm-petrel

Leach's storm-petrel

Madeiran storm-petrel

Cormorant
Phalacrocorax carbo

Status: Resident; common; **Voice:** Guttural croaks at nest and roost; otherwise silent; **Length:** 80–100cm; **Wingspan:** 130–160cm; **Habitat:** Breeds colonially, mainly around coasts in western Europe but on inland lakes elsewhere; overwinters mainly around sheltered coasts but also on inland waters; **Behaviour:** Often seen swimming and diving, or perched on posts with wings outstretched

Large, robust waterbird. Adult looks dark at a distance; at close range, has scaly appearance due to oily greenish-brown feathers on upperparts having dark margins. Bill large and dark with hooked tip. Race *carbo*, from northwest Europe, has yellow base to bill and white throat. Race *sinensis* has white throat but also shows white feathering on nape and sides of head. Both races have white thigh patches in breeding season. Much of white feathering lost outside summer months. Juvenile brown and scaly with paler underparts.

Shag
Phalacrocorax aristotelis

Status: Resident; common; **Voice:** Grunts and clicks; **Length:** 65–80cm; **Wingspan:** 90–105cm; **Habitat:** Rocky coasts; **Behaviour:** Performs head- and neck-rubbing courtship display; constantly adorns untidy nest with fresh seaweed

Smaller than superficially similar cormorant and seldom seen in similar habitats. Sexes similar. In poor light adult looks all dark. At close range breeding birds have oily-green plumage, bottle-green eyes, yellow gape and upturned crest. In winter crest and sheen are lost or less obvious. Juvenile pale brown with white chin; Atlantic birds have brown underparts but those from Mediterranean have white on belly. In flight shows proportionately shorter and more rounded wings than cormorant and faster wingbeats.

Pygmy Cormorant
Phalacrocorax pygmeus

Status: Resident; rare; **Voice:** Croaking calls at nest; otherwise silent; **Length:** 45–55cm; **Wingspan:** 80–90cm; **Habitat:** Shallow, reed-fringed lowland lakes; **Behaviour:** Usually seen swimming low in the water, or perched on dead branches with wings outstretched or at roost

Small cormorant with compact proportions. Sexes similar. Compared with cormorant, head and neck look proportionately short and tail looks proportionately long; these features are most noticeable in flight. Adult has mostly dark plumage except for chocolate-brown head. In breeding plumage shows white flecks on head, breast and mantle. In winter adult has whitish throat. Juvenile has brownish upperparts and paler underparts, belly and throat looking almost white.

Cormorant

WINTER ADULT

ADULT, RACE *CARBO*

Shag

SUMMER ADULT

Pygmy cormorant

SUMMER ADULT

Gannet
Morus bassanus

Status: Resident; common; **Voice:** 'Arr', 'urrah', heard at colonies; otherwise silent; **Length:** 87–100cm; **Wingspan:** 165–180cm; **Habitat:** Breeds colonially on islands and inaccessible cliffs; otherwise at sea; **Behaviour:** Gathers in large numbers when feeding is good; plunge-dives to feed

Large size and black and white plumage distinctive. Looks all white except for yellow-buff head, black wingtips and dark legs. Feet webbed; at close range, pale blue visible along toes. Bill dagger-like and pale blue-grey. Juvenile dark brown, speckled with pale spots; acquires white adult plumage over five years, upperwing and back being the last to lose immature feathering. Has deep, powerful wingbeats in direct flight; also glides on oustretched wings.

White Pelican
Pelecanus onocrotalus

Status: Summer visitor/partial resident; local; best seen in northern Greece in spring; **Voice:** Grunts, growls and mooing calls heard at nest; otherwise silent; **Length:** 140–170cm; **Wingspan:** 275–290cm; **Habitat:** Shallow, lowland lakes and river deltas; **Behaviour:** Feeds co-operatively; flocks seen circling above breeding grounds or on migration

Large, white waterbird, capable of sustained thermalling and gliding. Often seen swimming in flocks, when adult plumage looks all white except for black wingtips. In good light plumage seen to be tinged yellowish. Bill large and very long. Throat sac yellow to orange and shows bare patch of pink skin around eyes. Robust legs and webbed feet orange-yellow. Juvenile has brownish plumage and yellow throat sac. From below adult shows black flight feathers contrasting with otherwise white plumage. Juvenile shows brown flight feathers and brown leading edge to wing.

Dalmatian Pelican
Pelecanus crispus

Status: Summer visitor/partial resident; rare; **Voice:** Hissing and grunting calls heard at colony; otherwise silent; **Length:** 160–175cm; **Wingspan:** 280–290cm; **Habitat:** Shallow freshwater lakes; **Behaviour:** Sometimes engages in co-operative group feeding; soars and glides with ease

Similar to white pelican but slightly larger. White plumage has blue-grey tinge; back-curled mane formed by curly feathers. Bill long and large; throat sac orange-yellow in breeding season but pink at other times. Legs grey in all plumages. In flight, adult seen from below has uniformly greyish-white plumage, easily separating it from white pelican. From above, primary flight feathers are black, contrasting with otherwise pale plumage. Juvenile has more uniformly greyish-white underwing in flight than white pelican.

Gannet

JUVENILE

ADULTS

White pelican

Dalmatian pelican

Bittern
Botaurus stellaris

Status: Resident/summer visitor; rare; **Voice:** During breeding season, male utters deep, resonant booming, 3–4 times in 5–6 seconds; otherwise silent; **Length:** 70–80cm; **Wingspan:** 125–135cm; **Habitat:** Reedbeds; rarely in other wetland habitats – except during cold weather; **Behaviour:** Shy; best seen at reedbed reserve with hides

Large, robust bird with beautifully mottled and marbled buffish-brown plumage. Darker streaks, barring and arrow-shaped markings afford excellent camouflage. Sexes similar. Neck long but often held in hunched posture. Cap and nape dark, and shows dark moustachial stripe. Bill large, dagger-like and yellowish. Legs and feet yellowish-green with very long toes. When alarmed adopts motionless, upright posture with head and neck stretched skywards. In flight looks owl-like, with long and broad brown wings; trailing legs and forward-pointing head and bill clearly visible.

American Bittern
Botaurus lentiginosus

Status: Autumn vagrant, mostly to northwest Europe; **Voice:** Croaking call sometimes uttered in flight; otherwise silent in region; **Length:** 70–80cm; **Wingspan:** 110–120cm; **Habitat:** Wetlands with abundant emergent vegetation; **Behaviour:** Ventures into open more than bittern

Superficially very similar to bittern. Sexes similar. Adult has brown, streaked plumage, generally darker above than below. Throat white, well marked with large, reddish-brown streaks. Cap reddish-brown, not blackish as in bittern. Has conspicuous black face patches and, in flight, striking black flight feathers; these two features absent in bittern. Bill dull yellow; legs yellow-green. Juvenile similar to adult but lacks black facial markings, acquired in first winter.

Little Bittern
Ixobrychus minutus

Status: Summer visitor; locally common; **Voice:** Mostly silent but frog-like calls heard during breeding season and 'kerk' flight call; **Length:** 35–38cm; **Wingspan:** 53–56cm; **Habitat:** Reedbeds and other well-vegetated wetlands; **Behaviour:** Flies readily and can be flushed

Smallest member of heron family in the region. Male has black-tipped yellow bill, greyish face, black cap and orange-buff, streaked underparts. Back and flight feathers black, contrasting with buffish-white wing coverts forming pale panel. Upperwing features most striking in flight, which comprises jerky, rapid wingbeats and prolonged glides. Female has subdued version of male's plumage, with reddish-buff face and underparts, and streaked, brown back. Juvenile heavily streaked.

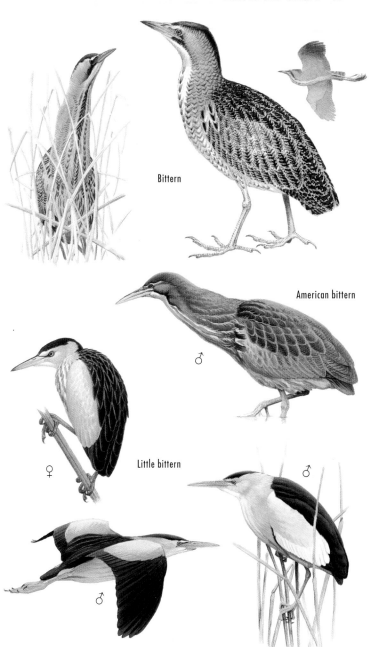

Bittern

American bittern

♂

Little bittern

♀

♂

♂

Night Heron
Nycticorax nycticorax

Status: Summer visitor; local; **Voice:** Raven-like 'kwaak' flight call; **Length:** 60–65cm; **Wingspan:** 105–110cm; **Habitat:** Wetlands; **Behaviour:** Most active after dark; long lines of flying birds often leave for feeding grounds at dusk

A dumpy and very distinctive heron. Sexes similar. Adult has black bill, black crown and large red eyes. Face, neck and underparts pale grey; whitish on forecrown and around base of bill. Back black and wings grey, the contrast most noticeable in flight. In breeding plumage sports long white head plumes. Legs yellowish except at start of breeding season, when pinkish. Immature has black-tipped yellow bill and dark-brown plumage adorned with large pale spots. Underparts streaked.

Squacco Heron
Ardeola ralloides

Status: Summer visitor; local; overshooting vagrants can be seen north of breeding range in spring; **Voice:** Harsh croaks heard in breeding season; otherwise silent; **Length:** 45–47cm; **Wingspan:** 80–90cm; **Habitat:** All sorts of wetlands; **Behaviour:** Generally solitary, feeding by stealth in shallow wetland margins

Sexes similar. In breeding plumage, standing bird looks mainly orange-buff with reddish tinge to back. Crown and nape streaked, feathers on lower nape being long and plume-like. Underparts white. Bill greenish with black tip, and eyes yellow. Legs greenish-orange. In flight looks remarkably white, showing pure white wings and back. Non-breeding adult has dull-brown upperparts and streaked head and neck. Still strikingly white in flight. Bill yellowish with black tip. Juvenile similar to non-breeding adult.

Cattle Egret
Bubulcus ibis

Status: Resident; common; **Voice:** During breeding season utters barking 'aak' and other calls; otherwise silent; **Length:** 48–52cm; **Wingspan:** 90–95cm; **Habitat:** Cultivated land and grassland, often alongside animals; also follows ploughs; **Behaviour:** Feeds more actively than other egrets; flocks follow herd animals to watch for frogs and insects

A stocky white bird with a characteristic bulging throat. Sexes similar. Plumage pure white except during brief period of breeding season, when feathers on nape, mantle and breast show warm, buffish tinge. Bill dagger-like and proportionately large; at height of breeding season pinkish-orange but otherwise yellow. Legs dull yellowish-green except, briefly, during breeding season, when pinkish-orange. In flight wings broad and rounded, and legs trailing; neck held in hunched-up posture, giving large-headed appearance.

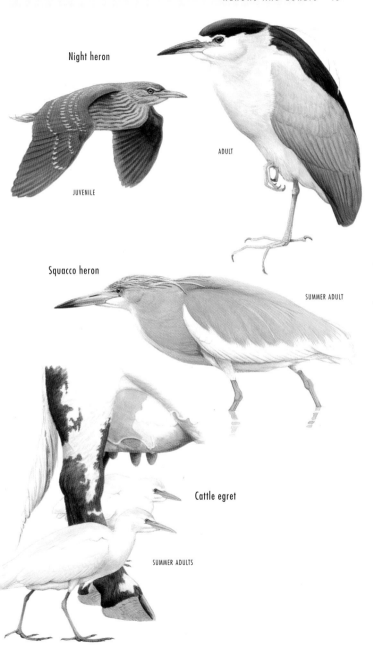

Night heron

JUVENILE

ADULT

Squacco heron

SUMMER ADULT

Cattle egret

SUMMER ADULTS

Little Egret
Egretta garzetta

Status: Resident/summer visitor; locally common; **Voice:** Harsh 'khaah' and other grating sounds heard at colony; otherwise mostly silent; **Length:** 55–65cm; **Wingspan:** 88–95cm; **Habitat:** Shallow lakes and wetlands; also coastal lagoons and saltpans; **Behaviour:** Waits motionless for fish to pass by; sometimes shuffles feet in front of it to disturb prey

The most common pure white, heron-like bird in Europe. Slender and elegant appearance, with long neck. Bill long, dark and dagger-like. Bare skin at base of bill yellowish in breeding season but otherwise darker. Also sports long head plumes in breeding season. Legs long and black, contrasting with plastic-yellow feet. Appearance similar throughout year. In flight shows broad, rounded wings and long, trailing legs; head and neck held hunched up.

Great White Egret
Egretta alba

Status: Resident; local; **Voice:** Grating 'kraak' heard at colony and roost; otherwise silent; **Length:** 85–102cm; **Wingspan:** 140–170cm; **Habitat:** Extensive wetlands and large, reed-fringed lakes; **Behaviour:** Nests colonially but solitary at other times; less active than smaller egrets

Largest white heron-like bird of the region, size of grey heron. Plumage pure white at all times; shows long, lacy plumes on lower back in breeding season. Bill black in breeding season but yellow at other times; has patch of yellow skin at base of bill at all times. Legs long; yellow in breeding season on adult but dark greenish-yellow at other times and in juvenile. In flight shows long, broad wings and long, trailing legs; head and neck held in hunched posture.

Grey Heron
Ardea cinerea

Status: Resident; common; **Voice:** Call a loud and harsh 'frank'; young birds at nest give pig-like squeals; **Length:** 90–98cm; **Wingspan:** 175–195cm; **Habitat:** Wetlands; sometimes on coasts; **Behaviour:** Will stand motionless for hours on end, when resting or feeding

Large and elegant waterbird. Adult head, neck and underparts mostly whitish, except for black feathering on neck and head; has black, trailing tuft of feathers on head. Bill large, dagger-like and yellow. Back and upperwings grey except for flight feathers; black and white carpal feathers appear as black 'shoulder' on resting bird. Legs long and yellowish-green. Juvenile similar to adult but underparts more grubby and streaked; black and white head markings less distinct. In flight grey herons look huge with long, broad and rounded wings. Wingbeats slow and leisurely, and head and neck held kinked and pulled in. Legs held outstretched with toes together.

Little egret

SUMMER ADULTS

Great white egret

SUMMER ADULTS

Grey heron

ADULT

JUVENILE

Purple Heron
Ardea purpurea

Status: Summer visitor; locally common; spring vagrant to northwest Europe; **Voice:** 'Kraank' call sometimes, but mostly silent; **Length:** 78–90cm; **Wingspan:** 120–150cm; **Habitat:** Extensive wetlands, especially in dense reedbeds; **Behaviour:** Retiring; flies low over reeds and soon drops back into cover

Slightly smaller than grey heron, with more slender head and neck. Adult plumage appears mostly purplish-grey. Head and neck orange to buff, with black stripe along length down each side. Long breast feathers appear streaked, and underparts look dark on standing bird. Upperparts purplish-grey. Juvenile appears more uniformly buffish-brown. In flight, adult upperwings look purplish-brown with black flight feathers; underwings look grey, except for dark-maroon band forming leading edge. In flight, head held in snake-like kink, and long, trailing legs show hind toes cocked upwards.

Black Stork
Ciconia nigra

Status: Summer visitor/resident; rare; **Voice:** Variety of soft calls; also non-vocal bill clattering at nest; **Length:** 95–100cm; **Wingspan:** 145–150cm; **Habitat:** Forested wetlands; **Behaviour:** Shy and retiring, especially when nesting; often seen in flight

Size, shape and colour make this species unmistakable. Sexes similar. Seen from behind, plumage of adult looks all black; in good light, oily sheen also visible. From other views, white underparts can be seen. Legs long and red, and bill long, dagger-like and red; also shows ring of bare red skin around eye. In flight has huge, broad wings that look square-ended, with 'fingers' of primaries showing; plumage all black except for white underparts extending to innerwing. Juvenile plumage browner; legs and bill dull greenish.

White Stork
Ciconia ciconia

Status: Summer visitor; locally common; **Voice:** Mostly silent; produces non-vocal bill clapping at nest; **Length:** 100–115cm; **Wingspan:** 155–165cm; **Habitat:** Feeds in wetlands and fields adjacent to towns and villages; **Behaviour:** Easy to see in breeding season, nesting on rooftops or churches; huge numbers migrate through Bosphorus and Straits of Gibraltar

Unmistakable, given size and markings. Sexes similar. When standing, head, neck, back and underparts white; can look rather grubby. Wingtips black. Bill long, dagger-like and bright red. Legs long and red. In flight soars impressively on long, outstretched wings that look square-ended and have 'fingers' of primaries projecting. Body white except for black flight feathers when seen from above and below. Juvenile similar but colour of bill and legs duller.

Purple heron

Black stork

White stork

Glossy Ibis
Plegadis falcinellus

Status: Summer visitor; local; **Voice:** Crow-like 'kra-kra' sometimes heard near nest, but mostly silent; **Length:** 55–65cm; **Wingspan:** 80–95cm; **Habitat:** Wetlands; **Behaviour:** Probes for invertebrates in the shallows; has distinctive flight silhouette, and small groups tend to fly in a trailing line

Waterbird with distinctive shape, even in silhouette. Pinkish bill large, long and curved downwards, and head rather large and bulbous in proportion to long neck. Plumage mostly rich chestnut-maroon. In poor light can look all black, but in bright light shows green or purplish sheen to wings and back. Breeding birds have white line from base of bill around eye. Non-breeding birds have pale streaks on head and neck. In flight head and neck held outstretched and legs trail.

Spoonbill
Platalea leucorodia

Status: Resident; local; **Voice:** Mostly silent; occasional grunting sounds at nest; **Length:** 80–90cm; **Wingspan:** 115–130cm; **Habitat:** Shallow lakes, coastal lagoons; **Behaviour:** Birds fly in long lines with rapid wingbeats

Resting birds often have bill tucked in and so can be mistaken for little egrets. Feeding birds distinctive, and identified by bill shape and feeding method, when bill is swept from side to side. Sexes similar. Adult plumage all white, but can look rather grubby; shows buffish-yellow on breast in breeding season and long plumes on nape. Legs long and black, and bill long and flattened with spoon-shaped tip. In flight carries head and neck outstretched and legs trailing. Immature has black wingtips.

Greater Flamingo
Phoenicopterus ruber

Status: Resident; locally common; **Voice:** Flocks utter 'kaa-haa' calls; **Length:** 125–145cm; **Wingspan:** 140–165cm; **Habitat:** Shallow brackish lagoons, and saline lakes; **Behaviour:** Groups feed in close formation and are very noisy

Large and unmistakable bird both standing and in flight. Sexes similar. Adult plumage mainly pale pink but can look very washed out. Black-tipped pink bill is downcurved and banana-shaped. Neck very long and usually held in 'S' shape. Body compact and rounded. Legs very long and pinkish-red. In flight, wings show black flight feathers and rosy-pink coverts; head and neck held outstretched and legs trailing. Juvenile is pale grey-brown with dark legs and black-tipped grey bill.

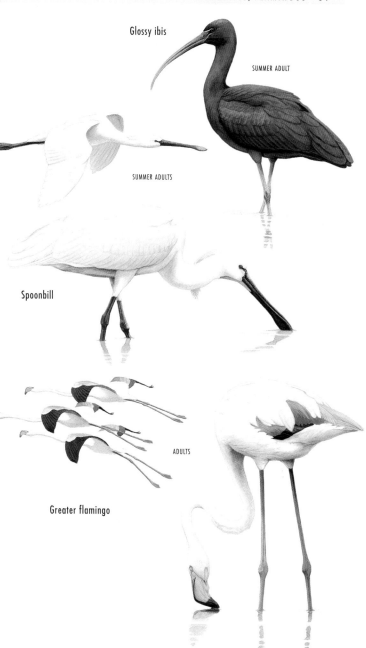

Glossy ibis

SUMMER ADULT

SUMMER ADULTS

Spoonbill

ADULTS

Greater flamingo

Mute Swan
Cygnus olor

Status: Resident; common; **Voice:** Hoarse trumpeting, snorting and hissing calls; wing noise in flight; **Length:** 145–160cm; **Wingspan:** 210–235cm; **Habitat:** Freshwater wetlands and sheltered coasts; **Behaviour:** Males aggressive in spring and have spectacular displays

Commonest swan in the region. Sexes similar. Adult has all-white plumage although neck sometimes stained buffish. Bill is orange-red with large black knob at base. Juvenile buffish-brown with grubby-pink bill; acquires adult feathering during first winter. When swimming, neck is held in a more graceful 'S' shape than in other swans. Wingbeats deep and powerful. Sometimes flies in 'V' formation or diagonal lines.

Bewick's Swan
Cygnus columbianus

Status: Winter visitor; local; **Voice:** Varied, soft or loud musical, bugling calls; far-carrying; **Length:** 115–125cm; **Wingspan:** 180–210cm; **Habitat:** Breeds on remote tundra areas outside region; overwinters on flood meadows, saltmarshes and shallow lakes; **Behaviour:** Small family parties tend to stick together throughout winter

Smallest swan in Europe and invariably seen in flocks. Adult has all-white plumage. Legs black and bill black with irregularly shaped yellow patch at base; yellow does not extend beyond nostrils. Juvenile buffish-grey and has black-tipped pink bill, fading to white at base; distinguished from juvenile whooper swan by smaller size and bill size and shape, but mainly by association with adult birds.

Whooper Swan
Cygnus cygnus

Status: Rare breeding species; locally common in winter; **Voice:** Loud, trumpeting or bugling calls; **Length:** 145–160cm; **Wingspan:** 220–240cm; **Habitat:** Breeds on northern lakes and marshes; overwinters on flood meadows, stubble fields and lochs; **Behaviour:** Flocks fly in 'V' formations; family units stick together

Superficially similar to Bewick's swan but much larger and with proportionately longer neck. Adult has all-white plumage, black legs and black bill with yellow patch at base; area of yellow proportionately larger than on Bewick's; wedge-shaped and extending beyond nostrils. Juvenile pinkish-buff with black-tipped, pinkish bill, grading to white at base. Similar to juvenile Bewick's; best distinguished by larger size and association with adult birds.

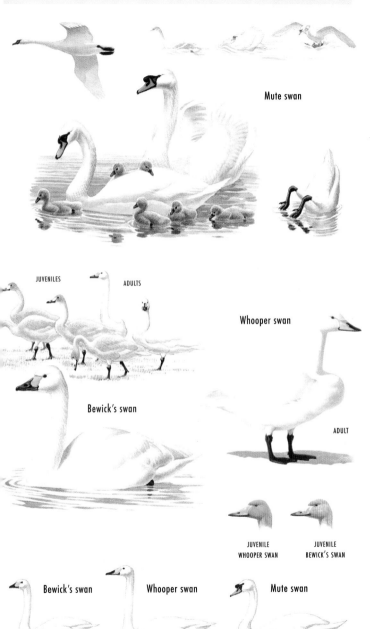

Mute swan

JUVENILES

ADULTS

Whooper swan

Bewick's swan

ADULT

JUVENILE
WHOOPER SWAN

JUVENILE
BEWICK'S SWAN

Bewick's swan

Whooper swan

Mute swan

Bean Goose
Anser fabalis

Status: Rare breeding species; local winter visitor; **Voice:** Calls include a nasal cackle; **Length:** 65–80cm; **Wingspan:** 150–175cm; **Habitat:** Breeds on tundra and in northern forests; in winter, on arable and stubble fields; **Behaviour:** Nervous in winter, favouring large, open fields where flock can easily spot danger

Adult identified by chocolate-brown appearance, particularly on head and neck, and proportionately long neck. Bill dark with variable orange markings: in race *rossicus,* orange limited to near bill tip, but in race *fabalis* orange much more extensive. Legs of both races orange. In flight upperwings look all dark. Lower back is brown, separated from white-edged brown tail by white band at base.

Pink-footed Goose
Anser brachyrhynchus

Status: Rare breeding species; locally common in winter; **Voice:** Musical disyllabic or trisyllabic honking; also high-pitched, sharp 'wink-wink'; **Length:** 60–75cm; **Wingspan:** 135–170cm; **Habitat:** Breeds on uplands or tundra; in winter, on fields, roosting on estuaries or lakes; **Behaviour:** In winter feeds on coastal feeds, flying inland in vast flocks at dusk

Smaller than superficially similar bean goose and with proportionately shorter neck and smaller bill. Adult bill dark with variable patch of pink, usually in the form of a band, near tip. Head and neck usually dark brown, breast and flanks paler brown and back greyish. Legs pink; duller in juvenile. In flight, wings pale grey except for darker flight feathers; back and tail paler than on bean goose.

PINK-FOOTED GOOSE

BEAN GOOSE

PINK-FOOTED GOOSE

Bean goose

RACE *FABALIS*

PINK-FOOTED GOOSE

WHITE-FRONTED GOOSE

Pink-footed goose

White-fronted Goose
Anser albifrons

Status: Mainly winter visitor; locally common; **Voice:** Flocks utter musical ringing, laughing and yodelling calls; hissing and yapping calls on ground and non-vocal 'creaking' wings on taking to air; **Length:** 65–78cm; **Wingspan:** 130–165cm; **Habitat:** Breeds on boggy tundra; overwinters on water meadows and near estuaries; **Behaviour:** Easily frightened on feeding grounds, taking to the air in huge, noisy flocks

Large goose, which, as adult, has white forehead not extending above eye. Siberian race *albifrons* has pinkish bill, while Greenland race *flavirostris* has orange-yellow bill. Plumage looks generally grey-brown, with underparts paler, but with variable black bands and crescents on belly; undertail white. Juvenile similar but lacks white forehead. In flight looks comparatively long-winged.

Lesser White-fronted Goose
Anser erythropus

Status: Rare breeding species; local winter visitor; **Voice:** High-pitched yelping calls; **Length:** 55–65cm; **Wingspan:** 120–135cm; **Habitat:** Breeds on tundra; overwinters on meadows and fields; **Behaviour:** Vagrants to northwest Europe mix with white-fronted flocks

Superficially similar to white-fronted goose but more compact and appreciably smaller when seen side by side. Bill relatively small and pinkish-orange. White forehead extends above eye, which has conspicuous yellow eyering; white forehead absent in juvenile and eyering dull. Plumage mostly grey-brown with dark markings on otherwise paler belly. Undertail white. In flight has fast wingbeats.

Greylag Goose
Anser anser

Status: Resident/winter visitor; locally common; **Voice:** Clattering clamour in flight, less bugling than other grey geese; **Length:** 75–90cm; **Wingspan:** 150–180cm; **Habitat:** Arable land, marshes, lakes; **Behaviour:** Easily alarmed; flies on powerful wingbeats and flock sometimes engages in aerobatic dives and plunges

Large, stoutly built goose with mainly grey-brown plumage. Most adult birds seen in western Europe have orange bills; eastern birds have pinkish bills. Legs pink in all adult birds. Shows pale margins to feathers on back. Lower belly and undertail white. Some birds have a few dark feathers on belly. In flight shows grey on forewing, lower back and tail. Juvenile similar to adult but duller and appears more barred on upperparts.

White-fronted goose

ADULT

JUVENILE

Lesser white-fronted goose

ADULT

JUVENILE

ADULT

Greylag goose

ADULTS

COMPARING GREY GEESE

Seen at a distance grey geese can be a challenge to identify. Close attention should be paid to the overall colour of the birds in question, markings on the head, and leg and bill colour. In flight the degree of contrast between the dark flight feathers and the rest of the wing is crucial. The best way to learn grey goose identification is to observe feeding flocks of known species and then take careful note when they take to the wing.

BEAN GOOSE: Similar to pink-footed goose but longer-necked with more uniformly dark wings; white tail band narrower than on pink-footed goose

PINK-FOOTED GOOSE: Dark head and neck contrast with pale-grey back and mostly pale-grey upperwings; seen from below, head, neck and underwings appear uniformly dark; rump darker than greylag's

BEAN GOOSE: Larger and proportionately longer-necked than pink-footed goose; contrast between head and neck and rest of body never so noticeable as in pink-footed goose

PINK-FOOTED GOOSE: Striking contrast between brown head and neck and greyish back; bill appears dark at a distance but shows small, variable amount of pink

LESSER WHITE-FRONTED GOOSE: Superficially very similar to white-fronted goose but slightly smaller

LESSER WHITE-FRONTED GOOSE: Smaller than white-fronted goose, with more dainty bill and white on forehead extending back over eyes; yellow eyering diagnostic at close range

WHITE-FRONTED GOOSE: Flight feathers darker than rest of upperwing when viewed from above but contrast never as striking as in greylag and pink-footed geese; adult has black belly patches

WHITE-FRONTED GOOSE: White blaze on head limited to forehead and never extends over eye; adult has dark belly patches

GREYLAG GOOSE: Upperwings show contrast between pale-grey forewing panels and dark flight feathers; underwings also bicoloured

GREYLAG GOOSE: Bulky; appears uniformly grey-brown but head and neck slightly paler than rest of body; legs pink and bill pinkish-orange

Barnacle Goose
Branta leucopsis

Status: Winter visitor; locally common; **Voice:** Short, sharp bark; repeated as yapping chorus by flocks; **Length:** 60–70cm; **Wingspan:** 135–145cm; **Habitat:** Breeds on tundra; overwinters on coastal grassland and saltmarshes; **Behaviour:** Flies to and from feeding grounds in large flocks at dawn and dusk

A small, compact goose. Bill and eye black. Adults have white face and black neck. Back barred black and grey; underparts white. Legs and feet black. Juvenile has more blotched face and greyer chest. In flight looks very black and white; flight feathers black, and bird shows conspicuous white rump when seen from above.

Snow Goose
Anser caerulescens

Status: Winter vagrant from North America; white-phase birds recorded annually but beware escapes; **Voice:** Loud cackling honks in flight; **Length:** 70–75cm; **Wingspan:** 140–150cm; **Habitat:** Breeds on tundra; overwinters on wetlands and grasslands; **Behaviour:** Birds usually found among winter flocks of other geese, notably white-fronted

Relatively small but distinctive goose, seen in two colour phases. Sexes similar but male larger than female. Adult white phase is pure white except for black primaries and greyish upperwing primary coverts. Adult blue phase has white head and neck and variable amounts of white on otherwise dark bluish-grey body plumage. Immature white phase has pale greyish-brown upperparts and dirty-grey underparts. Immature blue phase has brownish plumage, paler on underparts. Both colour phase juveniles have greyish legs and bill and black primaries. Immatures of both phases resemble adults by first spring. Beware confusion with escapes from captivity, including domestic white goose and Ross's goose; latter superficially similar but appreciably smaller with relatively short, stubby bill.

Bar-headed Goose
Anser indicus

Status: Vagrant from Asia; most sightings probably escapes (feral population in Norway); **Voice:** Honking calls uttered in flight; **Length:** 70–80cm; **Wingspan:** 140–150cm; **Habitat:** Grassland and wetlands; **Behaviour:** Gregarious goose; in Europe usually seen in flocks of Canada or wild grey geese

Distinctively marked and attractive goose. Sexes similar. Adult has mainly pale grey-brown plumage on body. Head white except for two dark, transverse bars on crown. Neck dark brown with bold white stripe down side. Bill and legs orange-yellow. Juvenile similar to adult but lacks bars on head, crown being greyish-brown not white. Plumage acquires adult characteristics by first winter.

Barnacle goose

Snow goose

WHITE-PHASE ADULTS

Bar-headed goose

Canada Goose
Branta canadensis

Status: Resident; locally common; **Voice:** Loud, resonant honking calls, usually two notes 'gor-rronk'; also a variety of other trumpeting notes; **Length:** 90–100cm; **Wingspan:** 150–180cm; **Habitat:** Ornamental lakes, flooded gravel pits and nearby meadows; **Behaviour:** Flocks generally quite tolerant of observers

Europe's largest goose. Head and neck black, except for contrasting white patch on face. Plumage on back and underparts brown, except for white on undertail and black flight feathers; upperparts can look rather barred. Yellow-buff goslings follow parents. Juvenile birds duller than adults but soon indistinguishable.

Brent Goose
Branta bernicla

Status: Winter visitor; locally common; **Voice:** Deep, rolling bark; **Length:** 55–60cm; **Wingspan:** 110–120cm; **Habitat:** Breeds on tundra; overwinters on saltmarshes and coastal grassland; **Behaviour:** Large flocks feed on mudflats in winter, frequently taking to the air

Small, dark goose. Adult has all-black head and neck except for white neck patch. Back and wings dark grey-brown except for black flight feathers. Rear end white, most noticeable in flight, but tail dark. Legs and feet black. Race *bernicla* has dark belly; race *hrota* has pale-grey belly. Juvenile has pale-edged feathers on back and lacks white neck; acquires adult characteristics during winter.

Red-breasted Goose
Branta ruficollis

Status: Winter visitor; rare; **Voice:** High-pitched, disyllabic call; **Length:** 53–56cm; **Wingspan:** 115–135cm; **Habitat:** Breeds on tundra; overwinters on steppe or sometimes arable land; **Behaviour:** Vagrants to northwest Europe mix with brent or white-fronted geese

Small but beautifully marked goose. Sexes similar. Adult has complicated pattern of red, white and black on head, neck and breast. Back, wings and belly mostly black but shows conspicuous white stripe on flanks. Rear end white except for tail; white is most striking in flight. Juvenile similar to, but duller than, adult.

Canada goose

Brent goose

Red-breasted goose

Egyptian Goose
Alopochen aegyptiacus

Status: Feral population resident in eastern England; **Voice:** Mostly silent; **Length:** 65–73cm; **Wingspan:** 135–155cm; **Habitat:** Seldom far from water, usually in fields and marshes; **Behaviour:** Aggressive towards one another and other species

Superficially similar to ruddy shelduck but with distinctive markings. Adult has pinkish bill and legs. Head and neck pale except for dark patch through eye, and dark collar. Breast and underparts buffish-brown but with dark-chestnut patch on belly. Back usually rufous-brown but sometimes greyish-brown. Juvenile more uniformly buffish-brown, without clear markings on head or belly; legs and bill dull brown. In flight, adults show striking white forewing patches on both upper and underwing surfaces, green speculum and black flight feathers.

Ruddy Shelduck
Tadorna ferruginea

Status: Resident; locally common; **Voice:** Noisy; flight call 'ang' or rolling 'aarl'; **Length:** 61–67cm; **Wingspan:** 120–145cm; **Habitat:** Wetlands including river deltas; **Behaviour:** Hole-nesting species, burrowing underground where possible; seldom found far from water

Attractive and distinctive duck. Adult has dark bill, eyes and legs. Head and upper neck buffish with clear demarcation from orange-brown body. In breeding season only male has black collar separating buff and orange plumage; sexes similar in other plumage respects. At rest, black wingtips can be seen. In flight, wings strikingly black and white, the black being confined to the flight feathers. Juvenile similar to adult but duller.

Shelduck
Tadorna tadorna

Status: Resident; locally common; **Voice:** Male whistles; female utters deep, quick quacks; **Length:** 60–70cm; **Wingspan:** 110–130cm; **Habitat:** Mostly coastal on sandy and muddy shores; also inland on flooded gravel pits and marshes; **Behaviour:** Nests in holes; after breeding, huge flocks gather in traditional sites to moult flight feathers

Large and distinctively marked duck. Adult has bright red bill and legs. Head and upper neck dark green; can look all dark in some lights. Rest of plumage comprises patches of white and black with conspicuous orange-chestnut breast band. Only male has red knob at base of bill, while female shows pale feathering at bill base; sexes similar in other plumage respects. Juvenile mottled and marbled brown and white; shows dull-pink legs and bill. In flight, adult looks conspicuously black and white.

Egyptian goose

Ruddy shelduck

♂

Shelduck

♂

♀

Mandarin
Aix galericulata

Status: Feral birds resident; elsewhere sightings presumed escapes; **Voice:** Mostly silent; **Length:** 41–49cm; **Wingspan:** 68–75cm; **Habitat:** Wooded rivers and lakes; **Behaviour:** Sometimes perches in trees; nests in large tree-holes

Male extremely distinctive with long mane of dark feathers on cap and nape, broad, pale stripe above eye and radiating orange feathers on neck and breast. Underparts and back dark but flanks orange, and shows sail-like feathers at rear end; undertail white. Female mainly grey-brown with white belly and larger white spots on neck and breast. Shows conspicuous white 'spectacle' around eye, and white throat and base to bill.

Wigeon
Anas penelope

Status: Rare breeding species; locally common winter visitor; **Voice:** Male utters whistling 'whee-OO'; female gives grating purr; **Length:** 45–51 cm; **Wingspan:** 75–85cm; **Habitat:** Breeds on northern lakes and wetlands; in winter, on saltmarshes and coastal grassland; **Behaviour:** Flocks feed together in shallow water

Attractive dabbling duck. Male can look drab in dull light. In good light, reveals orange head with yellow forecrown. Breast pinkish, and back and flanks covered with soft grey vermiculations. Underparts white and stern black. In water appears to have black and white rear end. Female has mainly brown plumage with white belly and dark feathering around eye. In flight, male shows conspicuous white patch on upper surface of innerwing.

American Wigeon
Anas americana

Status: Autumn vagrant; **Voice:** Male has whistling call similar to wigeon; female generally silent; **Length:** 45–55cm; **Wingspan:** 80–85cm; **Habitat:** Vagrants favour estuaries and freshwater wetlands; **Behaviour:** Vagrants consort with wigeon flocks

Attractive dabbling duck, superficially similar in all plumages to corresponding plumages of wigeon. Male has pale-yellow crown, speckled brown face and green mask grading to dark on nape. Underparts pinkish-buff except for white belly, which extends to rear of flanks; undertail coverts black. Mantle pinkish-grey. Female mainly reddish-brown with mottled grey head. Immature birds and eclipse plumage similar to adult female. Birds of both sexes have dark legs and dark-tipped grey bill at all times. In flight both sexes show white wing patches and white axillaries on underwing (latter feature greyish in wigeon).

Mandarin

♂

♀

Wigeon

♀

♂

American wigeon

♂

Wood Duck
Aix sponsa

Status: All sightings presumed to be escapes; **Voice:** Mostly silent; **Length:** 40–50cm; **Wingspan:** 68–74cm; **Habitat:** Wetlands; **Behaviour:** Forages for food under cover of tree roots and overhanging branches, usually at dawn and dusk

Male unmistakable and showy, with red bill and green head showing white stripes. When swimming, deep red breast shows vertical white stripe; flanks buff and back dark. Female superficially similar to female mandarin, with grey-brown plumage and large white spots on breast and flanks. White 'spectacle' around eye extends down head, to a lesser extent than on female mandarin, and white at base of bill and chin less extensive.

Gadwall
Anas strepera

Status: Resident/winter visitor; locally common; **Voice:** Male utters nasal 'mair'; female gives quiet quack; **Length:** 45–55cm; **Wingspan:** 85–95cm; **Habitat:** Breeds on wetlands with open water; in winter, on lakes and marshes; **Behaviour:** Found in flocks outside breeding season, often with coots

At first glance a rather drab duck. Close views of male in good light reveal grey plumage comprising intricate vermiculations; bill dark grey and head, neck and back buffish-grey with conspicuous black stern. Female recalls female mallard with yellow bill and brown plumage. Both sexes easily identified when swimming if flash of white speculum is revealed. This feature very obvious in flight, when white underwing also noticeable.

Black Duck
Anas rubripes

Status: Autumn vagrant from North America; **Voice:** Quacking calls, similar to those of mallard; **Length:** 55–60cm; **Wingspan:** 85–90cm; **Habitat:** Vagrants often found on coasts in winter; **Behaviour:** Vagrants often stay for some time, feeding on coasts or open water

Large and robust dabbling duck, superficially similar to female mallard. Male has dark chocolate-brown body plumage with paler feather edges. Head and upper neck contrastingly pale grey-brown with clear demarcation from body. Tail all dark. Bill yellowish and legs orange. Eclipse male plumage similar to non-eclipse plumage but bill olive. Female similar to male but with olive bill and dull-brown legs. Juvenile similar to female. In flight all birds show striking white underwing contrasting with otherwise dark plumage. Speculum is violet and bordered with black, not white as in mallard.

Wood duck

♂

♀

Gadwall

♀

♂

Black duck

♂

Teal
Anas crecca

Status: Resident; common; **Voice:** High-pitched, chirping 'krick'; **Length:** 34–38cm; **Wingspan:** 58–65cm; **Habitat:** Shallow fresh water when nesting; flood meadows or saltmarshes in winter; **Behaviour:** Wary; when alarmed takes off almost vertically from the water; flight path swerving

The region's smallest duck. Male has attractive orange-brown head with large green patch from eye to nape, bordered with creamy-yellow stripe. Back and flanks show grey vermiculations; underparts white. Black-bordered, creamy-yellow patches on sides of stern. Female small, with mottled grey-brown plumage; best identified by size and association with male. In flight both sexes show green speculum and white underwing.

Green-winged Teal
Anas crecca carolinensis

Status: Autumn vagrant from North America; **Voice:** Male has bell-like call; female utters nasal quack; **Length:** 35–37cm; **Wingspan:** 60–64cm; **Habitat:** Freshwater wetlands and estuaries; **Behaviour:** Invariably seen with teal flocks

Tiny dabbling duck. Female indistinguishable from female teal of European race *A. c. crecca*. Male has chestnut-brown head with glossy green patch extending from eye backwards along side of nape. Breast pinkish-buff with darker spots. Underparts mostly white and flanks grey with intricate, fine markings; shows conspicuous and diagnostic white stripe on flanks (absent in male of *A. c. crecca*). Upperparts grey-brown. Shows creamy-yellow and black patches on undertail. Bill dark grey. Eclipse male similar to female but has orange base to bill. Female generally mottled brown with pale underparts. Juvenile resembles female in late summer. In flight all birds show green speculum.

Blue-winged Teal
Anas discors

Status: Autumn vagrant from North America; **Voice:** Generally silent; **Length:** 38–40cm; **Wingspan:** 60–62cm; **Habitat:** Freshwater wetlands; **Behaviour:** Favours dense cover; very retiring

Attractive dabbling duck, similar to garganey. Male has dull blue-grey head, darkest on crown; conspicuous white crescent in front of eye. Body generally mottled brown with dark spots; shows distinctive white patches near stern and black undertail coverts. Bill and legs dark. Eclipse male resembles female. Female mottled grey-brown. Recalls female teal but larger and with proportionately longer bill, usually showing conspicuous white patch at base. Head more uniformly marked than female garganey's. Juvenile similar to female. In flight both sexes show green speculum and pale-blue patch covering leading half of inner upperwing.

Teal

♂

♀

♂

Green-winged teal

Blue-winged teal

♂

♂

Mallard
Anas platyrhynchos

Status: Resident/summer visitor; common; **Voice:** Female gives familiar quack; male a weak nasal note; **Length:** 50–65cm; **Wingspan:** 80–100cm; **Habitat:** Almost anywhere with water; **Behaviour:** Very tame on urban lakes

Common and familiar duck. Male has yellow bill, green head showing sheen in good light, chestnut breast and otherwise mostly grey-brown plumage; shows black stern and white tail. Female has orange-yellow bill and rather uniform brown plumage. Eclipse male similar to female but more reddish on breast. In flight both sexes show white-bordered blue speculum.

Pintail
Anas acuta

Status: Resident/winter visitor; common in winter; **Voice:** Male utters quiet whistle; female gives short quacks; **Length:** 51–66cm; **Wingspan:** 80–95cm; **Habitat:** Open areas with shallow water; **Behaviour:** Often seen in pairs or small group in winter; rather shy

Male is an elegant duck with chocolate-brown head and white on underparts and on front of neck, forming narrow stripe up side of face. Flanks grey and black with elongated feathers. Stern buff and black, with long tail often characteristically cocked upwards. Female has dark-grey bill and largely brown plumage; has long-bodied appearance. In flight both sexes look particularly long-bodied.

Shoveler
Anas clypeata

Status: Resident/winter visitor; common; **Voice:** Quiet 'tuc' uttered by male; female quacks; **Length:** 44–52cm; **Wingspan** 70–85cm; **Habitat:** Shallow water; **Behaviour:** Easiest to see in winter, when small groups often gather to feed in the shallows, moving slowly forward sieving food from the mud with their bills

Unusual duck, the most distinctive feature of both sexes being the broad, flattened bill. Male has green head with sheen visible in good light. Bright orange belly provides striking contrast with otherwise white breast and flanks. Back and stern dark; bill black. Female mottled brown. Bill dark but with lower edges orange. In flight both sexes show blue forewing separated by white band from green speculum.

Mallard

♀

♂

Pintail

♂

♀

PINTAIL ECLIPSE ♂

SHOVELER ECLIPSE ♂

Shoveler

♂

♀

Garganey
Anas querquedula

Status: Summer visitor; common; **Voice:** Male utters characteristic mechanical-sounding rattle; female gives quiet quack; **Length:** 37–41cm; **Wingspan:** 60–65cm; **Habitat:** Shallow wetlands and flooded meadows; **Behaviour:** Generally unobtrusive; flight is direct and fast without teal's swerves and twists

Small duck, hardly bigger than teal. Male is distinctive with broad, white crescent-shaped stripe over eye leading back to nape. Cap dark but head and neck otherwise reddish-brown. Breast brown, flanks grey; shows long, trailing black, blue-grey and white feathers on back. Female similar to female teal, best distinguished by association with male. In flight both sexes show blue forewing and green speculum.

Red-crested Pochard
Netta rufina

Status: Resident/winter visitor; local; **Voice:** Mostly silent; **Length:** 53–57cm; **Wingspan:** 72–82cm; **Habitat:** Fresh water with extensive cover; in winter, on lakes and flooded gravel pits; **Behaviour:** Dives with great ease, up-ending in shallows like a mallard; usually seen in pairs or small flocks

Male is attractive and distinctive. Bill bright red. Head orange-brown and neck and body feathers mostly black except for grey-brown back and white flanks. Female has pink-tipped dark bill. Cap and nape dark brown; cheeks and throat conspicuously pale. Plumage otherwise brown. Eclipse male resembles female but retains red bill. In flight both sexes show pale underwing and broad, white stripes on upperwing.

Marbled Duck
Marmaronetta angustirostris

Status: Resident; rare; **Voice:** Mostly silent; **Length:** 40–42cm **Wingspan:** 63–67cm; **Habitat:** Well-vegetated shallow pools and lakes; freshwater and saline; **Behaviour:** Favours dense cover and rather retiring; seldom flies far when disturbed

An attractive duck, despite subdued colouring. Sexes similar. Plumage ground colour grey-brown, covered with pale-buff spots; these are particularly large and striking on breast, belly and back. Bill dark and shows dark smudge through eye. In flight has rather uniform brown wings.

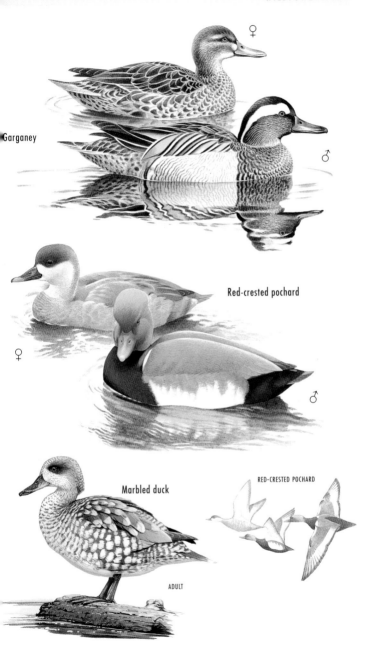

Garganey

♀

♂

Red-crested pochard

♀

♂

Marbled duck

ADULT

RED-CRESTED POCHARD

Ring-necked Duck
Aythya collaris

Status: Autumn vagrant from North America; **Voice:** Generally silent; **Length:** 40–45cm; **Wingspan:** 65–70cm; **Habitat:** Shallow freshwater lakes; **Behaviour:** In Europe usually consorts with tufted ducks; dives frequently

Striking and attractive diving duck. Superficially similar to tufted duck but readily separable with good views. Male has blackish head, neck, breast and back; brownish collar seldom visible in the field. Crown is peaked but not tufted. When swimming, flanks appear grey; separated from black breast by striking white vertical stripe. Bill has distinctive pattern with white band separating black tip from grey base. Female mainly brown, paler and mottled on face. In good light conspicuous white eyering and white line create 'spectacle'; bill has same pattern as male's. Juvenile similar to female. In all plumages birds show grey stripe on wings (stripe white in tufted duck).

Pochard
Aythya ferina

Status: Winter visitor/resident; local, more common in winter; **Voice:** Harsh, growling notes; **Length:** 42–49cm; **Wingspan:** 72–82cm; **Habitat:** Well-vegetated pools in summer, open water in winter; **Behaviour:** Mixes with tufted ducks in winter and spends much time diving for food

Male is attractive and distinctive. Bill relatively long and black with broad grey band across middle. Rounded head is reddish-orange and neck and breast black. Underparts and back grey with intricate vermiculations. Stern black. Female has mottled brown and grey-brown plumage, most grey on back. Bill pattern and head shape as male. Usually shows pale 'spectacle' around eye. In flight, wings of both sexes appear rather uniform; belly of female looks pale.

Ferruginous Duck
Aythya nyroca

Status: Resident; local; **Voice:** Female utters high-pitched, repeated 'karri'; **Length:** 38–42cm; **Wingspan:** 63–67cm; **Habitat:** Shallow, well-vegetated lakes and pools; **Behaviour:** Unobtrusive and retiring

Male has rather uniform chocolate-brown plumage with dark back and very conspicuous white stern. Bill grey with dark tip; eye has white iris. Female similar to male but duller with brown iris. Juvenile similar to female but lacks white stern. In flight looks slimmer than tufted duck and shows striking white wingbar; underwings pale.

Ring-necked duck

♀

♂

♀

Pochard

♀

Ferruginous duck

♂

Tufted Duck

Aythya fuligula

Status: Resident/winter visitor; common; **Voice:** Various harsh, growling notes; **Length:** 40–47cm; **Wingspan:** 68–73cm; **Habitat:** Open water, including rivers; **Behaviour:** Dives frequently and for extended periods, often swimming a long way underwater

Male is very distinctive, looking black and white at a distance. In good light dark feathering shows sheen. Bill is grey with white band towards end, and black tip. Iris yellow and head bears crest feathers, which can be raised. Female has mostly brown plumage, slightly paler on belly and flanks. Bill pattern similar to that of male, and iris yellow. Head bears short tuft of feathers, giving it a rather square outline. Some females have white patch at base of bill; this never as extensive as on female scaup. Eclipse male similar to female. In flight, both sexes show white wingbar.

Scaup

Aythya marila

Status: Local breeding species; locally common in winter; **Voice:** Harsh, grating 'karr-karr' while flying; **Length:** 42–51cm; **Wingspan:** 72–83cm; **Habitat:** Breeds on coastal tundra; overwinters in shallow, coastal waters; **Behaviour:** Shallow diver; feeding affected by state of tide

Male is superficially similar to male tufted duck. Can look black, grey and white at a distance, but rounded head has green gloss in good light. Bill grey with black nail at tip and yellow iris. Neck, breast and stern black, belly and flanks white and back soft grey with fine vermiculations. Female has mainly brown plumage but with yellow iris and conspicuous white patches at base of bill and on forehead and cheek. In flight both sexes show white wingbars.

Lesser Scaup

Aythya affinis

Status: Autumn vagrant from North America; **Voice:** Generally silent; **Length:** 40–45cm; **Wingspan:** 65–70cm; **Habitat:** Freshwater wetlands; **Behaviour:** Dives frequently

Buoyant diving duck. Very similar to scaup. At all times useful identification features include lesser scaup's smaller size, its proportionately smaller bill with only small black tip, and its peaked, not rounded, head. Male has dark head and neck, which, in good light, appear purple-glossed. Shows black breast and stern, grey, finely patterned back and pale flanks with faint fine patterning. Female essentially brown; pale feather edging can produce scaly appearance on back and flanks. Shows large white patch at base of bill. Juvenile and first-winter birds similar to adult female but with white on face reduced or absent. In flight all birds show broad white band on secondaries; on scaup white extends on to primaries.

ECLIPSE ♂

Tufted duck

♀

♂

Scaup

♀

♂

Lesser scaup

♂

COMPARING DUCKS IN FLIGHT

Ducks seen at a distance and in flight can often be frustratingly difficult to identify. Observers should concentrate on the overall body proportions, the relative size and the presence of any distinctive colours or patterns on the body and, more particularly, on the wing speculum. Female ducks are generally more of a challenge to identify than males, but fortunately a clue to their identity can often be gained from their association with males of their kind.

WIGEON: Compact and rather dumpy. Male shows conspicuous white patch on leading edge of inner upperwing and white belly; stern looks strikingly black and white. Female lacks conspicuous markings on wings but shows pale belly. Outside breeding season invariably seen in single-species flock

MALLARD: Both sexes show bright, iridescent blue speculum on innerwing, bordered on leading and trailing edges by narrow white border; underwings appear uniformly whitish. Body of female is uniformly brown and streaked, while that of male shows clear colour demarcations between head, neck and body

GADWALL: Body plumage of male appears uniformly grey except for black stern and bill; wings show diagnostic white speculum, defined and bordered by black. Female similar to female mallard but has pale belly and suggestion of white on speculum

TUFTED DUCK: Male in particular looks strikingly black and white, white appearing on belly and on extended wingbar. Female similar to male but contrast between dark and light elements of plumage less sharp

PINTAIL: Male's elongated shape is diagnostic; equally striking are black and yellow stern and dark head, contrasting with white sides to neck and white belly. Female also looks elongated but appears buffish-brown. Both sexes have indistinct speculum bordered by prominent white bands; underwings variably mottled with brown

♀

♂

SHOVELER: Male's green, white, orange and black body is striking, as is proportionately large bill; upper surface of innerwing shows blue leading edge separated from green speculum by white band. Female has front-heavy proportions of male but uniformly mottled brown plumage; underwings appear whitish

♂

♀

TEAL: Tiny duck, which, when alarmed, rises almost vertically from water. Head of male can look dark when seen against sky; it contrasts with paler, grey body plumage. Female appears uniformly grey-brown in flight. Both sexes show pale underwing and green speculum bordered by white on leading and trailing edges

♀

♂

GARGANEY: Poor flight views can lead to confusion with teal but male's striking head pattern is diagnostic. Pattern on male's upperwing similar to that of male shoveler with pale-blue leading edge separated from green speculum by white band. Female's wing pattern similar to male's but colours less intense; body plumage brown but paler on belly

♂

♀

POCHARD: Appears bulky and thick-set. Male distinctive with grey wings and belly, black stern and neck and reddish head. female's pattern less contrasting than male's but head and neck always dark and clearly demarcated from paler belly and wings

♂

♀

Eider

♂

♀

Eider

Somateria mollissima

Status: Resident; **Voice:** Male utters humorous 'ah-whooo' during breeding season; otherwise silent; **Length:** 50–71cm; **Wingspan:** 80–105cm; **Habitat:** Coastal waters, usually close to shore; **Behaviour:** Females nest on undisturbed beaches and grassland; young are led to sea immediately on hatching

Distinctive coastal duck with dumpy body and wedge-shaped bill following line of forehead. Mature male is unmistakable, with black and white markings on body; also shows lime-green markings on head and pink flush to breast. Full plumage not acquired until fourth year. Female has mottled brown plumage, looking rather barred on flanks. In flight both sexes look heavy and ponderous with slightly drooping neck. Flies low over the water in lines.

Spectacled Eider

Somateria fischeri

Status: Rare winter vagrant; **Voice:** Generally silent; **Length:** 54–56cm; **Wingspan:** 85–90cm; **Habitat:** Breeds on tundra; otherwise in Arctic seas; **Behaviour:** Similar to eider

Male has black breast and underparts. Upperparts mainly white except for dark rump; flight feathers black. Head shows black 'spectacle' line around eye bordered in front and behind by dull lime-green patches of feathers. Bill orange-pink. Female has essentially brown plumage with darker barring. Head shows conspicuous pale patch around eye, corresponding to 'spectacle' of male; bordered at front by dark feathering on lores. Bill dark grey. Eclipse male and juvenile similar to adult female. Immature male takes three years to acquire full adult plumage.

Eider

ADULT MALE, BREEDING

ADULT MALE, ECLIPSE

IMMATURE MALE, FIRST WINTER

IMMATURE MALE, FIRST AUTUMN

JUVENILE

Spectacled eider

King Eider
Somateria spectabilis

Status: Winter visitor; scarce; **Voice:** Male utters cooing calls during courtship; otherwise mostly silent; **Length:** 48–63cm; **Wingspan:** 85–100cm; **Habitat:** Breeds on Arctic tundra; in winter, on northern coasts; **Behaviour:** Gathers in flocks for winter, feeding in sheltered coastal waters

Mature adult male is striking and unmistakable. Red bill is expanded at base into basal knob. Head proportionately large with square outline; marked with pale blue-grey and green, the areas of colour outlined in black. Rest of body plumage black and white; shows two sickle-shaped 'sails' on back. Female similar to female eider with mottled and barred brown plumage; bill proportionately smaller and shows pale patches on cheeks and around eye.

Steller's Eider
Polysticta stelleri

Status: Winter visitor/resident; locally common; **Voice:** Mostly silent; non-vocal whistling sound made by wings in flight; **Length:** 43–47cm; **Wingspan:** 70–75cm; **Habitat:** Breeds on Arctic tundra; in winter, on sheltered coasts; **Behaviour:** Extremely sociable outside breeding season, flocks feeding off rocky shores and diving with ease

Small eider with comparatively small bill. Mature adult male is unmistakable. Looks mainly black and white at a distance. At closer range rounded head has green feather patches on forehead and rear of crown; eye emphasised by black patch and has black under chin and as collar. Body plumage mainly black and white but has pinkish-orange tinge to belly, variable in intensity, and a circular black mark on side of flanks, visible at water level when swimming. Female has dark-brown plumage, but bill size and head outline similar to male.

Harlequin Duck
Histrionicus histrionicus

Status: Resident; rare (Iceland only); **Voice:** Occasionally utters high-pitched squeals but otherwise mostly silent; **Length:** 38–45cm; **Wingspan:** 63–69cm; **Habitat:** In summer, on fast-flowing rivers; in winter, around coasts; **Behaviour:** Favours roughest possible water at all times

Male is attractive and distinctive. Plumage mainly a mixture of blue and deep red with bold white stripes and spots on head and body. Female has more subdued, dark-brown plumage with white patch between base of bill and eye, and white spot behind eye. Eclipse male similar to female. Flies low over the water with fast, whirring wingbeats.

King eider

♂

♀

Steller's eider

♀

♂

Harlequin duck

♀

♂

Common Scoter

Melanitta nigra

Status: Rare breeding species; locally common in winter; **Voice:** Mostly silent but male utters quiet whistles in breeding season; **Length:** 44–54cm; **Wingspan:** 80–90cm; **Habitat:** Breeds on upland moors and tundra; overwinters around coasts; **Behaviour:** Dives well and swims buoyantly, favouring inshore waters in winter

Classic sea duck that can look all dark at a distance. Male has black plumage with black and yellow bill. Female has dark-brown plumage but much paler cheeks that show up well even at a distance or in flight. Invariably seen in flocks outside breeding season. Migrating flocks seen flying low over water, sometimes in lines but also in more tightly bunched packs with trailing stragglers.

Surf Scoter

Melanitta perspicillata

Status: Winter vagrant from North America; **Voice:** Mostly silent; **Length:** 45–55cm; **Wingspan:** 80–90cm; **Habitat:** Breeds on tundra and taiga forest; overwinters on coastal waters; **Behaviour:** Invariably seen with common scoters; vagrants usually stay for several months

Attractive diving duck. All birds show proportionately large, flat-topped head and proportionately large bill that slopes at angle continuous with that of forehead. Male is all black except for white nape patch and white on forehead; eye has white iris. Bill pattern diagnostic: mainly orange but with larger white patch at base, inside which is smaller black patch. Orange legs sometimes revealed on swimming birds when roll-preening. First-winter male has bill pattern of adult male but plumage similar to female. Female uniform brown except for pale patches on head, one at base of bill, other behind pale eye; pale nape patch seen in some birds. Juvenile similar to female but paler.

Velvet Scoter

Melanitta fusca

Status: Rare breeding species; locally common in winter; **Voice:** Male utters whistling call in breeding season and female has grating call; silent at other times of year; **Length:** 51–58cm; **Wingspan:** 90–100cm; **Habitat:** Breeds on coastal moors and tundra; overwinters in coastal waters; **Behaviour:** In winter often seen with common scoters

Male has all-black plumage but is readily identified, even when among common scoters, by conspicuous white eye and white patch below eye. Bill black and yellow. Female has brown plumage with white patches between eye and base of bill and behind eye. In flight both sexes show extremely conspicuous white wing patches; these are occasionally visible on swimming birds.

Common scoter

♀

♂

Surf scoter

♂

Velvet scoter

♂

Long-tailed Duck
Clangula hyemalis

Status: Resident/winter visitor; locally common; **Voice:** Very vocal, males having musical calls; **Length:** 40–47cm + male tail length; **Wingspan:** 73–79cm; **Habitat:** Breeds on tundra; overwinters on sea coasts; **Behaviour:** Forms restless flocks in winter, often favouring the roughest water

 An attractive seaduck with a distinctive outline. Plumage a mixture of black, white and brown but varies throughout year. Male has dark bill with pink band and long central tail feathers, often cocked upwards. In summer, head, neck and breast dark except for white patch around eye. Shows brown back and white underparts. In winter male has much more white in plumage, face having buff flush and dark cheeks. Female lacks male's long tail and has grey bill. In summer upperparts mostly brown and underparts white. In winter body brown but head white with dark markings.

Barrow's Goldeneye
Bucephala islandica

Status: Resident; very local (Iceland only); **Voice:** Grunting calls accompany courting male's display; otherwise silent; **Length:** 42–52cm; **Wingspan:** 67–85cm; **Habitat:** Breeds on Arctic lakes and rivers; in winter on coastal Arctic lakes and rivers and also inshore seas; **Behaviour:** In spring males display with much head-bobbing and splashing

Similar to goldeneye but distinguished, even in silhouette, by steep, rounded forehead and relatively short, broad bill. Male has dark head with purple gloss and white crescent shape in front of yellow eye. Underparts mainly white and upperparts and stern dark; back shows small patches of white. Female has dark-brown head; eye yellow. Body plumage grey-brown, underparts paler. In flight both sexes show less white on innerwing than goldeneye.

Goldeneye
Bucephala clangula

Status: Winter visitor/resident; locally common; **Voice:** Creaking display call but otherwise silent; **Length:** 42–50cm; **Wingspan:** 65–80cm; **Habitat:** Breeds beside northern, wooded lakes; in winter on lakes and reservoirs, occasionally on coasts; **Behaviour:** Winter flocks dive frequently; nests in tree-holes and perches in trees

Superb diving duck with peaked-cap profile to head, readily seen even in silhouette. Male has dark head with greenish sheen, white circular patch at base of bill and yellow eye. Body plumage mostly white except for dark back and stern. Female has reddish-brown head and dark-grey bill with pink patch near tip. Body plumage mainly grey-brown except for paler underparts and white neck. In flight both sexes have white patches on upper surface of innerwing.

♂

♀

WINTER ♀

Long-tailed duck

WINTER ♂

JUVENILE

FIRST-WINTER MALES

♀

Barrow's goldeneye

♂

♀

Goldeneye

♂

Smew
Mergus albellus

Status: Rare breeding species; more widespread in winter;
Voice: Mainly silent; **Length:** 38–44cm; **Wingspan:** 55–70cm;
Habitat: In breeding season favours wooded lakes;
overwinters on lakes, reservoirs and sheltered coasts;
Behaviour: Nests in tree-holes; forms small flocks in winter

Small sawbill duck with narrow bill bearing serrated
edges. Male is distinctive and attractive with mainly
white plumage but with black lines on body, around eye and
on back; at close range, fine grey markings visible on flank.
Female has grey-brown plumage, reddish-brown cap and
white cheeks and chin. Immature drake resembles female. In
flight both sexes show white bars on wings.

Red-breasted Merganser
Mergus serrator

Status: Resident; locally common; **Voice:** Mostly silent;
Length: 52–58cm; **Wingspan:** 70–85cm; **Habitat:** Breeds on
northern lakes and rivers; in winter, mainly in coastal waters
Behaviour: Overwinters on large, ice-free lakes as well as
around coasts

Slim-bodied duck with long, narrow sawbill. Male has
red bill, legs and eyes. Head dark green with untidy
tufts on nape. Neck white and breast reddish-brown.
Underparts grey and finely marked, and back black and
white. Female has red bill and reddish head. Rest of body
plumage mainly grey-brown, although underparts paler. In
flight both sexes show white on innerwing; less extensive on
female and divided by black bar.

Goosander
Mergus merganser

Status: Resident; locally common; **Voice:** Ringing calls
uttered by displaying male; otherwise silent; **Length:**
58–66cm; **Wingspan:** 82–96cm; **Habitat:** Breeds beside
northern lakes and rivers; in winter, favours lakes, reservoirs
and sheltered coasts; **Behaviour:** Swims buoyantly and dives
well and frequently; bobbing and water-rushing feature in
spring display

Large sawbill duck. Male is attractive and distinctive.
At a distance can look black and white. At closer range
and in good light head has greenish gloss and white on body
plumage suffused with pink. Bill red; lower back and tail grey.
Female similar to female red-breasted merganser but has
more elegant, reddish-brown head. Throat and neck white
and body plumage mainly grey-brown with paler underparts.
In flight, female shows undivided white speculum and male
has white innerwing.

Smew

♀

♂

Red-breasted merganser

♂

♀

Goosander

♀

♂

White-headed Duck

Oxyura leucocephala

Status: Resident; rare; **Voice:** Mostly silent; **Length:** 43–48cm; **Wingspan:** 62–70cm; **Habitat:** Shallow, well-vegetated lakes and pools; both freshwater and brackish; **Behaviour:** Often swims with tail cocked in the air; when diving stays submerged half a minute or more

A stifftail duck, superficially similar to ruddy duck but larger. Male is distinctive with white head, black cap and eye and disproportionately large blue bill with strangely swollen base. Body plumage mainly brown. Female has brown body plumage and bill similar in shape to male's but dark grey in colour. Head shows dark-brown cap down to level of eye and white face with dark line running from base of bill.

Ruddy Duck

Oxyura jamaicensis

Status: Introduced to Britain but now resident there; localised; **Voice:** Mostly silent; **Length:** 35–43cm; **Wingspan:** 53–62cm; **Habitat:** Well-vegetated ponds, lakes and reservoirs; **Behaviour:** Dives frequently like a little grebe; retiring during breeding season

A so-called stifftail duck that often lives up to its name by raising its relatively long tail in the air. Male has mainly orange-brown plumage but with black cap, white face and bright-blue bill; stern white. Female has mainly grey-brown plumage but similar, distinctive outline. Often shows pale cheeks broken by dark line from base of bill. Seldom seen in flight.

White-headed duck

♂

♂

Ruddy duck

♀

♂

WINTER ♂

Black-shouldered Kite
Elanus caeruleus

Status: Resident; rare; **Voice:** Mostly silent but utters thin scream in alarm; **Length:** 31–35cm; **Wingspan:** 75–83cm; **Habitat:** Dry, open country with scattered trees; **Behaviour:** Perches on trees or telegraph poles for long periods

Small, pale raptor. Sexes similar. Seen perched, looks rather large-headed and short-tailed. Upperparts mostly pale grey and underparts white. Head looks superficially owl-like and has staring red eyes with black 'eyebrows'. Has black-tipped yellow bill and yellow legs. At rest black patch on innerwing shows as a black 'shoulder'. In flight, which is buoyant and graceful, black wingtips and black on leading edge of innerwing conspicuous. Often hovers or glides with wings in 'V' shape.

Red Kite
Milvus milvus

Status: Resident; common; **Voice:** Shrill, quavering 'weoo-weoo-weoo'; **Length:** 60–65cm; **Wingspan:** 155–185cm; **Habitat:** Typically associated with wooded valleys adjacent to areas of farmland or open country; **Behaviour:** Tends to feed on carrion and therefore at risk of poisoning

Attractive bird of prey with mainly reddish-brown plumage, paler, greyish head and deeply forked tail. Has black-tipped yellow bill and yellow legs. Sexes similar. In flight, soars effortlessly, often with wings slightly kinked forwards. Seen from below, body and leading edge of innerwing are reddish. Wings are long and show translucent pale-grey patch near tips; tail pale grey. Seen from above, tail is orange-red and brown innerwings contrast with dark flight feathers.

Black Kite
Milvus migrans

Status: Summer visitor; widespread; **Voice:** Gull-like whinnying call; **Length:** 55–60cm; **Wingspan:** 145–165cm; **Habitat:** Wooded lakes and open country; **Behaviour:** Skilled aeronaut; in some parts of region will visit rubbish dumps and markets

In flight most easily confused with female marsh harrier. Sexes similar. Plumage mainly dark brown and can look all black in poor light. Head rather paler than body. Has black-tipped yellow bill and yellow legs. Wings relatively long and broad and held flat when circling. Tail forked, but not as deeply as red kite's; constantly twisted in flight to assist control.

Black-shouldered kite

Red kite

Black kite

White-tailed Eagle
Haliaeetus albicilla

Status: Resident; local; **Voice:** Yelping call; **Length:** 70–90cm; **Wingspan:** 200–240cm; **Habitat:** Associated with sea coasts and extensive wetlands; **Behaviour:** Seldom flies very high; specialises in catching ducks and geese in winter

Largest raptor likely to be seen in northern Europe. In flight has immense wingspan with broad, parallel-sided wings, which are square-ended with primaries resembling splayed fingers. Tail relatively short and broad; white in adult birds but dark in juveniles. When seen perched, yellow legs and bill can be seen in adult; juvenile bill dark but yellow at the base. Adult head looks paler than body.

Lammergeier
Gypaetus barbatus

Status: Resident; rare; **Voice:** Mostly silent; **Length:** 100–115cm; **Wingspan:** 265–280cm; **Habitat:** Mountainous regions, often near gorges and ravines; **Behaviour:** Will drop bones from great height to get at marrow

Very distinctive bird of prey with very long and comparatively narrow wings and long, wedge-shaped tail. Seen in good light, adults show orange-buff head and underparts; wings and tail black. At close range, black patch around orange eye can be seen along with black moustache-like feathers. Juvenile has similar flight silhouette to adult but is all dark.

Egyptian Vulture
Neophron percnopterus

Status: Summer visitor; rare; **Voice:** Mostly silent; **Length:** 60–70cm; **Wingspan:** 155–180cm; **Habitat:** Mountainous regions; **Behaviour:** Can be seen rising to great heights on thermals from mid-morning

In flight, silhouette recalls a miniature lammergeier with its wedge-shaped tail; wings proportionately broader and shorter than this species. Sexes similar. Seen from below, adult has black flight feathers that contrast with otherwise rather grubby white plumage; at close range, black-tipped yellow bill, bald yellow face and yellow legs visible. Juvenile similar to adult in shape but all dark; full adult plumage acquired gradually over four years or so.

White-tailed eagle

Lammergeier

Egyptian vulture

Griffon Vulture
Gyps fulvus

Status: Resident; locally common; **Voice:** Utters croaking calls near nest or roost; silent in flight; **Length:** 95–105cm; **Wingspan:** 260–280cm; **Habitat:** Warm, mountainous regions; **Behaviour:** Able to soar for hours; dependent on rising thermals

Large vulture, adult with buffish-brown body plumage contrasting with dark flight feathers; contrast visible from above and below in flight and on perched birds. Sexes similar. When standing looks hunched up, with wings almost touching ground. Head and neck bald and whitish but sometimes stained; has collar of ruffled feathers. In flight looks small-headed and short-tailed. Wings long and broad, narrowing towards tips and showing pale barring against brown underwing coverts; soars with wings held in shallow 'V'. Juvenile similar to adult but underwing coverts rather pale with dark barring.

Black Vulture
Aegypius monachus

Status: Resident; rare; **Voice:** Mostly silent; **Length:** 100–110cm; **Wingspan:** 250–290cm; **Habitat:** Seen at towering heights over all sorts of broken terrain, especially near mountains; **Behaviour:** Takes precedence over other scavengers at carcasses

Huge raptor with immense wingspan. Flight silhouette distinctive with long, broad and parallel-sided wings, which are square-ended but show splayed 'fingers' of primary feathers; soars with wings held flat. Head appears relatively small and tail is usually slightly fanned. Sexes similar. Plumage mostly dark brown but invariably appears all black because of distance at which most birds are seen. Seen at close range, has huge, black-tipped bill and bald head and neck with ruffled collar of feathers. Juvenile difficult to separate from adult in the field.

Short-toed Eagle
Circaetus gallicus

Status: Summer visitor; locally common in south; **Voice:** Fluting calls by male, harsher notes from female; **Length:** 62–67cm; **Wingspan:** 170–185cm; **Habitat:** Dry, open habitats, with some maquis, garigue or scattered trees; **Behaviour:** Preys on snakes; usually hunts by hovering or quartering low over the ground

Large, pale raptor, usually seen hovering or using updraught, when underparts look very white. Wings broad and quite long in proportion to body size; tail narrow and square-ended. Darker head gives hooded appearance. Sexes have similar plumages but female is larger than male. May be confused with osprey, but does not show dark carpal patches.

Griffon vulture

Black vulture

Short-toed eagle

Marsh Harrier
Circus aeruginosus

Status: Resident/summer visitor; locally common; **Voice:** Plaintive, shrill 'kweeoo'; **Length:** 50–55cm; **Wingspan:** 115–130cm; **Habitat:** Reedbeds and wetlands; **Behaviour:** Usually seen in flight low over ground, often with legs dangling

 Graceful bird of prey with relatively long wings and long tail. Seen from above, male has dark-brown back and wing coverts that contrast with blue-grey flight feathers and tail. Wingtips black, and head and leading edge of innerwing pale grey-buff. Seen from below, underwing blue-grey except for black wingtips, body dark brown and tail grey. Female has mostly chocolate-brown plumage except for pale-buff forehead and cap, throat and leading edge to innerwing. Juvenile resembles female but pale markings less distinct.

Hen Harrier
Circus cyaneus

Status: Resident/winter visitor; widespread; **Voice:** Rapid, chattering 'ke-ke-ke' heard in nesting territory; otherwise silent; **Length:** 45–50cm; **Wingspan:** 100–120cm; **Habitat:** Breeds on northern and upland moors and bogs; overwinters in lowland, open terrain, often coastal; **Behaviour:** Flight pattern leisurely with long glides; holds wings in 'V'

Elegant and graceful bird of prey. Male has mainly pale grey plumage, feathers on breast and belly being palest of all. Wingtips contrastingly black, and shows conspicuous white rump in flight. At close range and when perched reveals yellow iris, black-tipped yellow bill and yellow legs. Female has brown plumage with owl-like facial disc and streaked underparts; shows conspicuous white rump in flight and strongly barred tail and underwing. Juvenile similar to female.

Pallid Harrier
Circus macrourus

Status: Summer visitor/partial resident; local; **Voice:** Whistling calls uttered near nest; otherwise generally silent; **Length:** 44–46cm; **Wingspan:** 100–15cm; **Habitat:** Grassland; **Behaviour:** Usually seen in buoyant, low-level flight

Similar in all plumages to corresponding plumages of Montagu's and hen harriers. In flight all birds show more pointed wingtips than other harriers due to very short first and second primaries. Male appears uniformly pale grey, often almost white, in flight except for conspicuous black wingtips. Lacks male hen and Montagu's harriers' dark-hooded appearance. Legs, base of bill and iris yellow. Female similar to female hen and Montagu's harriers; facial pattern is more contrasting than on those species. Juvenile not readily separable from juvenile Montagu's harrier but facial marking more contrastingly dark and light.

Marsh harrier

♂

♀

Hen harrier

♂

♀

Pallid harrier

♂

Montagu's Harrier
Circus pygargus

Status: Summer visitor; locally common; **Voice:** High-pitched 'yik-yik-yik' over breeding ground; otherwise silent; **Length:** 40–45cm; **Wingspan:** 105–120cm; **Habitat:** Uses variety of habitats during breeding season including wetlands, arable fields, young plantations, heaths and moors; **Behaviour:** Flies low over the ground, often very slowly

Both sexes superficially similar to hen harrier but wings look proportionately longer and more pointed. Male has mainly pale-grey plumage, palest on breast and belly. Seen from below, shows extensive black wingtips, two black wingbars and fainter, reddish wingbars on coverts; seen from above, has black wingtips, single black wingbar and white rump, less conspicuous than rump on male hen harrier. Female very similar to female hen harrier and best separated by smaller white rump and wing shape. Juvenile similar to female but, seen from below, body and wing coverts reddish-orange.

Goshawk
Accipiter gentilis

Status: Resident; locally common; **Voice:** Rapid, hoarse 'gek-gek-gek' at nest; otherwise silent; **Length:** 50–60cm; **Wingspan:** 125–150cm; **Habitat:** Extensive forests, often pine or beech; **Behaviour:** Shy; solitary outside breeding season

Large, dashing hawk, the female similar in size to buzzard. Smaller male can be confused with female sparrowhawk but note goshawk's bulkier body, shorter tail relative to body size and longer wings, often held in an 'S' curve. Seen from below, both sexes look pale with grey barring on body, wings and tail; fluffy white feathers at base of tail often conspicuous. Plumages of both sexes rather similar, with grey-brown upperparts and prominent pale supercilium above staring yellow eye. Feet and legs yellow with black talons. Juvenile has streaked underparts and less uniform upperparts.

Montagu's harrier

♂

♂

♀

Goshawk

Sparrowhawk
Accipiter nisus

Status: Resident; common; **Voice:** Harsh 'kek-kek-kek-kek'; **Length:** 30–40cm; **Wingspan:** 55–75cm; **Habitat:** Mixed woodland, farmland with hedgerows; increasingly in urban areas; **Behaviour:** Often seen in low-level, dashing flight

When soaring, relatively short, rounded wings and long tail are apparent. Male considerably smaller than female and has blue-grey upperparts and whitish underparts, bearing strong reddish-orange barring on body and underwing coverts. Undertail feathers white and tail barred. Female has grey-brown upperparts and whitish underparts with grey-brown barring. At close range both sexes show yellow legs and black-tipped yellow bill; iris of male orange, that of female yellow. Juvenile similar to female but with streaked underparts.

Levant Sparrowhawk
Accipiter brevipes

Status: Summer visitor; local; best seen on migration; **Voice:** Harsh screaming call uttered near nest; **Length:** 33–36cm; **Wingspan:** 65–75cm; **Habitat:** Warm, dry woodland and farmland; **Behaviour:** Often circles at low levels before dropping to catch insects or lizards

Dashing raptor, superficially similar to sparrowhawk. Male seen in flight appears very pale underneath except for pinkish flush to breast, black wingtips and dark barring on tail. At rest, head and back appear uniformly blue-grey; shows white throat, white vent and faint pinkish barring on breast and belly. Iris red. Female similar but barring on underparts more prominent. When seen in flight from below, black wingtips contrast with otherwise pale wings. Juvenile recalls female but has teardrop-shaped dark spots and streaks on breast and belly; underwings show dark barring.

Honey Buzzard
Pernis apivorus

Status: Summer visitor; common; **Voice:** Thin, mournful call, seldom heard; **Length:** 50–60cm; **Wingspan:** 135–160cm; **Habitat:** Breeds in mature woodland; **Behaviour:** Frequently soar over forests with characteristically flat wings

Invariably seen in flight and seldom on ground or perched. Sexes similar. Colour rather variable but usually dark brown above and pale underneath with dark barring. Seen from below in flight, wings are long and broad, tail is relatively long and head proportionately long and cuckoo-like. Shows pale throat but heavy barring from neck to base of tail; tail itself has several dark bars and conspicuous dark terminal band. On wings flight feathers have dark tips and are barred, as are coverts. Dark patches on forewing are characteristic. At close range pale head, yellow eyes and yellow legs can be seen.

Sparrowhawk

♂

♀

Levant sparrowhawk

♂

Honey buzzard

Buzzard
Buteo buteo

Status: Resident; common; **Voice:** Mewing 'peeioo'; **Length:** 50–55cm; **Wingspan:** 115–130cm; **Habitat:** Hilly country, open farmland with adjacent woodland; **Behaviour:** Often seen perched in the open

Medium-sized bird of prey. Sexes similar. Colour extremely variable but almost always some shade of brown. Soars on broad, rounded wings held in a 'V', with barred tail fanned out. Upperparts, including wings, usually dark brown, although flight feathers contrastingly dark in paler birds. Seen from below, wings and tail barred, the trailing edge of wings and terminal edge of tail noticeably dark. Some birds show dark collar and dark carpal patches. At close range black-tipped yellow bill and yellow legs visible Occasionally birds with almost pure white plumage are seen.

Rough-legged Buzzard
Buteo lagopus

Status: Resident; local; **Voice:** Similar mew to buzzard's but louder and lower; **Length:** 50–60cm; **Wingspan:** 120–150cm; **Habitat:** Nests on tundra; in winter, on marshes, moors and downs; **Behaviour:** Very dependent on small mammals for food, so numbers and distribution variable

Superficially similar to buzzard in silhouette but slightly larger and with proportionately longer wings and tail. Like this species, soars on raised wings, but also regularly hovers. Sexes similar. Seen from below, typically shows dark and white pattern: has dark belly patch, dark carpal patches on wings and tail with faint barring towards tip and broad, dark terminal band. Seen from above, conspicuous pale base to tail appears as white rump. Seen perched, dark belly often noticeable and head can look pale, especially in young birds.

Long-legged Buzzard
Buteo rufinus

Status: Resident/summer visitor; rare; **Voice:** Mewing call similar to buzzard's; **Length:** 50–65cm; **Wingspan:** 130–150cm; **Habitat:** Arid mountainous terrain and semi-desert; **Behaviour:** Perches in open more than other buzzard

Large, rufous-looking but generally pale buzzard. Sexes similar. Adult plumage variable but perched birds generally show pale head and breast; latter separated from pale vent and undertail by broad rufous band across belly. Mantle rufous and flight feathers dark. Seen from below in flight, shows reddish-brown underwing coverts and dark carpal patches; flight feathers white but with contrasting black tips to primaries and black trailing edge to secondaries From above reddish-brown mantle and upperwing coverts contrast with dark flight feathers. Juvenile similar to adult but with faint barring on tail.

Buzzard

Rough-legged buzzard

Long-legged buzzard

Lesser Spotted Eagle
Aquila pomarina

Status: Summer visitor; rare; **Voice:** High-pitched yapping call; **Length:** 57–65cm; **Wingspan:** 135–160cm; **Habitat:** In European breeding range, favours forests adjacent to wetlands; **Behaviour:** Often seen in low-level, laboured flight as well as soaring; perches on posts by feeding areas

Comparatively small eagle but with proportionately long, parallel-sided wings, which appear rather square-ended in soaring flight with 'fingers' of primaries clearly visible. Sexes similar. From below can look all dark; in good light flight feathers always darker than brown body feathers in both adults and juveniles, a good feature for separating from greater spotted eagle. Seen from above, adult shows tail and flight feathers darker than body feathers, narrow white band on base of tail and white 'shafts' on inner primaries. Juvenile similar to adult but has numerous white spots on inner flight feathers.

Greater Spotted Eagle
Aquila clanga

Status: Summer visitor/partial resident; rare; **Voice:** Yapping call near nest; **Length:** 62–75cm; **Wingspan:** 160–180cm; **Habitat:** Forest and scattered woodland close to wetland; **Behaviour:** Feeds on carrion but also catches prey in active low-level flight

Appreciably larger than lesser spotted eagle, but this not always easy to see in distant, solitary birds. Best feature for separation in flight seen from below is greyish flight feathers, which appear paler than rest of feathering on wings and body (converse true in lesser spotted eagle). Sexes similar. Seen from above, adult plumage looks all dark; that of juvenile shows heavy white spotting on wing coverts and inner flight feathers with white 'shafts' on all primaries.

Booted Eagle
Hieraaetus pennatus

Status: Summer visitor; locally common; **Voice:** Various whistling and cackling calls; **Length:** 45–50cm; **Wingspan:** 100–130cm; **Habitat:** Wooded mountain slopes, open hilly country; **Behaviour:** Vocal near nest site; sometimes hunts in pairs

The smallest European eagle, occurring in a pale and dark form. Sexes similar. Pale form has pale underparts and wings except for dark flight feathers, dark-grey tail and greyish-buff head. Dark form varies from red-brown to blackish-brown, with buff tail darkening towards tip. Both dark and pale forms show a pale 'V' on upperparts formed by median upperwing coverts. May be confused with buzzard, but primary feathers in outstretched wings appear as typical eagle 'fingers'.

Lesser spotted eagle

JUVENILE

ADULT

Greater spotted eagle

JUVENILE

ADULT

Booted eagle

PALE FORM

DARK FORM

Golden Eagle
Aquila chrysaetos

Status: Resident; widespread; **Voice:** Mostly silent, but some yelping calls, rarely heard; **Length:** 76–89cm; **Wingspan:** 190–227cm; **Habitat:** Mountainous regions, lowland forests and marshes where human habitation is absent; **Behaviour:** Elaborate aerial displays seen in winter and early spring

Large eagle with long tail and long, broad wings held in a shallow 'V' when soaring and gliding. Looks dark from below but shows buff, grey and dark-brown markings from above with paler head. Strong wingbeats are followed by one to two-second glides in normal flight, but prey may be surprised by a steep dive, or low-level glide. Immatures have white wing patches and white tail with dark terminal band. Adult plumage attained after five to seven years.

Spanish Imperial Eagle
Aquila adalberti

Status: Resident; rare; considered by some authorities to be race of imperial eagle; **Voice:** Repeated, harsh barking call; **Length:** 75–85cm; **Wingspan:** 180–215cm; **Habitat:** Open woodland and fields; **Behaviour:** Spends much of the day sitting unobtrusively in trees

Immense and impressive raptor. Seen in flight, wings look relatively long and parallel-sided; tail not normally fanned. Adult can look all dark but in good light shows dark-brown plumage and white markings on scapulars and leading edge of innerwing; crown and nape are pale buff. Juvenile has pale-brown plumage except for dark flight feathers and tail; shows heavy white spotting on upper surface of flight feathers and, in good light, teardrop spots on wing coverts.

Imperial Eagle
Aquila heliaca

Status: Resident; rare; **Voice:** Deep raven-like 'gahk'; **Length:** 75–84cm; **Wingspan:** 180–215cm; **Habitat:** Mediterranean steppe; mixed lowland habitats with some tall trees; **Behaviour:** Spends much time sitting on low perch, but makes feeding forays at high altitude

Immense, relatively long-winged raptor with white scapular patches. Adult is a very dark bird showing creamy-buff nape and greyish tail with a dark terminal band. Wings are long and narrow and held flat when soaring, but may be slightly raised with a flat tip when gliding. Tail appears long and narrow in adults, but juveniles show a more spread tail when soaring. Juvenile brownish-red, fading to paler buff-brown with streaked breast.

Golden eagle

FIRST WINTER

ADULT

ADULT

Spanish imperial eagle

Imperial eagle

Bonelli's Eagle
Hieraaetus fasciatus

Status: Resident; local; **Voice:** Shrill, piping calls; **Length:** 65–70cm; **Wingspan:** 150–170cm; **Habitat:** Mountainous and hilly country in Mediterranean region; sometimes marshes; **Behaviour:** Often hunts in pairs, using the same hunting areas every day

Adults are distinctive with very pale belly, dark terminal band to long tail, and contrasting dark underwings; lesser underwing coverts are whitish and flight feathers greyish at base, giving distinctive pattern, but general effect is of dark wings. Variable pale patch shows on upper back. Wingbeats are quick and shallow, with wings held level and slightly forwards when soaring. When gliding, wings are gently arched and show straight rear edge. Juveniles are pale pinkish-brown below and darker on back.

Osprey
Pandion haliaetus

Status: Summer visitor; widespread; **Voice:** Shrill piping and yelping calls; **Length:** 55–69cm; **Wingspan:** 145–160cm; **Habitat:** Rivers, lakes, coastal areas; **Behaviour:** Feeds on fish; dives at great speed

Large, long-winged bird of prey, looking very pale below. Dark primaries and carpal patches give the underwing a distinctive pattern; the pale head has a dark eye band, and females and juveniles have a darker breast band on a buff background. The long tail has a broad, dark terminal band and three to four narrower dark bands.

Merlin
Falco columbarius

Status: Resident; common; most widespread in winter; **Voice:** Shrill 'kek kek kek'; **Length:** 25–30cm; **Wingspan:** 60–65cm; **Habitat:** Moorland, upland bogs; lowland heaths, coastal marshes in winter; **Behaviour:** Flies low over ground, surprising small birds which it then pursues acrobatically

The smallest European bird of prey, with a neat, light outline. Wings appear short and relatively broad, but tail looks long and square-ended. Resembles small peregrine. Male greyish-blue above with reddish-buff underside. Female noticeably larger than male, dark brown above and strongly patterned below. Juvenile resembles female but is darker with white patches on nape.

Bonelli's eagle

Osprey

Merlin

♀

♂

Lesser Kestrel
Falco naumanni

Status: Summer visitor/resident; local; **Voice:** Rasping two- or three-note calls and trilling notes at colonies;
Length: 29–32cm; **Wingspan:** 58–72cm; **Habitat:** Mediterranean region; cultivated country, villages;
Behaviour: Nest colonially and often hunt together; hover less than other kestrels

Small falcon with narrow wings and a longish, slender tail. Male strongly coloured with unspotted chestnut back, blue-grey innerwing and hood and pale-grey tail with dark terminal band. Female slightly larger and has chestnut colouring with dark spotting on the feathers; tail more barred than in male and primaries dark. Juvenile resembles female. In all stages claws are pale, not dark as in kestrel.

Kestrel
Falco tinnunculus

Status: Resident; common; **Voice:** Piercing 'kee-kee-kee', especially at nest site; **Length:** 33–39cm; **Wingspan:** 65–75cm; **Habitat:** Cultivated country, heaths, moorland, roadsides and towns; **Behaviour:** Hovers in fixed position on rapidly beating wings; drops vertically on to prey

When hovering has characteristic long-tailed silhouette and downward-looking head. Male is colourful with spotted brick-red back, black primaries and grey tail and head. Female more uniform with heavily spotted chestnut plumage, barred tail and brownish streaked head. At a distance sexes can appear similar. Juvenile resembles female but is more streaked on the underside.

Hobby
Falco subbuteo

Status: Summer visitor; common; **Voice:** Sharp, scolding 'kew kew kew kew kew'; **Length:** 28–35cm; **Wingspan:** 75–90cm; **Habitat:** Open habitats, marshes, heathlands; **Behaviour:** Expert at catching large insects on the wing, usually high up

Powerful, fast-flying falcon. In flight the wings look long and pointed, and the tail appears short, giving the impression of a large swift. The white cheeks and moustachial stripes show well in sitting birds, as do the red 'trousers' and vent. Streaked underside looks dark in flight. Males and females are almost identical, apart from the smaller size of the male, but juveniles are browner with pale feather edging and a pale crown, and they lack the red colour.

Lesser kestrel

♂

♀

Kestrel

♂

♀

Hobby

Red-footed Falcon
Falco vespertinus

Status: Summer visitor; locally common; **Voice:** Highly vocal; 'kew kew kew' flight calls; **Length:** 28–31cm; **Wingspan:** 65–75cm; **Habitat:** Open heaths, steppe, marshland; **Behaviour:** Often perches on posts, from which short forays are made to catch insects; most active at dusk

Small falcon resembling a short-tailed kestrel at a distance. Male is distinctive with dark-grey plumage, pale, silvery primaries, deep rufous-red vent and thighs, and red feet, eyering and cere; immature male similar to adult male but has paler underparts and pale face and throat. Female has orange or pale-yellow crown and underside, and barred, dark-grey upperparts. Juvenile streaked below and has darker, blotched upperparts and barred tail, and like female has dark eye patches resembling highwayman's mask.

Lanner Falcon
Falco biarmicus

Status: Resident; rare; **Voice:** Similar to, but quieter version of, peregrine's call; **Length:** 43–52cm; **Wingspan:** 95–115cm; **Habitat:** Mediterranean region; dry open country, mountains **Behaviour:** Often hunts in pairs, covering vast areas; remains in its large territory all year

Similar to peregrine, but slightly slimmer with longer tail and uniformly broad wings with more rounded wingtips. Male has rusty nape and dark blue-brown mantle with pale, spotted underside. Larger female similar but has buff nape and more boldly spotted underside. In both sexes moustachial stripe less pronounced than in peregrine. Juvenile darker brown above than adult and more buff below with heavier brownish-black streaks. Flight feathers look pale on underwing.

Saker Falcon
Falco cherrug

Status: Resident; rare; **Voice:** Harsh 'kek kek kek' or screaming 'giak giak giak'; **Length:** 48–57cm; **Wingspan:** 110–125cm; **Habitat:** Open cultivated country, steppe, lightly wooded areas; **Behaviour:** May be seen circling high up on straight wings; may attack prey from low-level flight

Sexes similar, although female is larger than male. Adult greyish-brown above with pale-fringed feathers on mantle. Head is noticeably pale with lightly streaked crown. Underside streaked, with boldest markings on flanks and 'trousers'. Most individuals show contrast on the underwing between pale flight feathers and darker coverts, although some very pale birds occur, where this is not obvious. Juvenile generally darker than adult, with bolder markings on the underside.

Red-footed falcon ♂ ♀

Lanner falcon ♂

Saker falcon

Eleonora's Falcon
Falco eleonorae

Status: Summer visitor; locally common; **Voice:** Hoarse, kestrel-like chatter; not often heard; **Length:** 36–42cm; **Wingspan:** 90–105cm; **Habitat:** Mediterranean sea cliffs and headlands; **Behaviour:** Preys mainly on young songbirds; active usually very late or early in the day

Appears rather slender and dainty but is actually larger than hobby. Sexes similar. Tail longer than on other small falcons. Wings long and slender, giving angular outline in flight. Pale and dark forms occur, but pale form three times more numerous. Dark phase looks almost black in flight; pale phase shows pale cheeks, dark moustachial stripe and dark, streaked underside. Underwing shows contrasting dark coverts and paler primaries in both phases. Juvenile similar to light phase but has buffish underparts and heavy streaks.

Gyr Falcon
Falco rusticolus

Status: Resident; local; **Voice:** A hoarse 'kee-a kee-a kee-a'; **Length:** 55–60cm; **Wingspan:** 125–155cm; **Habitat:** Arctic tundra, high mountains; high Arctic seabird colonies; **Behaviour:** Flies low over ground to flush birds out

Very large falcon, lacking any striking facial markings. Sexes similar. Some birds, mostly from high Arctic, are almost pure white, but dark lead-grey and brownish birds also occur in southern part of range. Southern birds have heavily barred plumage with pale patches and pale forehead, darker eye patch and moustachial streak. The white underparts are heavily marked with spots and streaks, and underwing shows almost translucent panels contrasting with darker coverts. Adult white high Arctic forms have almost no spots except on mantle, although dark tips to primaries can be seen; juvenile of this form are similar to adults but have black 'teardrop' marks on underparts.

Peregrine Falcon
Falco peregrinus

Status: Resident; widespread; **Voice:** Shrill 'kek kek kek kek'; **Length:** 39–50cm; **Wingspan:** 95–115cm; **Habitat:** Open, upland habitats; sea cliffs, coasts in winter; **Behaviour:** Nest on cliff ledge using abandoned nest of other species

Large falcon with a compact body shape and broad-based, pointed wings. Shallow wingbeats with springy wingtips are characteristic, as is the dramatic high-speed stoop for prey from a great height. Sexes similar. Adult is steely-grey above with paler grey rump. Underside is pale with dark barring. Facial patterning bold with dark moustachial stripes. Juvenile slightly slimmer and browner, with pale feather edging on mantle and bold streaking below; facial markings less distinct than on adult and cere grey-blue rather than yellow as in the adult.

DARK PHASE

Eleonora's falcon

PALE PHASE

TE PHASE

DARK PHASE

yr falcon

Peregrine falcon

COMPARING BIRDS OF PREY

Identifying raptors (birds of prey) in flight is decided challenging even for an experienced observer. Absolute size often hard to gauge and colours can be difficult to detect whe the bird is seen in silhouette against the sk Concentrate on size relative to nearby birds of know species, the relative proportions of body, wings an tail, and any distinctive habits. Even seasoned rapt watchers have to accept that a significan proportion of sightings must remain unidentifie

GRIFFON VULTURE: Easily told by immense size and flight silhouette. Broad wings can look narrow-tipped in gliding flight. Compared to eagles, tail looks proportionately short; neck appears bulging and head tiny

RED KITE: Forked, reddish tail and white wing patches are best identifiers

GOLDEN EAGLE: Much larger than buzzard, with longer wings and tail and powerful bill on well-protruding head. Soars on wings raised in shallow 'V'

MARSH HARRIER (male): Note wing pattern and rusty body. Like all harriers, soars and glides on raised wings

SHORT-TOED EAGLE: Medium-sized, pale eagle that frequently hovers on updraughts over open hillsides. Has distinct barring on tail and underwing but lacks dark carpal patches

MARSH HARRIER (female Brown, often with yello head and wing markin

BUZZARD: Large raptor with broad wings raised in shallow 'V' when soaring. Has different wing pattern from honey buzzard, which has longer neck and tail, and soars on flat wings

MONTAGU'S HARRIER: Male similar to male hen harrier but note dark bars on wings. Female very similar to female hen harrier but wings narrower

♂

OSPREY: Long wings bowed when gliding and soaring. Underbody white with large, black patches at bend of wing

GOSHAWK: Size difference between this species and sparrowhawk not always apparent but flight looks heavier. Wings proportionately broader and tail shorter than sparrowhawk's

HONEY BUZZARD: Head and neck look proportionately long and narrow and generally paler than body. Typically shows dark carpal patches, extensive barring on wings and diagnostic pattern on tail. Generally soars on flat wings

♂

HEN HARRIER: Male has white underparts, grey head and upper breast, black wingtips and dark trailing edge. Female difficult to distinguish from female Montagu's, but note head pattern

ĦOTED EAGLE: Size of buzzard. Pale ■rm (shown here) shows ⬛gnostic contrast ■ween pale head, body ⬛d underwing coverts and dark ⬛ght feathers. Dark form recalls ⬛ck kite without forked tail. ⬛aring birds often ⬛d wings curved ⬛ghtly forwards

♀

GYR FALCON:
Recalls peregrine
but looks much bulkier,
with proportionately broader
wings and thick-set body. In direct
flight, wingbeats much slower and
more leisurely than peregrine's

RED-FOOTED FALCON:
Plumage varies according
to age and sex. Flight
pattern extremely variable:
sometimes hawks for
insects like hobby but also
hovers like kestrel

♂

PEREGRINE FALCON:
Large falcon with thick-
set body, broad-based,
pointed wings and rather
short tail. Note large
'moustache' and
white cheeks

LESSER KESTREL: Slightly smaller than
kestrel. Hovers less frequently and
wingbeats much more rapid
in level flight

ELEONORA'S FALCON:
Easily recognised by elegant,
long-tailed, long-winged silhouette. In
vicinity of nesting cliffs often performs
incredible aerobatic feats

MERLIN: Smallest falcon, with shorter wings than other species and bold, dashing flight. Male has blue-grey upperparts and black tail band

♀

♂

SPARROWHAWK: Has short, rounded wings and long tail. In flight rapid wingbeats are interspersed with glides

HOBBY: wings long, narrow and pointed. Silhouette not unlike swift. Streaked black underparts and reddish undertail coverts are characteristic

KESTREL: Most characteristic feature is persistent hovering; often seen over roadside verges

Willow Grouse

Lagopus lagopus lagopus

Status: Resident; widespread; **Voice:** A hoarse, rattling 'ko-ah ko-ah-ko-ah'; **Length:** 37–42cm; **Wingspan:** 55–66cm; **Habitat:** Mixed forests on mountain slopes, willow scrub; **Behaviour:** Mostly keeps to dense cover; male has strange, laughing call

Plump gamebird with liver-red to grey-brown plumage in summer and white plumage in winter. Male has red wattle over eye which is more prominent in spring, when white plumage is lost from the head first; by the end of summer he is more uniformly brown, but retains white primaries and black tail feathers, which are most obvious in flight. Female white in winter, but more tawny brown in summer than male and lacks red wattle.

Red Grouse

Lagopus lagopus scoticus

Status: Resident; confined to Britain, where locally common **Voice:** Hoarse, rattling 'ko-ah ko-ah ko-ah'; **Length:** 55–66cm **Wingspan:** 55–66cm; **Habitat:** Treeless heather moorland, mountain slopes; **Behaviour:** Most often seen when flushed from dense heather

Plump gamebird that appears uniformly dark brown both on the ground and in flight; the wings are dark grey-brown. Male rich reddish-brown with red wattles and white-feathered legs. Female pale buff-brown with pale feathered legs, but lacks male's wattles over the eyes. Juvenile buff-brown all over with pale feather margins.

Ptarmigan

Lagopus mutus

Status: Resident; widespread; **Voice:** Hoarse rattling 'karrrrr k k k k k k'; **Length:** 34–36cm; **Wingspan:** 54–60cm; **Habitat** Open, stony tundra, high treeless mountain slopes; **Behaviour:** Forms flocks in winter to feed

Slightly smaller than willow grouse, which it resembles in winter, but male has black lores in addition to red wattles; female appears all white in winter. Both sexes show black outertail feathers in flight. Plumage changes gradually through spring and summer, as snow melts, to more mottled grey-brown in male and buff-brown in female. White primaries are retained in the wings, showing prominently in flight. Newly hatched young are downy and mottled buff-brown, and juveniles are warmer brown with darker, scalloped feather edges.

Willow grouse

WINTER ♂

SUMMER ♂

Red grouse

♀

♂

♂

Ptarmigan

WINTER ♂

SUMMER ♂

Hazel Grouse
Bonasa bonasia

Status: Resident; local; **Voice:** High-pitched whistle, recalling goldcrest; **Length:** 35–37cm; **Wingspan:** 48–54cm; **Habitat:** Extensive mixed and coniferous forests; **Behaviour:** Very secretive; prefers damp gullies but may be found perching in tree

Compact gamebird with grey rump and grey tail ending in a black and white band. Male has black chin patch, red wattle over the eye and a short crest; female has warmer brown coloration overall. Head and neck of male are finely barred and the underside is more heavily marked with chestnut and brown blotches; female generally less boldly marked.

Black Grouse
Tetrao tetrix

Status: Resident; local; **Voice:** Males make cooing calls and a sudden loud 'shoo-eesh'; females cackle; **Length:** 40–55cm; **Wingspan:** 65–80cm; **Habitat:** Woodland close to bogs and heather moors; **Behaviour:** Males display in the open in spring; otherwise sit quietly high up in trees

Almost all-black male, the size of a domestic hen, has white wingbars, white shoulder patches, white underwings and white undertail coverts. Black tail has distinctive lyre shape and is used in the communal display. Female, often known as a greyhen, is warm brown above and grey-brown below with strong barring and speckling all over. Tail shallowly forked. Juvenile similar to female but smaller and duller with pale central streaks on the feathers of the upperparts.

Capercaillie
Tetrao urogallus

Status: Resident; local; **Voice:** Very loud popping sounds, followed by 'drum roll'; various grunts and gulps; **Length:** 60–87cm; **Wingspan:** 87–125cm; **Habitat:** Coniferous forests with bogs and shrubby areas; **Behaviour:** Found on ground in early morning taking grit

Largest grouse, with male about 40 per cent larger than female. Both sexes are very bulky with broad wings and tails, and strong, heavy bills. Male appears dark blackish-grey at a distance, but has glossy green chest and dark-brown wing coverts and upper mantle. Large white patches on shoulders and whitish speckles on flanks and tail break up overall dark effect. Female has rufous-brown upperparts with chestnut patch on chest and paler brown underside. Most of plumage is heavily barred with black above and black and white below. Juvenile resembles female but smaller and duller; young males develop distinctive plumage in their first winter, but do not reach full size until the next year.

Hazel grouse

♂

lack grouse

♂

♀

♀

♂

♂

Capercaillie

♀

Chukar

Alectoris chukar

Status: Resident; locally common; introduced to Britain; **Voice:** Short 'chuck' sounds; louder rhythmic call when flushed; **Length:** 32–34cm; **Wingspan:** 47–52cm; **Habitat:** Dry, rocky mountain slopes, stony plains; **Behaviour:** Usually found in small groups; when flushed flies low and drops down quickly

Compact, rounded gamebird with strongly patterned head and flanks, and red legs and bill. Sexes very similar throughout the year, showing grey head and grey-brown upperparts, and grey chest merging into sandy underside. White flanks boldly barred with black and chestnut stripes and black eyestripe extends down neck to join on the chest, forming dark necklace. Juvenile similar to adult but head and flank markings less distinct.

Rock Partridge

Alectoris graeca

Status: Resident; rare; **Voice:** Four-note call and various shorter contact notes uttered by members of covies; **Length:** 32–35cm; **Wingspan:** 46–53cm; **Habitat:** Dry, treeless mountain slopes, often south-facing; **Behaviour:** Spends most of its time on the ground searching for food

Very similar in appearance to the chukar but chin and throat pure white, not creamy-buff, and black necklace extends through the eyes and down to the base of the bill. Sexes similar. Stripes on flanks narrower and neater in appearance than on chukar, and chest and upperparts greyer. General impression at a distance is of a very sharply defined set of markings.

Red-legged Partridge

Alectoris rufa

Status: Resident; widespread; **Voice:** Harsh repetitive 'kchoo kchoo-kchoo kchoo'; **Length:** 32–34cm; **Wingspan:** 45–50cm; **Habitat:** Open country, farmland, lowland heaths; **Behaviour:** Often seen in small groups

Compact gamebird with overall greyish-brown colouring but strongly marked flanks and head. Sexes similar but males larger. Head grey and rest of upperparts and chest greyish-brown, with more distinct grey band on lower chest. Necklace meets over bill and surrounds the white throat patch, and there is a bib of black streaks. Flanks strongly barred with black and chestnut stripes on a white background. Juvenile lacks adult's head pattern and flank markings.

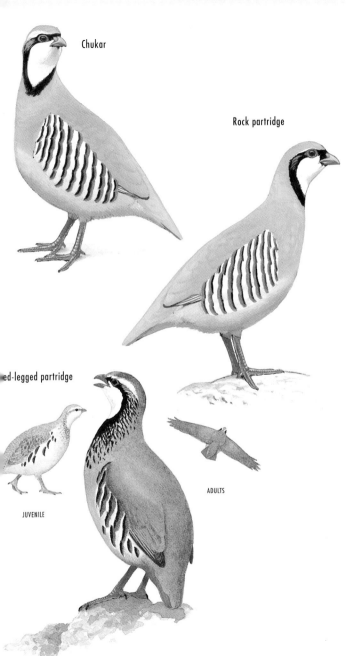

Chukar

Rock partridge

ed-legged partridge

JUVENILE

ADULTS

Barbary Partridge
Alectoris barbara

Status: Resident; rare; **Voice:** Repetitive 'kchek kchek' and other harsh calls; also curlew-like call in flight; **Length:** 32–34cm; **Wingspan:** 46–49cm; **Habitat:** Dry, open habitats with low bushes at low altitudes and mountains up to 3,000m **Behaviour:** Remains concealed in low vegetation and will not fly unless approached very closely

Very similar to red-legged partridge, but lacks that species' striking facial markings. Sexes similar. Face and throat grey; there is a collar of white spots on a dark chestnut background but no necklace. Most distinctive feature is the crown of dark chestnut with a light-grey supercilium. Upperparts grey-brown with pinkish tinge and flanks less boldly marked than in red-legged partridge with bars of black, buff and white.

Black Francolin
Francolinus francolinus

Status: Resident; rare; **Voice:** Harsh shrill 'kek kek kek kek-ek-ek'; **Length:** 33–36cm; **Wingspan:** 50–55cm; **Habitat:** Low lying shrubby areas near water; dried-up river beds; **Behaviour:** Stays in thick cover and is difficult to flush

In flight this partridge-sized bird shows dark outertail feathers and rich brown, dark-barred wings. Male has mostly black head and underside with white ear coverts and white flecks on flanks. Wings dark brown with black feather centres and tail finely barred with black and white. Broad chestnut collar. Female has pale head, chestnut patch on neck, and overall brown plumage with black arrow marks on all feathers. Juvenile resembles female but has dull plumage and faint markings.

Grey Partridge
Perdix perdix

Status: Resident; widespread; **Voice:** Harsh 'keirr-ik keirr-ik' at night, 'pitt pitt pik pirr pik' calls when alarmed and fleeing **Length:** 29–31cm; **Wingspan:** 45–48cm; **Habitat:** Lowland grassland, cultivated areas; **Behaviour:** Runs for cover when alarmed; often seen in small groups

This bird looks very rounded, its head appearing round with no neck. Underparts mostly grey. From a distance upperparts look brown and plain, but on close inspection they are finely marked with darker brown and buff. Facial colouring brick red, contrasting with grey underside. In flight distinctive rusty outertail feathers are seen. Adult has dark chestnut horseshoe-shaped patch on underside which is larger in male than female. Juvenile is browner than adult and lacks horseshoe mark.

Barbary partridge

Black francolin

♂

Grey partridge

♀

♂

JUVENILE

Pheasant
Phasianus colchicus

Status: Resident; common; **Voice:** Male has two-note crow, females have quieter contact notes; **Length:** 53–89cm; **Wingspan:** 70–90cm; **Habitat:** Woodland, copses, farmland, large gardens and orchards; **Behaviour:** Spends much time on ground, but roosts in trees at night

Male has brightly coloured, iridescent plumage, with red wattles and glossy green head, some showing well-developed 'ear tufts'. White collar is present in some races. Tail is very long and barred. Purplish-chestnut plumage shows scalloped pattern, due to bold markings on each feather. Female has paler, brownish-buff plumage with strong pattern on upperparts and flanks. Barred tail is shorter. Juvenile resembles female, but with duller, less strongly marked plumage.

Lady Amherst's Pheasant
Chrysolophus amherstiae

Status: Resident; naturalised in Britain only; **Voice:** Hissing 'su-ik-ik-ik' calls at dusk roosts; **Length:** 60–120cm; **Wingspan:** 70–85cm; **Habitat:** Mixed woodland with dense undergrowth; **Behaviour:** Always secretive; gathers in large groups in winter

Very long-tailed pheasant with blue-grey legs and feet. Male is strikingly marked with dark glossy green and white, and a colourful yellow rump with red at base of tail. Wing coverts have bluish sheen in good light. Females are smaller with cinnamon-brown plumage and black barring on all feathers. Juvenile similar to adult but duller, without rufous colouring on crown.

Golden Pheasant
Chrysolophus pictus

Status: Resident; naturalised in Britain only; **Voice:** Male utters crowing call during breeding season; otherwise both sexes rather silent; **Length:** male 85–115cm; female 65–85cm **Wingspan:** 65–75cm; **Habitat:** Mountain woodland and scrub in natural range (China); birds introduced into Europe favour conifer plantations; **Behaviour:** Very secretive

Large, well-marked pheasant. Adult male has mainly orange-red body plumage except for yellow on crown and areas of blue and green on mantle and wings; shows conspicuous barring on nape. Tail broad and extremely long; brown with intricate pattern of fine black lines. Adult female has roughly similar proportions to male. Body plumage mainly buffish-brown with dark barring. Juvenile similar to adult female but with shorter tail.

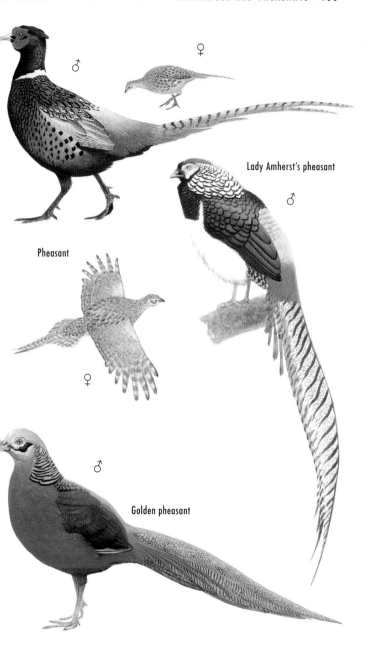

♂

♀

Lady Amherst's pheasant

♂

Pheasant

♀

♂

Golden pheasant

Common Quail

Coturnix coturnix

Status: Summer visitor; common; **Voice:** Oboe-like 'wet-my-lips', repeated frequently; **Length:** 16–18cm; **Wingspan:** 32–35cm; **Habitat:** Lowland grassland, agricultural land, pastures; **Behaviour:** Quiet and unobtrusive; feeds on insect

The smallest of the gamebirds and very difficult to see usually observed when flushed, when rounded shape, small head and pale underside are easy to see. Male mostly yellowish-brown with dark brown barring on upperside, rufous chest and dark-streaked flanks. Head markings vary, but usually shows some dark-chestnut markings on the crown, through the eye, and on the cheeks and throat. Female resembles male but has less striking head markings; juvenile similar to female but has barred and spotted, not streaked, flanks.

Andalusian Hemipode

Turnix sylvatica

Status: Resident; rare; **Voice:** At dawn female gives deep 'ho hoo hoo' resembling distant cattle; **Length:** 15–16cm; **Wingspan:** 25–30cm; **Habitat:** Dry, sandy areas with grass and scattered bushes; **Behaviour:** Very elusive; flies only short distance if flushed

Small, secretive, quail-like bird with rusty-red breast and boldly black-spotted flanks. Crown is brown and finely barred, and has a creamy stripe; upperparts brown with darker brown bars and cream streaks. Female more striking marked than male, with overall browner colouring. Juvenile very similar to male, but at close range shows more spots on the chest and white spots on upperparts.

Common quail

♀

♂

ndalusian hemipode ♀

Water Rail
Rallus aquaticus

Status: Resident; locally common; **Voice:** Harsh squealing and grunting sounds; nocturnal 'kipp kipp' call; **Length:** 22–28cm; **Wingspan:** 38–45cm; **Habitat:** Reedbeds, marshes, well-vegetated river and lake shores; **Behaviour:** More often heard than seen; usually well concealed in dense reedbeds

Secretive waterbird with mostly dark-brown colouring above and plain slate grey-blue below. Dark flanks strongly barred and tail noticeably white beneath. Slender bill red and slightly downcurved. Sexes similar, but female is a little smaller than male with slightly shorter bill. Juvenile browner on underside and has brown bill. In flight the long legs and toes trail conspicuously.

Spotted Crake
Porzana porzana

Status: Summer visitor; locally common; **Voice:** Far-carrying 'dripping tap' call – 'hwitt hwitt'; **Length:** 22–24cm; **Wingspan:** 37–42cm; **Habitat:** Sedges and rushes bordering lakes, ponds and rivers; **Behaviour:** Secretive; solitary

Small, compact waterbird, which at a distance appears all dark grey-brown or greenish-brown, but in good light looks spotted. Undertail pale buff; short, pointed bill red at base with yellowish-orange tip, and legs and feet bright olive green. Female resembles male but has less grey on face and underparts, with slightly more spotting. Juvenile resembles female but lacks any grey tones, and has less spotting and duller, olive-coloured legs.

Little Crake
Porzana parva

Status: Summer visitor; rare; **Voice:** Low accelerating croaking sounds, ending in a trill; **Length:** 18–20cm; **Wingspan:** 34–39cm; **Habitat:** Reedbeds and swamps with still water and floating vegetation; **Behaviour:** Secretive; walks on floating vegetation

Small waterbird resembling tiny water rail but with shorter, yellowish bill. Male olive-brown above with feathers showing dark centres and buff margins; at close range scapulars and mantle show some pale streaks. Face and underside slate blue or grey with pale streaking on rear flanks and undertail coverts, which are not as striking as in water rail. Female pale buff beneath rather than grey, and has whitish face with faint barring under tail. Juvenile similar to female but paler below; shows white supercilium and pale mottling on chest and flanks; barring on underside is darker than in female.

Water rail

Spotted crake

♂

Little crake ♂

Baillon's Crake
Porzana pusilla

Status: Summer visitor; rare; **Voice:** Rasping sounds resembling a finger scratching a comb; **Length:** 17–19cm; **Wingspan:** 33–37cm; **Habitat:** Swampy areas, streamsides, pond margins; **Behaviour:** Secretive; swims readily

Very small waterbird, the size of a house sparrow, with colouring resembling a water rail. Upperparts rufous brown with irregular whitish spots and streaks; feathers have dark centres. Face and chest deep slate blue and unmarked, but rear flanks and underside as far as tail black with white barring. Legs dark flesh or dull olive, and bill green. Female almost identical to male but throat and chest region paler grey. Juvenile has same-coloured upperparts as adults, but buff-coloured below, and bill brownish.

Corncrake
Crex crex

Status: Summer visitor; rare; **Voice:** Far-carrying, rasping 'crex crex' or 'crake crake'; **Length:** 27–30cm; **Wingspan:** 46–53cm; **Habitat:** Hay meadows, driest areas of marshes; **Behaviour:** Very secretive; keeps to dense cover

Similar in size to water rail but with shorter, yellowish-brown bill and noticeably long rusty wings when seen in flight. Flight pattern is weak and legs dangle; flies low, quickly drops into cover and then runs to safety. Adult upperparts grey-brown with dark centres to feathers forming broken lines running the length of the body. Neck and supercilium greyish, but underside mostly brownish-buff turning to reddish-brown with white barring on flanks. Sexes identical apart from lack of grey on neck and face of female. Juvenile resembles female but is paler, with light spots on wing coverts and grey legs. Legs flesh-coloured, darker in juveniles than adults, and eyes are pale brown.

Moorhen
Gallinula chloropus

Status: Resident; common; **Voice:** Varied, loud calls, including harsh 'krreck' and rhythmic 'kipp kipp kipp'; **Length:** 32–35cm; **Wingspan:** 50–55cm; **Habitat:** Wetlands, including urban park lakes, rivers, small ponds; **Behaviour:** May gather in large groups after breeding

At a distance adult appears all black with red shield on face and yellow tip to bill. Horizontal white line along flanks and black and white pattern under constantly flicked tail make confusion with any other waterbird unlikely. Sexes similar. In good light plumage black only on head; rest of upperparts very dark brown and underside is deep slate grey. Juvenile brownish with paler flanks and chest, white chin and throat, and buff rather than white lateral line. Undertail pattern as in adult.

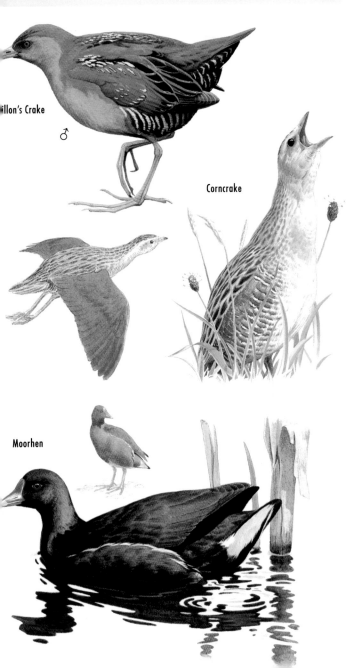

illon's Crake

♂

Corncrake

Moorhen

Purple Gallinule
Porphyrio porphyrio

Status: Resident; rare; **Length:** 45–50cm; **Wingspan:** 90–100cm; **Habitat:** Marshes, reedbeds, tracts of bulrush, brackish swamps; **Behaviour:** Uproots tubers and rhizomes of water plants to feed on central pith; swims and dives quite easily

Chicken-sized waterbird. Sexes similar. Adult has uniform violet-blue plumage with brighter blue face and red eyes, legs and bill. Undertail all white and exposed frequently when bird is nervous. After breeding, bill is duller and has dark patches. Birds from the western Mediterranean are bluest; Egyptian race has green tinge on scapulars and back, and Middle Eastern race has green head and is paler blue. Juvenile grey, with dull-red bill and legs and white throat.

Coot
Fulica atra

Status: Resident; common; **Voice:** Loud repetitive 'kowk' and explosive shrill 'pitt'; **Length:** 36–38cm; **Wingspan:** 70–80cm; **Habitat:** Larger ponds and lakes, canals, urban park lakes; **Behaviour:** Aggressive; very confident on urban park lakes

Rounded, sooty-black water bird, adult with gleaming white bill and facial shield and red eye. At close range head and neck seen to be most intensely black, while flanks greyer. In flight, wings appear to have pale margin. Sexes identical, although male is larger than female. Juvenile dull brown with pale face and throat, and yellowish-grey bill.

Crested Coot
Fulica cristata

Status: Resident; rare; **Voice:** Two-note 'clukuk' and a metallic 'croo-oo-k'; **Length:** 38–42cm; **Wingspan:** 75–85cm; **Habitat:** Large water bodies with plenty of marginal vegetation; **Behaviour:** Intolerant of human presence; forms large flocks in winter

Slightly larger than coot but in other respects very similar. Sexes identical. Adult has red knobs over facial shield which can be seen at close range; at a distance they are not especially obvious and in winter they are smaller and duller than during the breeding season. In flight, wings lack white edge to secondaries seen in coot. Juvenile drab brownish-black with paler chin and throat, and white centre to belly. Legs and feet of both adults and juveniles slate blue.

Purple gallinule

Coot

Crested coot

Crane
Grus grus

Status: Scarce breeding species; locally common in winter; **Voice:** Loud bugling calls, plus 'kroo-krii kroo-krii' calls by pairs; **Length:** 110–130cm; **Wingspan:** 200–230cm; **Habitat:** Marshes, farmland, large boggy clearings in northern forests **Behaviour:** Elaborate dancing display may be seen throughout the year; possibly mates for life

Very large bird of upright posture, which moves in a steady and measured way on the ground. Sexes similar. In flight shows long wings of even width with black flight feathers, and long extended neck and trailing legs. Adult plumage mostly grey but head much darker, appearing black at a distance, with white band extending back from red eye and red crown. Chest and parts of back have pale rufous tinge, and tail and overhanging cloak of secondaries darker. Juvenile paler grey than adult with unpatterned head and grey, rather than black, legs.

Demoiselle Crane
Anthropoides virgo

Status: Rare summer visitor; easiest to see in Cyprus on migration; **Voice:** Grating, honking flock calls uttered on ground and in flight; **Length:** 80–100cm; **Wingspan:** 170–180cm; **Habitat:** Steppe and upland grassland; **Behaviour:** Invariably seen in flight

Tall, long-legged and elegant bird. Superficially similar to crane but appreciably smaller. Sexes similar. Adult has mainly pale blue-grey plumage. Shows black from throat and neck to breast and broad black supercilium bordering grey crown. White nape plumes arise from behind eye, iris of which is red. Black flight feathers mostly hidden at rest but conspicuous in flight. Legs dark and bill yellowish. Juvenile has grubby brownish-grey plumage and lacks adult's head and neck patterns.

Crane

moiselle crane

Little Bustard
Tetrax tetrax

Status: Resident; locally common; **Voice:** Snorting 'knerr' or 'prritt' calls, various grunts and whistles; **Length:** 40–45c **Wingspan:** 105–115cm; **Habitat:** Open grassy plains, large arable fields, grassy airfields; **Behaviour:** Strong flier; easily disturbed

 Pheasant-sized bird with sturdy legs and small head o long, thick neck. Overall body colour speckled grey-brown with white underside. Male has strongly patterned black and white head and neck with grey throat. Female lacks male's black and white patterning, but has coarse speckling on back. In flight both sexes show white wings wit black-tipped primaries and primary coverts, and black and white tail rim. Juvenile similar to female.

Great Bustard
Otis tarda

Status: Resident; rare; **Voice:** Mostly silent but may give short, barking, alarm note; **Length:** 75–105cm; **Wingspan:** 190–260cm; **Habitat:** Open grasslands, lowland areas, wide river valleys and plains; **Behaviour:** Shy; keeps to open plain

Europe's heaviest bird; male weighs twice as much as female. In breeding season displaying male has bulgin neck and cocked tail, which makes it appear even larger. Breeding male also has strong chestnut chest band and whi moustachial 'whiskers' extending back from base of bill. Outside breeding season, male resembles female apart from his greater size. Female head and neck grey with upperpart cinnamon-brown but strongly barred with black; underside white, giving three-coloured grey, brown and white appearance. Juvenile resembles female but has buff neck.

Oystercatcher
Haematopus ostralegus

Status: Resident/summer visitor; common; **Voice:** Shrill piping calls, loud 'kubeek kubeek' alarm call; **Length:** 40–45cm; **Wingspan:** 80–86cm; **Habitat:** Rocky shores, estuaries, large stony rivers, stony lake shores; **Behaviour:** Roosts communally in winter; large flocks feed along coast

Large, unmistakable wader. Sexes similar. Adult has striking black and white plumage, red eyes, orange-pink bill and red-pink legs. In winter, adult acquires white chin stripe on otherwise black neck. Newly fledged juvenile is exceptionally well camouflaged to resemble lichen-covered rocks. First-winter bird paler than adult, with large white throat patch.

Little bustard

♂

♀

Great bustard

♂

♀

Oystercatcher

SUMMER

WINTER

JUVENILE

Black-winged Stilt
Himantopus himantopus

Status: Summer visitor; locally common around Mediterranean; **Voice:** Varied short, nasal, bleating calls; **Length:** 35–40cm; **Wingspan:** 67–83cm; **Habitat:** Coastal lagoons, shallow lakes, saltpans; **Behaviour:** Moves graceful on dry land; may submerge head when probing for food in deep water

Very long-legged wader with entirely black and white plumage. Wings and mantle black and underside whit but degree of black on head variable. In flight white rump and long white wedge on back show clearly, as do trailing pink legs. Head may be all white or show varying amounts o black. Sexes very similar except that breeding female usual shows pure white head and neck. Juvenile paler on mantle than adult, with sepia tinges to the darker feathers.

Avocet
Recurvirostra avosetta

Status: Summer visitor; locally common; **Voice:** Varied calls including a ringing 'pleet pleet'; **Length:** 42–46cm; **Wingspan** 77–80cm; **Habitat:** Estuaries, coastal lagoons, saltpans, shallow lakes; **Behaviour:** Uses upcurved bill to sweep through liquid mud in search of food; can swim

Unique large wader with strongly upcurved bill, long blue-grey legs and black and white plumage. Sexes similar. Plumage predominantly white with black head and nape and black panels on the wings that appear as oval panels in flight. From below avocet looks all white in flight apart from black wingtips. Juvenile resembles adults excep that black element of adult plumage brownish instead.

Stone Curlew
Burhinus oedicnemus

Status: Summer visitor; widespread; **Voice:** Curlew-like flight call, and various high-pitched whistling and shrill wader-like calls at night; **Length:** 40–44cm; **Wingspan:** 77–85cm; **Habitat:** Dry, open areas, semi-desert, arable lan heaths; **Behaviour:** Nocturnal; rests during the day; flies off low when flushed

Stocky wader with large, staring black and yellow eye and stout, almost gull-like bill, which is black at tip. Sexes similar. Plumage mostly sandy brown with darker streaks; underside pale. At rest, wings show white bar and dark lower edge; in flight, wings appear black with paler panels. Tail relatively long. When standing tarsus joint is prominent, giving rise to family's common name of 'thick-knee'. Juveniles resembles adult but less boldly marked.

Black-winged stilt

♂

♀

Avocet

Stone curlew

Collared Pratincole
Glareola pratincola

Status: Summer visitor; locally common in south; **Voice:** Tern-like calls and short rhythmic nasal calls; **Length:** 24–27cm; **Wingspan:** 60–68cm; **Habitat:** Dry open habitats with shallow pools, large saltmarshes; **Behaviour:** Gregarious at all times

Resembles small plover on the ground but recalls tern in flight. Sexes similar. Upperparts dark sandy or olive brown with darker primaries and tail feathers. Wings look dark-tipped in flight, and rump white. Underside divided into pure white belly, light-olive chest and buff throat clearly demarcated by thin black necklace stretching from eye to eye under chin. Gape of bill bright red. Outside breeding season, adult has less distinct necklace and more spotted throat and chest. Juvenile looks more scaly than adult due to pale margins to feathers; necklace absent.

Black-winged Pratincole
Glareola nordmanni

Status: Summer visitor; rare; vagrant to northwest Europe; **Voice:** Churring calls at nest; squeaky call in flight; **Length:** 25cm; **Wingspan:** 60–65cm; **Habitat:** Steppe grassland, usually close to water; **Behaviour:** Hawks for insects

Superficially similar to collared pratincole. Sexes similar. Plumage essentially dark sandy brown, palest on underparts. Has creamy-buff throat outline bordered by black and white lines. Shows forked tail and white rump. Upperwings uniformly dark sandy brown, lacking white trailing edge and contrasting dark wingtip seen in collared pratincole. Underwing all dark, lacking reddish-brown underwing coverts of collared pratincole. Winter adult (not seen in region) and juvenile have pale feather margins on upperparts, giving scaly appearance, and less clearly defined throat markings. All birds have essentially dark bill with only limited amount of red at base.

Cream-coloured Courser
Cursorius cursor

Status: Vagrant; rare; **Voice:** Generally silent; **Length:** 22–24cm; **Wingspan:** 51–57cm; **Habitat:** Arid open ground and semi-desert; **Behaviour:** Freezes at first signs of danger, then runs

Unmistakable and rather atypical wader with upright stance, proportionately long legs and rather short, downcurved bill. Sexes similar. Adult has uniformly pinkish-buff plumage, palest on belly and undertail. Head pattern distinctive. In flight note dark underwing, white trailing edge to wing and black and white bands at tip of tail. Bill dark and legs yellow. Juvenile recalls adult but has dark scaly markings and spots on upperparts and breast; head pattern of adult absent.

Collared pratincole

Black-winged pratincole

Cream-coloured courser

Little Ringed Plover
Charadrius dubius

Status: Summer visitor; widespread; **Voice:** Loud 'kiu' flight call and plaintive 'krree-u krree-u'; **Length:** 14–15cm; **Wingspan:** 42–48cm; **Habitat:** Dry open habitats, gravel bed, lake shores, dry river beds; **Behaviour:** Secretive when nesting; performs distraction display if disturbed at nest

Small, slender wader. Sexes similar. Adult has dull-brown upperparts and pure white underparts with strongly patterned head. Bright yellow eyering stands out well against black cheeks. Bill all black and legs dull orange-brown. When seen in flight the lack of any wingbar at all times is diagnostic. Juvenile looks like faded version of adult with indistinct head and chest markings.

Ringed Plover
Charadrius hiaticula

Status: Resident; locally common; **Voice:** A quiet 'tooip' whistle, and a louder alarm 'te-lee-a te-lee-a'; **Length:** 18–20cm; **Wingspan:** 48–57cm; **Habitat:** Seashores, estuaries, large lake shores, tundra; **Behaviour:** Found in small groups; feeds actively, running along the shore

Small, stocky wader with mostly plain colouring but striking facial markings. Upperparts of adult grey-brown and underparts pure white. In summer, legs and bill base orange; in winter legs darker and bill all dark with yellow base to lower mandible. Head strikingly marked with black cheeks and black line over brow; has black chest ring. In winter, black fades and looks worn. Sexes similar, although some females have less distinct black markings than males. Juvenile resembles adult, but has scalloped upperparts due to pale feather edges, and partial brownish collar. Striking white wingbars show well in flight in both adults and juveniles.

Kentish Plover
Charadrius alexandrinus

Status: Summer visitor/resident; locally common around Mediterranean; **Voice:** Short 'kip' or 'peep' sounds; **Length:** 15–17cm; **Wingspan:** 42–58cm; **Habitat:** Lagoons, estuaries, saltpans; **Behaviour:** Uses inland sites with sparse vegetation

Small, pale plover with comparatively large head and short tail. Adult has incomplete neck ring and shows less black on head than ringed plover. In breeding season, male has chestnut crown and black patch on forehead; female has grey-brown crown and no black patch. In winter, male resembles female with both becoming duller in appearance. Bill and legs black, and both sexes appear longer-legged than ringed plover. Juvenile plainer than adult with greyer upperparts.

Little ringed plover

Ringed plover

Kentish plover

Greater Sand Plover

Charadrius leschenaultii

Status: Vagrant from Asia; rare; **Voice:** Utters soft, trilling call; **Length:** 23–25cm; **Wingspan:** 55–60cm; **Habitat:** Breed on steppe and semi-desert; at other times mainly coastal; **Behaviour:** Vagrants sometimes feed alongside ringed plover

Small but stocky plover. At all times bill is outsized compared to those of other, similar species. Male in breeding plumage has generally sandy-brown upperparts and white underparts. Shows conspicuous brick-red chest band extending around side of nape to rear of supercilium. Face white except for dark patch through eye to ear coverts. Forehead white and crown reddish-buff. Female in breeding season similar to male but with washed-out colours. Winter adults of both sexes recall winter-plumage Kentish plover but note dumpy, longer-legged appearance with proportionately large bill. Juvenile recalls winter adult but shows pale margins to feathers on upperparts.

Caspian Plover

Charadrius asiaticus

Status: Spring vagrant from Asia; rare; **Voice:** Soft, plaintive whistle; **Length** 18–20 cm; **Wingspan** 55–60cm; **Habitat:** Dry steppe grassland and semi-desert; **Behaviour:** As dotterel

Small, well-marked plover, superficially similar to dotterel. Male in breeding season has dark-grey cap, white face and throat and dark ear coverts. Mantle and back brown. Shows brick-red chest band, bordered with black on lower margin; rest of underparts white. Legs dull grey and bill black. Female in breeding plumage recalls male but colours far less intense. In winter, adults of both sexes recall washed out and grubby plumage of breeding female. Juvenile similar to winter adult but with pale feather margins on upperparts. All birds show faint white wingbar in flight.

Dotterel

Charadrius morinellus

Status: Summer visitor/passage migrant; local; **Voice:** Soft 'pweet pweet' flight calls and trilling calls on ground; **Length** 20–22cm; **Wingspan:** 57–64cm; **Habitat:** Dry, open mountain plateaux; overwinters on arid grasslands; **Behaviour:** Prefers to run rather than fly from danger

Distinctly patterned wader with no real affinity for water. In breeding season adult has broad white supercilium and thin black and white chest band. Crown very dark, framed by white eyestripes that meet on nape; face whitish and rest of upperparts and neck grey-brown. Chest rich chestnut with darker centre, and undertail region white. Female generally brighter and more distinctive than male. In winter, colours fade to more uniform buff-brown with less markedly white supercilium. Juvenile resembles winter adult but has pale feather margins, giving a scalloped appearance.

Greater sand plover

SUMMER ♂

WINTER

aspian plover

SUMMER ♂

♀

Dotterel

JUVENILE

♂

Killdeer

Charadrius vociferus

Status: Late-autumn vagrant from North America; rare; **Voice:** Utters characteristic 'kill-dee' call; **Length:** 24–25cm; **Wingspan:** 60–62cm; **Habitat:** Favours areas of short grassland; **Behaviour:** As ringed plover

Recalls outsized ringed plover but always looks more slender and longer-bodied with proportionately longer legs; chest band pattern diagnostic. Sexes similar. Adult in breeding plumage has dark sandy-brown upperparts and mainly white underparts. Dark ear coverts, narrow eyestripe and malar stripe separated from brown crown by white supercilium. Shows white forecrown and neck. Pattern of two black chest bands distinctive. Red eyering visible only at very close range; legs relatively long and yellowish. Tail extends well beyond wingtips at rest and shows orange-brown at base. Non-breeding adult similar to breeding adult but with pale margins to feathers on upperparts. Juvenile similar to non-breeding adult but with colours washed out. In flight all birds look long-tailed and show conspicuous white wingbar.

Spur-winged Plover

Hoplopterus spinosus

Status: Summer visitor; locally common; **Voice:** Shrill 'peey-peey-k peey-k' and lapwing-like calls; **Length:** 25–27cm; **Wingspan:** 65–80cm; **Habitat:** Lakesides, marshes, river deltas, dry grassland; **Behaviour:** Often seen in small flocks or pairs

Sexes similar. Adult has mainly black and white underparts and buff wing coverts and back. Face and shoulders white, and in flight mostly white underwing shows clearly, contrasting with black tips to primaries and black belly. Upperwing has white panel between black primaries and buff mantle. Rump white; tail has broad black terminal band. Juvenile resembles adult but has pale margins to dark feathers, giving scalloped appearance.

Grey Plover

Pluvialis squatarola

Status: Passage migrant/winter visitor; locally common; **Voice:** Whistling 'pleeoo-wee'; **Length:** 27–30cm; **Wingspan:** 71–83cm; **Habitat:** Breeds on Arctic tundra; overwinters on estuaries and mudflats; **Behaviour:** Territorial on winter site

Has much greyer speckled upperparts than golden plover, with no golden tinge. In summer, male striking black below with pale head and white shoulders, and white-flecked upperparts. Female duller than male and has greyish cheeks and grey-brown upperparts. Winter adult more evenly marked with dark grey, speckled plumage. In flight, underwing pattern shows distinctive black armpits against a white background at all times. Juvenile resembles winter adult but with pale buff wash to plumage.

Killdeer

WINTER

Spur-winged plover

WINTER

SUMMER

Grey plover

WINTER

Golden Plover
Pluvialis apricaria

Status: Resident; common; **Voice:** Mournful, whistling 'pyuu' or 'pyuu pu'; **Length:** 26–29cm; **Wingspan:** 67–76cm; **Habitat** Breeds on moorlands, bogs; overwinters on lowland pastures **Behaviour:** Forms flocks outside breeding season

Plump wader with short bill and rounded head and spangled golden-brown upperparts. In summer, male has black face and black underside separated from upperparts by broad white border. In flight shows white underwings contrasting with black belly. Female similar to male but black on underside restricted to belly; face greyer than on male and white border to black areas less distinct. Northern birds have far more black than southern birds. In winter sexes similar with no black on the underside and more uniform plumage overall. Juvenile paler above than adult and greyer below, lacking adult's golden tinge.

American Golden Plover
Pluvialis dominica

Status: Vagrant from North America; annual; **Voice:** Flight call a sharp 'kew-ip'; **Length:** 24–25cm; **Wingspan:** 60–70cm; **Habitat:** Short grassland; **Behaviour:** As golden plover

Similar to golden plover but has proportionately longer legs and slimmer body, and dark-grey (not white) axillaries and underwing coverts. Breeding male has black underparts and spangled golden upperparts. Black on face and throat separated from dark crown and nape by broad white border. Breeding female similar to male but dark underparts less complete. Non-breeding adults and first-autumn birds grey-brown, spangled golden on mantle and back. Dark crown gives 'capped' appearance.

Pacific Golden Plover
Pluvialis fulva

Status: Vagrant from North America; rare; sometimes seen in breeding plumage in late spring; **Voice:** Calls include a spotted redshank-like 'chew-it'; **Length:** 24–25cm; **Wingspan** 60–70cm; **Habitat:** Favours areas of short grassland; **Behaviour:** As golden plover

Similar to golden plover but distinguished by pale-grey axillaries and underwing coverts, more slender body and proportionately longer legs. Subtle plumage differences and longer legs and neck help separate from American golden plover. At close range, three primaries project beyond tertials at rest (four in American golden plover). Breeding male has dark underparts and golden spangled upperparts, these separated by white band from forecrown to flanks. Undertail coverts white (black in American golden plover). Breeding female similar to male but black underparts less complete. Winter adults and first-autumn birds similar to winter golden plover but note dark cap and dark ear coverts.

Golden plover

WINTER

SUMMER

American golden plover

FIRST AUTUMN

Pacific golden plover

SUMMER ADULT

White-tailed Plover
Chettusia leucura

Status: Vagrant from Asia; very rare; **Voice:** Lapwing-like rasping, choked call; **Length:** 27–28cm; **Wingspan:** 65–70cm; **Habitat:** Damp grassland and margins of shallow fresh water; **Behaviour:** Feeds on insects

Long-legged plover. Sexes similar. Breeding adult has buffish-brown plumage, palest on face and belly. Cap greyish-buff; shows red eyering. Legs yellow, bill dark. Black primary tips extend beyond white tail. Non-breeding adult similar but colours less intense. In flight, adult shows striking pattern of buff, white and black on upperparts and conspicuous white rump and tail. Juvenile recalls non-breeding adult but has pale-edged dark feathers on mantle.

Sociable Plover
Chettusia gregaria

Status: Autumn vagrant from Asia; rare; **Voice:** Generally silent; **Length:** 28–30cm; **Wingspan:** 70–75cm; **Habitat:** Breeds on arid steppe; at other times cultivated ground; **Behaviour:** Vagrants usually join lapwing flocks

Elegant, lapwing-sized plover. Sexes similar. Breeding adult plumage essentially grey-buff to pinkish-buff but with striking head pattern comprising black cap, white supercilium, black eyestripe; latter defined below by diffuse area of white. Dark patch on belly grades from black at front to chestnut at rear; undertail white. Legs and bill dark. Juvenile recalls winter adult but plumage colours less uniform because pale feather margins give scaly appearance. In flight, all birds have striking upperwing pattern recalling that of juvenile Sabine's gull: black wingtips, white secondaries and buffish back and wing coverts forming three distinct triangles of colour. Underwing white with black primaries. Tail white with black patch near trailing edge.

Lapwing
Vanellus vanellus

Status: Resident; common; **Voice:** Shrill 'peeoo-wit' and other more scratchy sounds; **Length:** 28–31cm; **Wingspan:** 75–85cm; **Habitat:** Wet grassland, marshes, pastures; **Behaviour:** Very agile in the air, displaying over its territory at the start of the breeding season

Adult has a long black crest and glossy green upperparts. Underparts all white apart from rich orange undertail coverts, which show well when bird dips its head during feeding. Male is more boldly marked than female and has longer crest. At a distance, lapwing appears all black and white; in flight shows long, broad, black and white wings with white tips to three outer primaries. In winter, feathers have pale margins, giving scalloped appearance to mantle; cheeks buff rather than white. Juvenile resembles winter adult; crest shorter and chest browner.

White-tailed plover

Sociable plover

WINTER

Lapwing

Knot
Calidris canutus

Status: Winter visitor; locally common; **Voice:** Short, slightly nasal 'kwett' in winter; fluting calls on breeding grounds; **Length:** 23–25cm; **Wingspan:** 50–60cm; **Habitat:** Breeds on high Arctic tundra; overwinters on coasts; **Behaviour:** Remains very close to the water's edge

Stocky wader with a medium-sized straight bill. Sexes similar. In summer, adult has orange-red underside and white undertail coverts. Upperparts mostly buff and strongly patterned with chestnut and yellow patches; the largest feathers have black and white markings on them contributing to overall mottled effect. In winter, adult loses all red and brown colours, becoming grey-buff all over apart from mostly white underparts. Juvenile very similar to winter adult but has warmer brown or pinkish-buff wash with no grey tints. Larger feathers have thin black and white terminal bands, giving delicate scalloped pattern to upperparts. In flight all ages and plumages show thin white wingbar and grey rump.

Sanderling
Calidris alba

Status: Winter visitor; common; **Voice:** Loud 'plitt' flight call; short frog-like trill in display; **Length:** 20–21cm; **Wingspan:** 36–42cm; **Habitat:** Breeds on high Arctic tundra; overwinters on sandy shores; **Behaviour:** Distinctive method of feeding on sandy shores, running in and out of the surf snatching morsels of food from the sand as a large wave retreats

Small wader with relatively short, straight bill. In breeding plumage has rusty-red upperparts with black markings on larger feathers, giving mottled appearance at a distance. Chest rusty red and black, clearly demarcated from pure white underside. In winter, adult looks all white at a distance, but at close range is seen to have pale-grey upperparts with white fringes to feathers. Juvenile strongly marked above with black and white on upperparts, and with warm-buff tinge to the mantle and neck areas. All ages and plumages have black legs and bill, with broad white wingbar seen in flight.

Knot

JUVENILE

SUMMER

WINTER

WINTER

JUVENILES

Sanderling

MER

WINTER

Little Stint

Calidris minuta

Status: Summer visitor/passage migrant; local; **Voice:** Short 'tip' contact note and 'svee svee svee' display on breeding grounds; **Length:** 12–14cm; **Wingspan:** 28–35cm; **Habitat:** Breeds on tundra; migrants favour muddy, brackish margins; **Behaviour:** Active feeder

The smallest European sandpiper, all ages of which have black legs and short black bill. Most often seen on passage in Europe. Sexes similar. In summer plumage, upperparts mostly rusty red with dark feather centres. Centre of crown looks darker and there is yellowish 'V' mark on mantle. In winter plumage mostly grey-buff above and white below. Larger feathers have dark central shafts. Juvenile resembles summer adult but paler, with white 'V' on reddish-brown upperparts and white underparts.

Temminck's Stint

Calidris temminckii

Status: Summer visitor/passage migrant; rare; **Voice:** Ringing 'tirrr'; **Length:** 13–15cm; **Wingspan:** 30–35cm; **Habitat:** Nests in tundra and mountainous Arctic regions; overwinters on seashores and marshes; **Behaviour:** If startled shoots upwards rapidly and flies off on jerky flight path

Very small sandpiper with short legs and slightly elongated appearance. Sexes similar. Breeding bird greyish-buff above with some feathers showing dark centres and chestnut fringes; never as rusty red above as breeding-plumage little stint, and some adults in summer show a few worn grey winter feathers on mantle. Winter adult grey-brown above with white underparts; grey extending further down chest and more clearly demarcated than in winter little stint. Clay-coloured legs also separate this species from little stint. Juvenile warm buff above with pale edges to larger feathers.

Red-necked Stint

Calidris ruficollis

Status: Late-summer vagrant from Siberia; very rare; **Voice:** Flight calls include 'krrrp' and soft squeak; **Length:** 14–15cm; **Wingspan:** 36–38cm; **Habitat:** Vagrants likely to favour freshwater pools; **Behaviour:** As little stint

Similar to little stint and semipalmated sandpiper in most plumages. All birds have proportionately shorter bill and legs than little stint but longer wings and tail. Sexes similar. Adult in breeding plumage has mainly grey upperparts and white underparts but head appears rufous due to striking red throat and reddish-brown cap; supercilium and base of bill whitish. Some feathers on back also reddish-brown; red elements of plumage absent in non-breeding adult. Juvenile similar to non-breeding adult but reddish-brown on crown and mantle; lacks distinct white 'V' marking seen in juvenile little stint.

JUVENILE

Little stint

SUMMER

SUMMER

Temminck's stint

JUVENILE

Red-necked stint

FIRST AUTUMN

Curlew Sandpiper
Calidris ferruginea

Status: Autumn passage migrant; local; **Voice:** Clear, ringing 'krillee' in flight; **Length:** 18–20cm; **Wingspan:** 38–45cm; **Habitat:** Breeds on Arctic tundra; migrants mainly coastal; **Behaviour:** Seen in mixed flocks of small waders

Sexes similar. Underside rich red in summer with dark upperparts. Scapulars have dark centres and lighter patches, giving mottled effect. Fresh plumage looks 'mealy' at first due to pale feather edges, but as these become worn the darker colours show through. Winter adult pale grey above with pale feather margins and light streaking on upper chest; underparts pure white. Juvenile has buff-orange tint on upperparts and chest, and pure white underside. In all plumages, long black legs, rounded body and long, black, curved bill are best identification features.

Least Sandpiper
Calidris minutilla

Status: Autumn vagrant from North America; rare; **Voice:** Utters high-pitched 'kreep' call; **Length** 11–12cm; **Wingspan** 34–35cm; **Habitat:** Vagrants likely to favour coasts and shallow freshwater margins; **Behaviour:** Active feeder

Tiny, extremely active wader. Similar in size and proportions to little stint but distinguished by subtle plumage differences and yellow legs. Sexes similar. Breeding adult has grey-brown upperparts; shows chestnut on cap, ear coverts and on some feathers of back and mantle. Neck and breast grey-brown but underparts otherwise white. Bill black, short and slightly downcurved. Non-breeding adult lacks breeding adult's elements of chestnut in plumage. Juvenile and first-autumn birds have buffish-brown upperparts washed with reddish-brown on back, mantle, crown and ear coverts. In flight all birds show narrow white wingbar.

Semipalmated Sandpiper
Calidris pusilla

Status: Autumn vagrant from North America; rare; **Voice:** Trilling 'churrp'; **Length:** 14–15 cm; **Wingspan:** 35–36cm; **Habitat:** Vagrants likely to favour coasts and coastal pools; **Behaviour:** Active feeder

Most easily confused with little stint. Most consistent distinguishing features include broad-based, blob-tipped bill; bill usually only slightly longer than that of little stint. Sexes similar. Slight palmations between toes visible only at close range. Breeding adult upperparts grey-brown suffused with reddish-brown on back and cap; underparts white. Non-breeding adult upperparts greyish; underparts white. Juvenile and first-autumn birds similar to winter adult but with reddish-brown feathering on mantle and back. Lacks clean white lines on back of juvenile little stint. Bill and legs black in all birds.

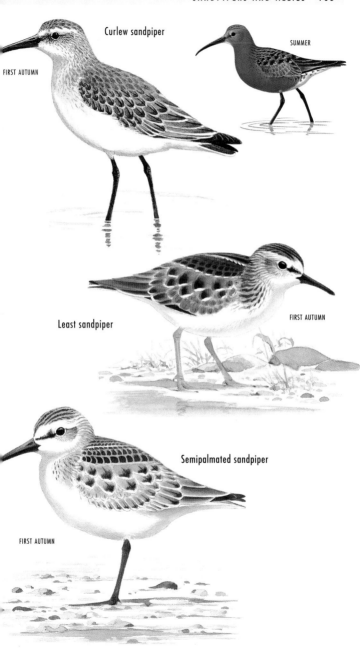

Curlew sandpiper

FIRST AUTUMN

SUMMER

Least sandpiper

FIRST AUTUMN

Semipalmated sandpiper

FIRST AUTUMN

Purple Sandpiper
Calidris maritima

Status: Resident; local: **Voice:** Short, variable, 'kewitt' call and agitated call on nest site; **Length:** 20–22cm; **Wingspan:** 40–44; **Habitat:** Breeds on tundra; overwinters on rocky shores; **Behaviour:** Approachable

The darkest small sandpiper, with only a thin white wingbar showing in flight. Sexes similar. Breeding adult has upperparts marked with black, chestnut and yellow on larger feathers, greenish-brown legs and dark bill. Winter adult dark grey above and paler grey below with dark streaks on breast. Legs yellow, bill yellowish-orange. Juvenile more distinctly patterned than adult due to pale fringes on darker feathers, and streaked underparts.

White-rumped Sandpiper
Calidris fuscicollis

Status: Autumn vagrant from North America; rare; **Voice:** Flight call a sharp 'tzeip'; **Length:** 15–16cm; **Wingspan:** 40–45cm; **Habitat:** Vagrants favour mudflats and coastal pools; **Behaviour:** Feeds in manner of dunlin

Small, active wader. Recalls winter-plumage dunlin but body proportionately more elongated and longer wings extend beyond tail at rest. Sexes similar. Bill medium length slightly downcurved towards tip and with dull-orange patch at base of lower mandible. White rump, seen in flight, is diagnostic for birds of this species' proportions. Summer adult has grey-brown upperparts with chestnut and black feathering on back and warm brown tone to crown and ear coverts. Adult in non-breeding plumage has grey upperparts and white underparts; adults in autumn often retain a few black feathers on back. Juvenile and first-autumn birds recall non-breeding adult but upperparts browner and with pale feather margins on mantle and back.

Dunlin
Calidris alpina

Status: Resident; common; **Voice:** Harsh, rolling 'krreee' in flight; longer display over nest site; **Length:** 16–22cm; **Wingspan:** 35–40cm; **Habitat:** Breeds on moor and tundra; overwinters on coasts; **Behaviour:** Active feeder seen in busy flocks

Small but striking wader in summer with black belly patch contrasting with mostly white underside. Sexes similar. Upperparts chestnut and black; neck and chest streaked and undertail region white. Winter plumage pale grey above and white below with slight grey streaking on upper breast and crown. Juvenile recalls moulting adult but black breast patch replaced by darker streaks and upperparts appear paler due to buff fringes to feathers. Bill length varies according to race but always black and slightly downcurved.

Purple sandpiper

SUMMER

WINTER

White-rumped sandpiper

FIRST AUTUMN

Dunlin

FIRST AUTUMN

SUMMER

WINTER

Baird's Sandpiper
Calidris bairdii

Status: Autumn vagrant from North America; rare; **Voice:** Trilling 'prrrt'; **Length:** 15–16cm; **Wingspan:** 40–45cm; **Habitat:** Vagrants favour short grass and coastal pools; **Behaviour:** Active feeder

Small, rather short-legged wader. Recalls dunlin but has shorter, straighter bill and elongated rear end due to long primary feathers. Sexes similar. Breeding adult has grey-brown upperparts, suffused on back with chestnut. Neck and breast grey-brown with clear division between these and white underparts. Non-breeding adult similar but plumage more uniformly grey-brown. Juvenile plumage similar to adult but upperparts, neck and breast essentially grey buff, pale feather margins on back giving scaly appearance. In flight all birds appear long-winged with only faint wingbar.

Pectoral Sandpiper
Calidris melanotus

Status: Autumn vagrant from North America; rare; **Voice:** Trilling 'chirrp'; **Length:** 20–22cm; **Wingspan:** 45–46cm; **Habitat:** Vagrants favour marshes and short grassland; **Behaviour:** Purposeful feeder

Small to medium-sized wader. Noticeably larger than dunlin, from which also distinguished by yellow (not black) legs, distinct pectoral band, proportionately longer neck and smaller head. Sexes similar. Breeding adult has grey-brown upperparts, darkest on back and on cap and with faint brown wash in these areas. Neck and breast grey and streaked, with distinct cut-off from white underparts. Non-breeding adult similar but without warm hues on upperparts. Juvenile recalls adult but upperparts, neck and breast warm buffish-brown and well marked. All birds show gently downcurved bill.

Sharp-tailed Sandpiper
Calidris acuminata

Status: Autumn vagrant from Siberia; very rare; **Voice:** Sharp 'preep'; **Length:** 18–20cm; **Habitat:** Vagrants found beside freshwater pools; **Behaviour:** Rather deliberate feeder

Similar to pectoral sandpiper. Sexes similar. Legs dull olive-yellow at all times; bill medium length, slightly downcurved, dark with dull-yellow base. Breeding adult warm brown above with pale underparts. Shows dark-brown cap, brown ear coverts, broad pale supercilium, dark spots and streaks on throat and distinct black arrow markings on flank and undertail coverts. Non-breeding adult similar but loses warm tint to brown of plumage and lacks arrow markings on underparts. Juvenile similar to non-breeding adult but with warm buff wash to breast and upperparts. In flight all birds show pale underwings, white on sides of otherwise dark rump, and only faint wingbar.

Baird's sandpiper

FIRST AUTUMN

Pectoral sandpiper

FIRST AUTUMN

Sharp-tailed sandpiper

FIRST AUTUMN

Broad-billed Sandpiper
Limicola falcinellus

Status: Summer visitor/passage migrant; scarce; **Voice:** Rasping 'chrreeeit' and mechanical-sounding 'swirr swirr swirr'; **Length:** 16–18cm; **Wingspan:** 34–37cm; **Habitat:** Breeds on bogs in sub-Arctic; **Behaviour:** Feeds with active, deliberate manner

Slightly smaller than dunlin, with longer body profile and more sharply downturned bill tip. In breeding and juvenile plumage, head shows pale stripes similar to snipe, and pale supercilium. Upperparts pale in early summer due to broad, pale feather fringes, but with wear bird becomes more richly coloured with chestnut and dark-brown upperparts, and dark streaking on upper breast. Winter plumage recalls dunlin but pale crown stripes still visible in good light and legs appear muddy grey-green.

Ruff
Philomachus pugnax

Status: Summer visitor/passage migrant; widespread in summer; **Voice:** Mostly silent; may make quiet drawn-out squeak; **Length:** 26–32cm (male), 20–24cm (female); **Wingspan:** 54–56 cm (male); 48–52cm (female); **Habitat:** Swamps, wet meadows and lake margins; **Behaviour:** Males perform elaborate dances at leks near nesting sites

Distinctive wader in breeding season. Great variation between sexes and individuals. Male has elaborate neck and head feathers, which may be any colour from black to white with red and brown shades in between; 'ruff' may be plain, barred or spotted, but male's legs, bill and warty face usually orange. Female's appearance also variable: mostly buff upperparts with varied darker mottling and streaking. Winter male loses ruff and resembles female; both sexes lose warm buff wash. Legs of adult orange, and bill dark at all times. Juvenile resembles female with warm buff colouring and olive-grey legs.

Buff-breasted Sandpiper
Tryngites subruficollis

Status: Autumn vagrant from North America; rare; **Voice:** Mostly silent; **Length:** 18–20cm; **Wingspan:** 45–46cm; **Habitat:** Vagrants favour short grassland; **Behaviour:** Feeds on insects and other invertebrates

Similar to small juvenile ruff but distinguished by buff throat and underparts, shorter, straighter bill and more scaly appearance to mantle and back. Sexes similar. Adult buff with dark spotting on crown; feathers on back darker but with pale margins. Juvenile similar to adult but back looks even more scaly. In flight all birds lack wingbar and pale sides on rump. Bill black and legs yellowish in all birds.

Broad-billed sandpiper

SUMMER

Ruff

♂

♀

♂

♂

FIRST AUTUMN

RUFF, FIRST AUTUMN

Buff-breasted sandpiper

Upland Sandpiper
Bartramia longicauda

Status: Autumn vagrant from North America; very rare;
Voice: Includes a plaintive 'quip-ip-ip-ip'; **Length:** 27–28cm;
Wingspan: 55–65cm; **Habitat:** Vagrants favour grassland and
fields; **Behaviour:** Feeds in deliberate manner

Recalls miniature, short-billed curlew in terms of
plumage but has yellowish legs and proportionately
very long wings and tail. Sexes similar. Adult has mottled
brown upperparts at all times. Head, neck and breast buffish
but with dark streaks; underparts otherwise white. Tail long,
with barring towards tip. Juvenile similar to adult but mantle
and back darker but with pale feather margins. Bill short,
straight and dark at all times. In flight all birds recall
miniature curlew but look proportionately longer-winged,
longer-tailed and shorter-billed.

Stilt Sandpiper
*Micropalama
himantopus*

Status: Summer/early-autumn vagrant from North America;
very rare; **Voice:** Mostly silent; **Length:** 18–20cm; **Wingspan:**
45–46cm; **Habitat:** Vagrants favour freshwater margins;
Behaviour: Often wades in fairly deep water

Recalls *Tringa* wader but has proportionately longer
legs than most species and long bill, which is
downcurved at tip. Sexes similar. Breeding adult has
extensive black streaking on head and neck and black barring
on underparts. Crown, lores and ear coverts suffused with
chestnut; dark feathers on back have brown margins. Shows
prominent white supercilium. Non-breeding adult has grey
upperparts, neck and breast; supercilium and underparts
white. Juvenile recalls winter adult but has buffish wash to
neck and breast and pale feather margins on mantle and
back. Bill black and legs yellow at all times. In flight, all
birds show white rump.

Woodcock
Scolopax rusticola

Status: Resident/winter visitor; common; **Voice:** Grunting
'oo-oorrt' call in flight, followed by a shrill squeak; **Length:**
33–35cm; **Wingspan:** 55–65cm; **Habitat:** Damp woodlands;
Behaviour: Very secretive; male performs 'roding' display
flight with jerky wingbeats on spring and summer evenings

Larger and more rotund than snipe, with red-brown
plumage. Sexes similar. Upperparts rufous-brown and
marbled with black and white; underside paler and barred
with dark grey-brown stripes. Wings and head have broad
pale bars, the whole effect affording excellent camouflage
on leafy woodland floor. Long bill is dark flesh colour,
becoming darker at tip. Juvenile similar to adult but
forehead spotted, not plain.

Upland sandpiper

FIRST AUTUMN

Stilt sandpiper

SUMMER

Woodcock

Snipe
Gallinago gallinago

Status: Resident; common; **Voice:** Sneeze-like call when flushed; rhythmic, repetitive 'tick-a tick-a' on breeding grounds; **Length:** 25–27cm; **Wingspan:** 37–45cm; **Habitat:** Bogs, wet meadows, upper reaches of saltmarshes; **Behaviour:** Males perform aerial displays in breeding season making a strange bleating sound with tail feathers; stands on posts and rocks to call

Very long-billed wader with distinctive patterned head and back. Sexes similar. Upperparts brown with pale stripes; larger feathers have dark centres and pale margins, giving scaly appearance. Flanks barred and underside greyish-white. Short tail also barred and has buff margin. Juvenile almost identical to adult in the field, but feather margins white rather than buff. Legs dull green and bill pale reddish-brown with darker tip in both adults and juveniles.

Great Snipe
Gallinago media

Status: Summer visitor/passage migrant; rare; **Voice:** Mostly silent, but gives short 'itch' call, and has chirping display call on territory; **Length:** 27–29cm; **Wingspan:** 42–46cm; **Habitat:** Marshy areas in mountains and lowlands; **Behaviour:** Normally only seen when flushed

Larger and plumper than snipe, with slightly shorter bill, longer legs, stronger barring on belly and more strongly patterned wing coverts. Sexes similar. In flight white outertail feathers and white wingbars are diagnostic; bird also appears larger than snipe, with more rounded body shape and wings. Flight pattern more laboured than snipe's and usually straight, not zigzagged; bird settles rather abruptly by dropping into cover. Juvenile almost impossible to distinguish from adult in the field, although usually less well marked. In winter, plumage becomes duller with loss of buff and cinnamon margins of larger feathers.

Jack Snipe
Lymnocryptes minimus

Status: Resident/summer visitor; rare; **Voice:** Brief sneezing sound when flushed, otherwise silent except for muffled, whistling display call near nest; **Length:** 17–19cm; **Wingspan:** 36–40cm; **Habitat:** Breeds on tundra bogs; overwinters on lowland marshes; **Behaviour:** Moves awkwardly on the ground with plenty of tail-bobbing and crouching

Small, short-billed snipe with conspicuous pale-yellow stripes running along back. Sexes similar. Overall impression is of greenish-brown, patterned back and boldly marked head. Shortish bill is yellowish with darker tip; legs and feet blue-green. Usually not possible to distinguish juvenile from adult in autumn.

Snipe

Great snipe

Jack snipe

Black-tailed Godwit

Limosa limosa

Status: Summer visitor/resident; widespread; **Voice:** Excited nasal, 'kee-wee-wee-wee' calls uttered near nest; **Length:** 36–44cm; **Wingspan:** 70–80cm; **Habitat:** Breeds on damp meadows, boggy areas; overwinters on estuaries, marshes; **Behaviour:** Wades in quite deep water and feeds by making deep probes into soft mud

Long-legged, slim wader with long, straight bill. Sexes similar. In breeding plumage, head and neck brick-red and upperparts and chest mottled with black, chestnut and grey, the colours forming broken bars on upper chest. Underside mostly grey-white. Amount of red coloration is very variable, some adult females being almost grey in summer. Icelandic race has deepest red coloration. Juvenile warm buff below with brown and buff plumage above. In winter, adult pale grey above with paler feather edges, and grey-white below. In flight all ages show tail that looks half black and half white, white wingbar and trailing black edge to wing.

Bar-tailed Godwit

Limosa lapponica

Status: Rare breeding species/widespread winter visitor; **Voice:** Nasal 'ke-vu' with variations for alarm or flight calls; **Length:** 33–42cm; **Wingspan:** 70–80cm; **Habitat:** Breeds on tundra; overwinters on muddy shores; **Behaviour:** Feeding methods similar to black-tailed godwit's, but bar-tailed generally more energetic

Superficially similar to black-tailed godwit, but shorter legged and stockier if seen in flight, lacking the distinctive wingbars and tail markings. Bill slightly shorter and has upwards tilt. In summer plumage, smaller male has dark rusty-red underside and mottled chestnut and dark-brown upperparts; larger female has warm-buff underparts and slightly paler upperparts. In winter both sexes are buff-grey above with white undersides. Grey feathers have dark central shafts giving slightly streaked effect above. Juvenile has browner coloration above than winter adult, with patterning similar to curlew.

Black-tailed godwit

SUMMER

WINTER

Bar-tailed godwit

SUMMER ♂

WINTER

Whimbrel
Numenius phaeopus

Status: Locally common breeding species/passage migrant; rare in winter; **Voice:** Seven-note trill in flight; brief curlew-like call in display; **Length:** 40–46cm; **Wingspan:** 75–85cm; Weight: 430–575g; **Habitat:** Tundra and moors in summer; coasts in winter; **Behaviour:** Often seen on estuaries in sma groups; readily takes flight

Smaller than curlew, with shorter legs. Bill also shorte and straighter apart from more sharply downcurved ti Sexes similar. Crown has two dark stripes and pale supercilium, but otherwise plumage rather plainer than curlew's. Juvenile resembles adult apart from pale-buff spot on crown and wing coverts.

Curlew
Numenius arquata

Status: Resident/winter visitor; widespread; **Voice:** Mournfu 'cour-lee'; also tuneful bubbling trill when displaying; **Lengtl** 50–60cm; **Wingspan:** 80–100cm; **Habitat:** Upland moors and bogs in summer; coasts and marshes in winter; **Behaviour:** Uses long curved bill to feed in soft mud and search among grass tussocks

Large wader with long downcurved bill. Female larger than male and has longer bill. Both sexes have similar mottled brown plumage with streaked underside and pale ventral region. In summer, fresh plumage has warmer yellowish tinge than in winter. Lower mandible pink-flesh-coloured in winter. Juvenile plumage very similar to adult's; juvenile male has significantly shorter bill than juvenile female.

Greenshank
Tringa nebularia

Status: Local breeding species/common passage migrant; rare in winter; **Voice:** Clear three-syllable 'chew chew chew' call; **Length:** 30–35cm; **Wingspan:** 60–70cm; **Habitat:** Breed on bogs and marshes; winters on coasts and lake shores; **Behaviour:** Sometimes runs after small fish, with its bill below the surface

Mostly grey wader with long green legs and slightly upturned bill. In summer grey upperparts have darker markings, forming pattern of bands along wings; arrow-shaped markings on breast and flanks give streaked effect. Ir winter, adult pale grey above with darker feather margins bordered with white; underside pure white. Juvenile looks browner than adult, with neater streaks on neck and breast. Bill slightly shorter and straighter in juveniles than adults. Ir flight, tail looks pale; white, wedge-shaped rump patch extends up the back in both adults and juveniles.

Whimbrel

Curlew

Greenshank

Spotted Redshank
Tringa erythropus

Status: Scarce breeding species/passage migrant; **Voice:** Shrill 'chu-witt' call, plus repetitive buzzing 'krruu-ee' utter in display; **Length:** 29–32cm; **Wingspan:** 55–65cm; **Habitat:** Bogs and tundra in summer; coasts and estuaries in winter; **Behaviour:** Wades in deep water and swims at times

Distinctive wader in summer with sooty-black plumag relieved only by pale margins to feathers on upperpart and long bill with red lower mandible. Female may have pal margins on some feathers on underside, giving scaly appearance. Winter adult pale grey above and white below; darker feather margins on upperparts give scalloped effect. Legs black in summer, red in winter. Juvenile similar to winter adult but browner overall in appearance. In flight, wedge-shaped white rump patch distinctive in all plumages.

Redshank
Tringa totanus

Status: Resident; common; **Voice:** Far-carrying and persiste 'klu-klu-klu' alarm call and two-syllable 'tu-hu'; **Length:** 27–29cm; **Wingspan:** 55–65cm; **Habitat:** Wet meadows, coastal marshes in summer; estuaries and shores in winter; **Behaviour:** When alarmed readily takes to the air with a ringing alarm call

Sexes similar. Mostly grey-brown wader with darker spots and streaks on upperparts in summer plumage; most conspicuous features are bright orange-red legs and base to bill. Extent of dark markings on grey background varies; northerly birds appear to have darkest markings. In winter appears almost uniformly grey-brown above and very pale below. Juvenile has red legs but lacks red base to bill. Shows dark streaks on underside and pale feather margins (mantle, giving slightly mealy appearance. In flight all birds show bright white trailing edge to wing and white rump. En(of tail barred and outer edges of wings dark.

Marsh Sandpiper
Tringa stagnatilis

Status: Passage migrant; rare; **Voice:** Clear, whistling 'kiew', repeated frequently; **Length:** 22–25cm; **Wingspan:** 50–55cm **Habitat:** Lake margins, marshes and sheltered shores; **Behaviour:** Wades to full depth of its legs

Slender, long-legged wader with straight, thin bill. Sexes similar. Pale winter plumage, mostly light grey above and almost white below, makes it stand out among other small waders. Darker shoulder patch contrasts with pale grey mantle. In summer, upperparts darker and more strongly patterned with blackish feather centres and pale margins; upper breast and neck streaked. Bill dark at all times but olive-green legs yellower in spring. Juvenile pure white below with browner upperparts than adults.

Spotted redshank

WINTER

SUMMER

SUMMER

Redshank

JUVENILE

Marsh sandpiper

SUMMER

Green Sandpiper
Tringa ochropus

Status: Resident/winter visitor; widespread; **Voice:** Shrill, three-note 'tuEEt-wit-wit' given in flight; **Length:** 21–24cm; 50–60cm; **Habitat:** Boggy areas in open woodland; streams, lake margins, watercress beds; **Behaviour:** Nervous and agitated bird, that will take flight readily if disturbed

From a distance looks almost black and white; similar impression when seen in flight, dark wings contrasting with white rump. Sexes similar. Upperparts dark olive-green with brownish tones, fading to grey-green on head. Shows white eyering and dull-white spots on back, and bright white underside. In winter, white spots are absent and underparts look even brighter than in summer. Juvenile has buff-brown spots on dark upperparts; neck and chest streaked. Both adults and juveniles have dark olive-green legs.

Solitary Sandpiper
Tringa solitaria

Status: Autumn vagrant from North America; rare; **Voice:** Calls include high-pitched 'cueep-cueep'; **Length:** 18–20cm; **Wingspan:** 56–58cm; **Habitat:** Vagrants found beside fresh water; **Behaviour:** Active; has bobbing feeding action

Similar to green sandpiper but smaller, with proportionately shorter legs and longer wings; in flight reveals dark rump (white rump seen in green sandpiper). Sexes similar. Adult in breeding plumage has dark olive-brown upperparts speckled with white spots. Head dark olive-brown but with striking, pale supercilium and eyering. Neck and breast olive-brown but underparts otherwise white. Outer margins of tail show conspicuous black and white barring. Non-breeding adult similar to breeding adult but lacks conspicuous white spotting on upperparts. Juvenile similar to adult in breeding plumage.

Terek Sandpiper
Xenus cinereus

Status: Summer visitor; scarce; rare vagrant to western Europe; **Voice:** Variable, rapid 'chu-du-du' call and other trilling sounds; **Length:** 22–25cm; **Wingspan:** 50–55cm; **Habitat:** Muddy lake shores, riverbanks; **Behaviour:** Active feeder, running and darting through shallow water

Recalls common sandpiper but has distinctive long, upcurved bill and steeply rising forehead when viewed in profile. Sexes similar. Adult plumage has dull-grey upperparts and dark 'V' shape visible on back in flight. Dark carpals partly visible when at rest. Legs short and yellow-green. Juvenile similar to adult but has dark markings on wing feathers, forming anchor shapes. In flight, pale underwing and lack of white rump and wingbars are useful for identification at all ages.

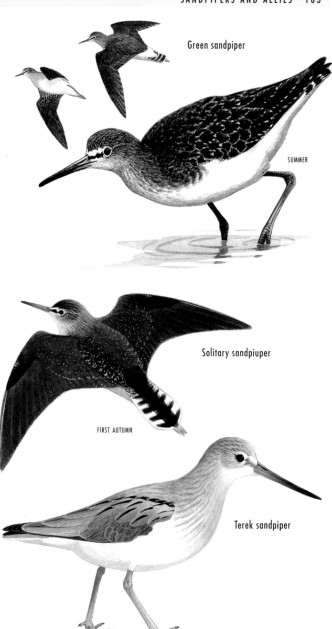

Green sandpiper

SUMMER

Solitary sandpiuper

FIRST AUTUMN

Terek sandpiper

Wood Sandpiper
Tringa glareola

Status: Summer visitor/passage migrant; common; **Voice:** Flight call a whistling 'jiff jiff'; utters rolling display call on breeding sites; **Length:** 19–21cm; **Wingspan:** 50–55cm; **Habitat:** Breeds in open forests with boggy areas; marshes and riversides on migration; **Behaviour:** Wades in shallow, well-vegetated water

Longer-legged and slimmer than common and green sandpipers. Sexes similar. Greyish with white-spotted plumage above and mostly white underparts, although less white visible than in other sandpipers. Neck and flanks streaked; legs and bill olive-green. Adult in worn plumage brownish-grey. Juvenile browner than adult, with streaked neck, chest and flanks. In flight all ages show narrow wings pale below (dark on green sandpiper), and tail with indistinct barring.

Greater Yellowlegs
Tringa melanoleuca

Status: Autumn vagrant from North America; very rare; **Voice:** Calls include loud 'tu-tu-tu'; **Length:** 30–32cm; **Wingspan:** 70–75cm; **Habitat:** Vagrants favour fresh water and coasts; **Behaviour:** Wades in stately manner

Similar to greenshank but legs diagnostically very long and usually bright yellow. Sexes similar. Breeding adult has greyish-brown upperparts marked with black, and white spotting on back. Head, neck and breast show dark streaks grading into dark crescent markings on flanks; underparts otherwise white. Non-breeding adult has grey back and mantle with pale margins to feathers. Head and neck pale but with dark streaking, most prominent on cap; underparts mostly white. Juvenile similar to non-breeding adult but with white spotting on upperparts. Bill greyish, long and slightly upcurved towards tip in all birds. In flight all birds show conspicuous white rump.

Lesser Yellowlegs
Tringa flavipes

Status: Autumn vagrant from North America; rare; **Voice:** Calls include sharp 'tiu-tiu'; **Length:** 24–25cm; **Wingspan:** 60–62cm; **Habitat:** Marshes and freshwater margins; **Behaviour:** Active feeder

Recalls outsized wood sandpiper. Sexes similar. Breeding adult has grey-brown upperparts, darkest on cap and back. Shows bold black feathering and white spangling on mantle and back; darker streaking on neck and upper breast. Underparts mainly white. Non-breeding adult similar but more uniformly grey-brown; lacks black and white elements to plumage. Juvenile and first-autumn birds similar to winter adult. All birds have dark, needle-like bill and yellow legs, and show white rump in flight.

Wood sandpiper

eater yellowlegs

FIRST AUTUMN

Lesser yellowlegs

FIRST AUTUMN

Spotted Sandpiper
Actitis macularia

Status: Autumn vagrant from North America; rare; **Voice:** Sharp 'weet-weet'; **Length:** 18–20cm; **Wingspan:** 38–40cm; **Habitat:** Freshwater margins; **Behaviour:** Same as common sandpiper

Very similar to common sandpiper except for spotted sandpiper's proportionately shorter tail. Distinguishe easily only in breeding plumage, when upperparts grey-brow and underparts white with conspicious dark spots. Sexes similar. Shows conspicuous white supercilium. Non-breedin adult has uniform grey-brown upperparts except for well-marked wing coverts; underparts white. Tail less well mark than that of common sandpiper. Juvenile upperparts grey-brown and underparts white. Similar to juvenile common sandpiper but has boldly marked tips to wing coverts and lacks that species' white markings on tertials. In flight, whi wingbar less obvious than common sandpiper's.

Common Sandpiper
Actitis hypoleucos

Status: Summer visitor/resident; widespread; **Voice:** Penetrating 'hee dee dee' call when flushed; song rhythmic and longer version of alarm call; **Length:** 19–21cm; **Wingspan:** 35–40cm; **Habitat:** Stony rivers and lake shores, sheltered seashores; **Behaviour:** Active, constantly bobbing up and down even when perched

Short-legged wader with elongated body, accentuated by crouching posture. Sexes similar. Adult upperparts appear plain grey-buff at a distance, but darker feather centres and pale margins give delicately patterned appearance close up; this less obvious outside breeding season. Underside white with small white patch extending in front of shoulder. Juvenile very similar to adult but with scaly appearance due to pale feather fringes. At all ages, le grey-green and bill dark brown with dull yellowish base.

Long-billed Dowitcher
Limnodromus scolopaceus

Status: Autumn vagrant from North America; rare; **Voice:** Calls include sharp 'kyik'; **Length:** 26–28cm; **Wingspan:** 45–50cm; **Habitat:** Vagrants favour freshwater margins; **Behaviour:** Feeds with 'sewing-machine'-like action of bill

Dumpy wader with extremely long bill. Recalls outsiz snipe in silhouette. Sexes similar. Breeding adult reddish-brown with pale supercilium, dark feathering on mantle and back, dark streaking on face and neck, and dar crescent markings on breast and flanks. Non-breeding adul has grey-brown upperparts; supercilium and underparts white. Juvenile and first-autumn birds recall non-breeding adult but show chestnut margins on mantle and back. Bill dark but greenish at base; legs greenish-brown in all birds.

Spotted sandpiper

FIRST AUTUMN

Common sandpiper

Long-billed dowitcher

FIRST AUTUMN

Turnstone
Arenaria interpres

Status: Resident; widespread; **Voice:** Short, nasal alarm calls uttered by feeding birds; longer urgent-sounding call given in flight; **Length:** 21–24cm; **Wingspan:** 49–55cm; **Habitat:** Breeds on coastal tundra; overwinters on seashores; **Behaviour:** Powerful bill used to flip over pebbles to find food; also forages among seaweed

Stocky, short-billed wader with striking breeding plumage. Male has bold black and white facial markings, rich chestnut upperparts with darker bands, pure white underside and orange legs. Female duller, with darker streaked head and less chestnut on upperparts. In winter, upperparts of both sexes become more uniform grey-brown with no chestnut; head and neck grey with faded black area. Juvenile resembles winter-plumage adult but dark feathers have buff edges, giving scaly appearance. In flight, wings show bold black, white and chestnut patterning at all ages.

Red-necked Phalarope
Phalaropus lobatus

Status: Summer visitor; rare; **Voice:** Calls include short 'kitt' or 'kirrik' sounds; **Length:** 18–19cm; **Wingspan:** 34–40cm; **Habitat:** Breeds on open tundra; overwinters at sea in tropical regions; **Behaviour:** Often spins on surface of water while feeding; also swims

Bill very thin and pointed. In summer, female has striking plumage, with rusty-red neck and upper chest, slate-grey head, white throat and paler grey chest. Upperparts dark grey with pale buff to white markings forming lines on back. Male plumage more subdued, having paler grey head and buff neck. Winter adult, rare in Europe, ashy grey above with broad white bands; looks black and white at a distance. Juvenile recalls male with washed-out summer plumage showing paler flanks and undersides, and no red on neck.

Grey Phalarope
Phalaropus fulicarius

Status: Summer visitor; rare; **Voice:** Sharp 'pik' alarm call; rolling 'prruut' uttered by female in summer; **Length:** 20–22cm; **Wingspan:** 37–44cm; **Habitat:** Breeds on tundra; overwinters at sea in tropical regions; migrants found on coasts; **Behaviour:** Feeds while swimming

Separated from red-necked phalarope by broader, less pointed bill, yellow-based in breeding season. Breeding female has brick-red underside and black head with white eye patch extending to back of head. Upperparts dark slate-grey with broad buff margins to large feathers. Male has more subdued and mealy colours than female. Winter adults of both sexes light grey above and white below, with black patch through eye. Juvenile grey-brown above with buff feather margins and dark bill. Shows dark eye patch and buff neck.

Turnstone

WINTER

SUMMER ♂

WINTER

JUVENILE

Red-necked phalarope

SUMMER ♀

Grey phalarope

ER

JUVENILE

SUMMER ♀

COMPARING IMMATURE SMALL WADERS

Many birdwatchers relish the prospect of scanning throug flocks of small waders in the autumn. The best advice for a prospective observer of immature small waders is to get t know the dunlin, since it is the yardstick by which all others a measured. This species is by far the commonest of its kind t occur around the coasts of Europe; it is also one of th most variable in terms of overall size and bill length.

TEREK SANDPIPER: Like adult, immature is easily recognised by long, upcurved bill; upperparts greyish with dark lines defining margins of mantle and small, dark patch on carpal joint of wings; bill mainly dark but yellowish at base; yellowish legs proportionately short and set rather far back along body

COMMON SANDPIPER: Shares distincti 'bobbing' feeding action with adu upperparts grey-brown and rath scalloped on back, contrasti markedly with wh underparts; neat divisio seen between white and do elements of plumage on ches legs yellowish and bill most dark but dull greenish at bas

GREEN SANDPIPER: Very similar to adult, with mostly dark upperparts and white underparts; at close range upperparts can be seen to be covered in small brown spots; legs greenish-yellow and bill mostly dark but dull greenish at base

WOOD SANDPIPER: Looks elegantly proportioned with mainly dark-brown upperparts and greyish-white underparts; good views reveal upperparts to be spangled with off-white to yellowish-buff spots, these being formed by scalloped margins to feathers; legs yellow and proportionately long; bill straight and rather short

DUNLIN: Unique among small European waders in this plumage in having dark streaking on flanks; bill and legs dark; shows warm wash to head and neck; brown feathers on back gradually replaced by grey feathers during moult during late autumn

CURLEW SANDPIPER: Superficially similar immature dunlin but appears longer-legged an plumage always look cleaner, with whi underparts an buffish wash upperparts; pale margins feathers on back give sca appearance; feeds in more delibera manner than dunli white rum seen in fligh

BROAD-BILLED SANDPIPER: Recalls miniature snipe or jack snipe with striking black and white stripes on head and back; bill dark and kinked at tip rather than downcurved; legs yellow and proportionately short; set rather far back on body

PURPLE SANDPIPER: Plump-bodied wader with yellowish legs; downcurved bill mostly dark but yellowish at base; like adult, seldom seen more than a few metres from waves on rocky shores; underparts whitish and upperparts mostly grey-brown; brown feather margins on back lost by first winter

LITTLE STINT: Tiny wader, often identified by its frantic feeding activity; white underparts contrast with darker upperparts; back shows brown feather margins and white 'V' on edge of mantle; crown looks brown; often shows orange-brown flush on 'shoulders'

TEMMINCK'S STINT: Recalls miniature common sandpiper; bill short and dark and legs yellow; pale underparts contrast with grey-brown upperparts; back appears scaly due to pale feather margins

RUFF: Warm brown tone to plumage is distinctive, as is scaly appearance on back created by feather margins; head appears disproportionately small for a wader; legs yellow and relatively long; bill dark and rather short

MARSH SANDPIPER: Even more elegantly proportioned than wood sandpiper with long, yellowish legs and long, needle-like bill; upperparts brown with varying amounts of darker and paler feathering; underparts white

Pomarine Skua
Stercorarius pomarinus

Status: Passage migrant; scarce; **Voice:** Harsh, gull-like 'kowk' or 'geck' anger calls and higher mewing contact calls. **Length:** 65–78cm; **Wingspan:** 113–125cm; **Habitat:** Breeds on high Arctic tundra, overwinters at sea; **Behaviour:** Harries other seabirds at sea for food

Large, gull-like bird with heavy bill, large head and barrel-shaped body. Wings long and broad at base, and tail relatively long with twisted streamers in full adult plumage. Sexes similar. Most adults occur as pale-phase birds and smaller number as dark phase. Pale-phase bird black-brown above and on upper chest and vent; belly white and nape pale yellow. Dark chest markings sometimes form complete band. Dark-phase bird has sooty-brown plumage all over. All birds show white wing 'flashes' in flight. Juvenile pale brown with darker brown barring; white wing flashes visible, but tail streamers are absent.

Arctic Skua
Stercorarius parasiticus

Status: Summer visitor; local; **Voice:** Utters a kittiwake-like 'kee-aah', and short 'kukk' calls; **Length:** 46–67cm; **Wingspan:** 97–115cm; **Habitat:** Breeds near coasts; overwinters at sea; **Behaviour:** Harries other birds to make them drop food

Falcon-like, with long, slender wings and long tail; has dashing, acrobatic flight when pursuing other birds. Sexes similar. Adult occurs in pale and dark phases. Dark-phase bird sooty-brown with darker cap and yellowish tone to sides of face. Pale-phase bird paler grey on mantle with grey-brown cap; flanks and ventral region light grey-brown and rest of underside, head and neck white; shows some straw-yellow around neck. All birds have black legs and bill, and all dark wings with pale-white flashes. Juvenile pale-phase bird has pale head and light-brown plumage with darker marking below, giving scaly appearance; dark-phase bird almost all dark with a slightly paler head.

Long-tailed Skua
Stercorarius longicaudus

Status: Summer visitor; rare; **Voice:** Short 'kreck kreck' calls and more drawn-out cackling calls for display; **Length:** 35–58cm; **Wingspan:** 92–105cm; **Habitat:** Breeds on tundra, overwinters at sea; **Behaviour:** As other skuas

Small skua, with narrow wings, long tail and slender body. Bill short but thick. Sexes similar. Adult has greyish-brown mantle and flanks, which contrast with darker wingtips and tail feathers. Cap black and sides of face and neck pale yellow; breast pale, darkening towards ventral region. Tail streamers sometimes absent in autumn migrants. Juvenile very dark with paler feather margins, giving a barred appearance; overall tone greyer than juvenile Arctic skua.

Pomarine skua

ADULT

JUVENILE

Arctic skua

JUVENILE

PALE-PHASE ADULT
CHASING KITTIWAKE

Long-tailed skua

JUVENILE

ADULT

Great Skua
Stercorarius skua

Status: Summer visitor; widespread; **Voice:** Utters harsh 'tu tuk' alarm calls and other fierce contact notes; **Length:** 53–66cm; **Wingspan:** 125–140cm; **Habitat:** Seabird cliffs ar islands in summer; overwinters at sea; **Behaviour:** Aggressi Bulky bird, reminiscent of juvenile gull but darker ar far more heavily built. Sexes similar. In flight, adult looks broad-winged and has short tail, sometimes with two slightly projecting central feathers. Dark wings have conspicuous white flashes, seen well in flight and when win are raised over head in display. Juvenile usually darker thar adult, but may show pale tips to larger feathers on upperparts. When standing, short legs and small feet are obvious; when swimming looks bulky and buoyant.

Mediterranean Gull
Larus melanocephalus

Status: Resident; locally common; **Voice:** Shrill, nasal calls, mostly heard in spring; **Length:** 36–38cm; **Wingspan:** 98–105cm; **Habitat:** Coasts and lagoons; mainly Mediterranean; **Behaviour:** As black-headed gull Sexes similar. From a distance adult can look all whi but close up reveals very pale grey mantle. In flight, wings seen to be pure white at the tips. Has red legs and dark-red bill. In summer plumage, adult has black head wit incomplete white eye ring giving impression of eyelids. In winter plumage, head is almost pure white, apart from smudges of dark grey and blackish patch behind eye. In firs winter has black terminal band on tail, black primaries, mostly grey secondaries and brownish-grey wing coverts. By second winter mostly pale grey on mantle but still shows black tips to primaries and partially black head.

Slender-billed Gull
Larus genei

Status: Resident; rare; **Voice:** Main call deeper version of black-headed gull's; **Length:** 42–44cm; **Wingspan:** 100–110c **Habitat:** Lagoons, deltas and lakes around Mediterranean, Caspian and Black Seas; **Behaviour:** Sometimes makes shallow dives, or dips into water with bill in flight Sexes similar. Adult similar to winter black-headed g without dark markings on head, but slightly larger th that species, with longer, broader wings and slower wingbea in normal flight. Often flies in 'V' formation. Summer adult has pale-grey mantle with white leading edge to wings and black-tipped primaries; white underside suffused with pink Long bill dark orange with dark tip; legs paler orange than black-headed gull's. Juvenile has pale-orange legs and bill, and buff and dark-brown wing coverts; shows tiny smudge o grey behind eye. If seen in mixed gull flocks, appears to hav small eye and proportionately longer bill.

Great skua

Mediterranean gull

BREEDING

NON-BREEDING

ender-billed gull

BREEDING

Little Gull
Larus minutus

Status: Resident/winter visitor; local; **Voice:** Harsh, short, tern-like calls; hoarse mewing calls uttered by juveniles; **Length:** 25–27cm; **Wingspan:** 70–77cm; **Habitat:** Breeds on lake shores and marshes; overwinters at sea; **Behaviour:** Remains offshore; seen near land only during gales

Smallest gull of the region, with vigorous tern-like flight. Sexes similar. Wings of adult black on undersid with white trailing edge. Mantle pale blue-grey, and rest of plumage white, suffused with pale pink. In summer, head is all black; in winter, adult has paler head with dark-grey cap and black spot behind eye. In breeding season, legs and bill are red; legs fade and bill darkens in winter. Juvenile has characteristic black zigzag on upperwing.

Sabine's Gull
Larus sabini

Status: Autumn passage migrant; scarce; **Voice:** Utters various grating cries and whistling calls; **Length:** 27–32cm; **Wingspan:** 90–100cm; **Habitat:** Arctic coastal lowlands; ope seas in winter; **Behaviour:** Erratic, buoyant flight; seeks inshore shelter from westerly storms

Smaller than kittiwake, with narrower wings, more deeply forked tail and buoyant, tern-like flight. Sexes similar. Summer adult has dusky-grey head with thin black lower border around neck; lower neck and underparts white Mantle grey, and tail and rump white; upperwing shows diagnostic triangular pattern of grey coverts, white inner primaries and secondaries, and black outer primaries. In winter, adult loses dark hood but retains dusky streaking on nape of neck. Bill black with yellow tip at all times; legs and feet blackish-grey. Juvenile nape, back and upperwing cover feathers warm brown with whitish margins; tip of tail dark.

Ivory Gull
Pagophila eburnea

Status: Winter vagrant; rare; **Voice:** Harsh calls uttered nea breeding colonies; otherwise silent; **Length:** 40–42cm; **Wingspan:** 110–115cm; **Habitat:** Breeds on Arctic cliffs; at other times usually found at edge of pack ice; **Behaviour:** Winter diet includes fish, carrion and faeces

High Arctic gull with almost pigeon-like expression. Sexes similar. Adult pure white although feathers at base of bill sometimes stained from feeding. Bill bluish but grading through yellow towards tip, which is red. Legs and feet black. Black eye outlined by narrow red eyering. Juveni and first-winter birds essentially white but with variable amounts of black spotting on upperwings and rump, and black tip to tail. Show variable amounts of greyish featherin between base of bill and eye. Bill usually dark and legs and feet black. Black eye surrounded by narrow dark eyering.

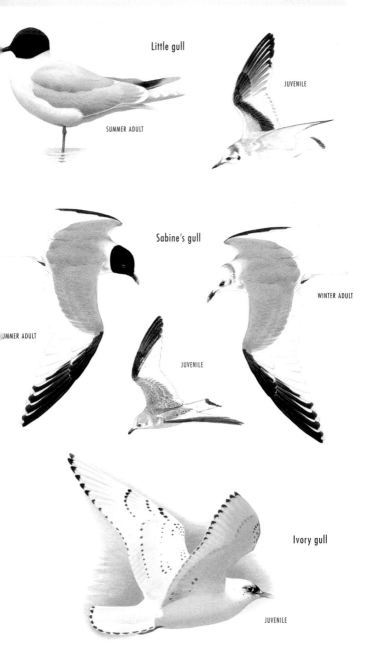

Little gull

JUVENILE

SUMMER ADULT

Sabine's gull

WINTER ADULT

SUMMER ADULT

JUVENILE

Ivory gull

JUVENILE

Ross's Gull
Rhodostethia rosea

Status: Winter vagrant; rare; **Voice:** Generally silent; **Length** 30–32cm; **Wingspan:** 85–95cm; **Habitat:** Breeds on boggy tundra; otherwise found at sea, usually in vicinity of pack ice edge; **Behaviour:** Vagrants often stay in same general location for extended periods

Small, long-winged gull, all ages of which have diagnostic wedge-shaped tail and proportionately small bill. Sexes similar. At rest, adult in breeding plumage has pale-grey upperparts and essentially white underparts. Pure white head is defined in extent by narrow black necklace. Head, neck and underparts suffused with rosy pink. In flight shows pale-grey upperwings with broad white trailing edge. Underwings smoky grey with white trailing edge and tail. Adult in non-breeding plumage loses pink suffusion and black necklace but similar in other respects. First-winter bird has similar proportions to adult. Has distinctive markings on wings best observed in flight, when pattern recalls that of first-winter kittiwake or first-winter little gull: shows distinctive black zigzag across whole of upperwing, behind which is white trailing edge. Tail white but black-tipped. Has dark smudging around eye, on nape and on ear coverts. Immature birds can take up to three years to acquire full adult plumage. All birds have black bill and red legs, colour being most intense in adult.

Black-headed Gull
Larus ridibundus

Status: Resident; common; **Voice:** Utters harsh screaming calls; very vocal near nests and when in feeding flocks; **Length:** 38–44cm; **Wingspan:** 94–105cm; **Habitat:** Sheltered seashores, lakes, marshes, urban parks, farmland; **Behaviour:** Opportunist feeder, taking wide range of foods

All non-juvenile plumages recognised in flight by white leading edge to wing with black border to primaries on upperwing; underside of wings dark grey with thinner white leading edge. Sexes similar. In summer, head of adult dark chocolate brown, colour extending to middle of head, but not down back of neck. In winter, head white with two blackish smudges around eye and on neck. Adult has red bill with dark tip, and dark-red legs; both features paler in winter. Juvenile buffish-white; subsequently, immature birds acquire grey mantle with brown and black wing coverts and black terminal tail band; legs and base of bill in immature birds dark flesh-coloured.

Ross's gull

FIRST WINTER

Black-headed gull

JUVENILE

FIRST WINTER

FIRST SUMMER

WINTER ADULT

SUMMER ADULT

Black-headed gull

FIRST WINTER

WINTER ADULTS

Audouin's Gull
Larus audouinii

Status: Resident; rare; **Voice:** Donkey-like calls and 'mew' calls similar to herring gull's; **Length:** 48–52cm; **Wingspan:** 127–138cm; **Habitat:** Remote Mediterranean headlands and islands; **Behaviour:** Graceful in flight

Elegant gull with proportionately slender wings and relatively large bill. Sexes similar. Adult very pale. In flight, mantle looks pale silvery grey with white trailing edge and black tips to primaries; inner primaries have a few white flecks. Bill mostly red with black and yellow tip. Legs black. Juvenile recalls juvenile lesser black-backed gull: mostly grey-brown with darker mantle and black bill. In second winter shows dark primaries, mostly grey mantle, and black terminal band to white tail; bill red with black and yellow tip

Common Gull
Larus canus

Status: Resident; common; **Voice:** Shrill 'keeow' and mewing 'gleeoo' calls; **Length:** 38–44cm; **Wingspan:** 110–125cm; **Habitat:** Coasts, freshwater lakes, marshes; **Behaviour:** Feeds at sea and on land, on insects and earthworms

Smaller and neater in profile than herring gull. Sexes similar. Adult has plain yellow bill, dark eye and red eyering. Wings show black primaries with white flecks in flight, and mantle grey. Head and body otherwise pure white during summer months. In winter, head and neck show grey-brown flecks, and bill duller, some individuals showing dark tip. Immature shows extensive brown in wings in first winter and broad black terminal tail band. In second winter wings almost completely pale grey. Immature bill black at first, then dull flesh colour before turning yellower in second winter.

Ring-billed Gull
Larus delawarensis

Status: Autumn vagrant from North America; rare; **Voice:** Generally silent; **Length:** 45–46cm **Wingspan:** 130–140cm; **Habitat:** Breeds beside inland wetlands; winters around coasts; **Behaviour:** Omnivorous

Similar to common gull but larger and separable with care. Immatures can recall immature herring gulls. Sexes similar. Breeding adult has white head, neck, underparts and tail. Back and upperwings grey and wingtips black. Bill more robust and proportionately larger than that of common gull; yellow with black sub-terminal band. Eye has yellow iris. Legs yellow. Non-breeding adult similar but acquires brownish streaking on head and nape. Leg and bill colour subdued. First-winter bird upperparts variably grey-brown but usually contrast with pale mantle and pale band of greater coverts and bases of inner primaries. Head and neck white but heavily spotted. Tail greyish with dark terminal band. Bill pink with black tip, and legs dull pink.

ADULT

JUVENILE

Audouin's gull

Common gull

SUMMER

Ringed-billed gull

WINTER ADULT

FIRST WINTER

Laughing Gull
Larus atricilla

Status: Vagrant from North America; very rare; **Voice:** Calls include laughing 'ha-ha-ha'; **Length:** 35–40cm; **Wingspan:** 100–120cm; **Habitat:** Vagrants usually on coastal habitats; **Behaviour:** Vagrants consort with gull flocks

Similar to Franklin's gull but larger and longer-winged. Sexes similar. Breeding adult has dark-grey mantle and upperwings with white trailing edge and black wingtips. Has black hood with white 'eyelid' markings. Neck, underparts and tail white. Bill and legs deep red. Non-breeding adult similar but loses dark hood. Bill and legs blackish. First-winter bird has grey back, grey-brown wing coverts and dark flight feathers with white trailing edge. Shows dark smudging around eye and on nape, and grey wash to neck. Underparts white and tail white with black tip. Legs and bill dark.

Franklin's Gull
Larus pipixcan

Status: Vagrant from North America; very rare; **Voice:** Vagrants to Europe silent; **Length:** 33–35cm; **Wingspan:** 90–95cm; **Habitat:** Vagrants usually favour coasts; **Behaviour:** Vagrants usually consort with black-headed gulls

Sexes similar. Breeding adult has grey back, white underparts and black hood with white 'eyelid'. Bill and legs deep red. In flight, upperwing dark grey with broad white trailing edge extending across primaries, separating grey from essentially black wingtips. Non-breeding adult similar but has broad black band on nape and rear of crown. Bill and legs dark. First-winter bird head markings similar to winter adult's. In flight, mantle and back dark grey, wings dark grey-brown with white trailing edge, and tail white with black tip. Bill and legs dark.

Bonaparte's Gull
Larus philadelphia

Status: Vagrant from North America; very rare; **Voice:** Utters plaintive, whistling calls; **Length:** 28–30cm; **Wingspan:** 95–100cm; **Habitat:** Vagrants favour coasts; **Behaviour:** Vagrants often consort with black-headed gulls

Small gull, recalling little gull. Sexes similar. Breeding adult has grey back, black wingtips, white neck and underparts and dark hood; shows white 'eyelid'. Bill dark and legs red. In flight, upperwings grey with white leading edge and black trailing edge along outer wing. Non-breeding adult similar but has white head with dark smudges above eye and on ear coverts. First-winter bird similar to non-breeding adult but has dark diagonal band on inner upperwing and black trailing edge along entire wing. Tail white with black tip.

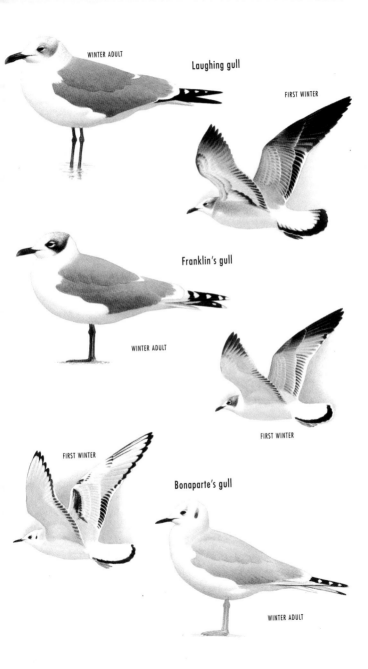

WINTER ADULT

Laughing gull

FIRST WINTER

Franklin's gull

WINTER ADULT

FIRST WINTER

FIRST WINTER

Bonaparte's gull

WINTER ADULT

Great Black-headed Gull
Larus ichthyaetus

Status: Vagrant; rare; **Voice:** Mostly silent; **Length:** 58–60cm;
Wingspan: 160–70cm; **Habitat:** Vagrants usually favour
coastal and freshwater habitats; **Behaviour:** Vagrants usually
consort with other large gulls

Large gull with massive bill and long yellow legs. Sexes
similar. Breeding adult has grey mantle and back with
black and white on projecting primaries. Underparts white.
Head has sooty-black hood except for white 'eyelid' and red
eyering. Bill yellow at base, grading to orange-red; has black
sub-terminal band. In flight shows mostly grey upperwing
with white leading and trailing edges, and broad white area
on primaries, tipped with black and white. Non-breeding
adult loses black hood and has dark smudging on nape and
behind eye. First-winter bird has dark-tipped pink bill, dark
smudging behind eye and on nape, and white underparts;
white tail dark-tipped.

Lesser Black-backed Gull
Larus fuscus

Status: Resident/summer visitor; widespread in winter;
Voice: 'Mew' calls; deeper and louder than herring gull;
Length: 52–67cm; **Wingspan:** 130–148cm; **Habitat:** Coasts,
marshes, agricultural land; **Behaviour:** Disperses widely out
to sea outside breeding season; some remain inland in winter

Occurs as three races in Europe, all with diagnostic
yellow legs. Sexes similar. Adult of western race,
graellsii, are slate grey on mantle; recalls dark herring gull,
but wingtips show less white on black primaries than this
species. Birds from Baltic (race *fuscus*) are black above,
recalling great black-backed gull but with only single white
spot on primaries. Scandinavian race *intermedius* shows
characteristics of both others. Juvenile darker than juvenile
herring gull, especially in flight. At successive moults, head
and body become whiter, and brown on wings becomes grey.

Great Black-backed Gull
Larus marinus

Status: Resident; common; **Voice:** deep barking 'owk uk-uk-
uk'; other wailing and squeaking calls; **Length:** 64–78cm;
Wingspan: 150–165cm; **Habitat:** Breeds on islands, beaches
and saltmarshes; mainly coastal in winter; **Behaviour:**
Ocassionally scavenges at rubbish dumps

Much bigger and bulkier than herring gull, with large
angular head, heavy bill and broad back. Sexes similar.
Summer adult has white head, neck, rump and tail. Back and
upperwing slaty black with white tips to primaries; underparts
white. Bill yellow with red spot on lower mandible. Legs and
feet pink. In winter, head and neck streaked with brownish-
grey. Immatures mottled dark brown and white, with whiter
rump and blackish terminal band to tail; bill black.

Great black-headed gull

BREEDING ADULT

FIRST WINTER

Lesser black-backed gull

SECOND WINTER

ADULT, RACE *GRAELLSII*

Great black-backed gull

ADULTS

JUVENILE

SECOND WINTER

JUVENILE

FIRST SUMMER

Herring Gull

Larus argentatus

Status: Resident; common; **Voice:** Utters long 'aahhoo' call and deep chuckling notes; **Length:** 55–67cm; **Wingspan:** 130–158cm; **Habitat:** All types of coastline, large lakes, rivers; **Behaviour:** Able to exploit a wide range of habitats and food sources

Sexes similar. In adult plumage, reached in fourth ye has silvery-grey mantle with black wingtips flecked with white. Large bill is yellow with orange spot near tip of lower mandible. Eye yellow and legs pink. Immatures mottl brown in first winter with dark eye and bill, and dirty-pink legs. In second winter have more grey in mantle, and iris paler. Before attaining full adult plumage black wingtips may look very pale, causing potential confusion with Icelar or glaucous gulls.

Yellow-legged Gull

Larus cachinnans

Status: Resident; common; **Voice:** Utters raucous 'aahhoo' calls and deep chuckling notes; **Length:** 55–67cm; **Wingspa** 130–158cm; **Habitat:** Mediterranean region, Black Sea; **Behaviour:** Most likely to be seen near harbours or feeding outfalls and refuse tips

Very similar to, and formerly considered a race of, herring gull; adult differs in having yellow legs and darker grey mantle when compared to western European herring gulls. Sexes similar. In winter, adult lacks dark mottling on head and neck, characteristic of herring gulls. all times bill is richer yellow and has larger red spot near t than herring gull. Three separate races of yellow-legged gu are recognised by experts; these are very similar, difficult to distinguish unless seen closely and are not considered here Immature birds brown as juveniles and in first winter; legs dark. Acquire adult's white head and body plumage, grey mantle and yellow legs through successive moults over subsequent two years.

SECOND WINTER

THIRD WINTER

SUMMER ADULT

Herring gull

ADULTS

FIRST AUTUMN

Yellow-legged gull

Iceland Gull

Larus glaucoides

Status: Winter visitor; scarce; **Voice:** Utters shrill version of herring gull's 'aahhoo' call; **Length:** 52–60cm; **Wingspan:** 130–145cm; **Habitat:** Breeds on Arctic islands; overwinters sea; **Behaviour:** Graceful flight, dipping quickly to pick up food, may submerge completely when plunge-diving

Smaller than herring gull, with more rounded head a smaller bill. Sexes similar. Absence of black on wingtips at all times is good identification feature but may lead to confusion with glaucous gull; Iceland gull is smaller and more graceful in flight, with more buoyant wingbeats. A rest, wingtips project beyond end of tail. Juvenile very simil to juvenile glaucous gull, but bill brown-grey, not pale pink. Canadian race of Iceland gull, known as Kumlien's gull, has dark-grey mark on tips of primaries.

Glaucous Gull

Larus hyperboreus

Status: Rare breeding species; scarce winter visitor; **Voice:** Short, high-pitched yapping and wailing calls; **Length:** 62–68cm; **Wingspan:** 150–165cm; **Habitat:** Breeds on small islands on Arctic and sub-Arctic coasts; overwinters on bays and harbours; **Behaviour:** Sometimes scavenges on rubbish tips

Larger than Iceland gull but usually smaller than grea black-backed gull. Sexes similar. Looks pale and whit winged at all times. Summer adult has pale-grey back and upperwings, otherwise plumage completely white, including wingtips. In winter, head and neck streaked brown. Pale eye yellow bill with red spot, and pink legs and feet seen at all times. Immature plumages white with uniform pale mottled brown gradually lost by moulting until all white by third yea bill pink with black tip.

Kittiwake

Rissa tridactyla

Status: Resident; common; **Voice:** Utters the musical cawing of its name, 'kit-ee-wak'; **Length:** 38–40cm; **Wingspan:** 95–120cm; **Habitat:** Breeds on sheer, high sea cliffs; open se in winter; **Behaviour:** Prefers the open seas outside breedin season; seen in buoyant flight passing headlands during gale

Slightly larger than black-headed gull but with more compact body and proportionately long wings. Sexes similar. Summer adult has bright white head, neck, underparts, rump and tail. Back and upperwing pale ashy blue-grey with neat black tip to wing. Winter adult has variable amounts of grey on nape. At all times of year bill pa yellow, and legs and feet brownish-black. Juvenile has diagnostic and conspicuous blackish zigzag across grey and white upperwing. Also shows blackish hind collar, black mar on face and dark tip to very slightly forked tail; bill black.

Iceland gull

FIRST WINTER

WINTER ADULT

SECOND WINTER

Glaucous gull

FIRST WINTER

WINTER ADULT

ADULTS

Kittiwake

WINTER ADULT

JUVENILE

COMPARING IMMATURE GULLS

When trying to identify any mystery gull, careful attent[?] should be paid to its overall size relative to nearby birds known species, its wing pattern and bill and leg colour. Outs[?] the breeding season gulls tend to form single-species floc[?] Immature small gulls are therefore likely to consort w[?] adults of their kind, which often helps identify them.

BLACK-HEADED GULL (first winter): Always shows white leading edge to wings and black trailing edge to primaries; seen from below latter are grey except for narrow white leading edge; brown upperwing coverts and black tail bar visible in flight; legs and bill dull pinkish-orange, bill with dark tip

LITTLE GULL (first winter): Distinctive upperwing pattern, with black angled bars, similar to that of immature kittiwake; recalls tern in size and flight; black on nape and crown striking, as is black tail bar; bill dainty and black

COMMON GULL (first winter): Well-marked with dark primaries and trailing edge to innerwing; mantle and rest of innerwing grey except for mottled brown wing coverts; tail white with broad, black terminal band; dark tipped bill dull pink

SLENDER-BILLED GULL (first winter): Superficially similar to first-winter black-headed gull, especially in upperwing pattern, but larger and with more attenuated proportions; in particular, forehead comparatively long, narrowing to join long (but not slender) bill; legs and bill dull pinkish-orange; bill has only small dark tip

MEDITERRANEAN GULL (first winter): Shows striking upperwing pattern comprising marbled brown wing coverts and black on primaries and on trailing edge of innerwing; tail black-tipped, and bill and eye patch look black at a distance

MEDITERRANEAN GU[?] (second winter): Similar to winter adult with mos[?] pure white wings except for black spots near tips primaries; black markings through eye and on na[?] give menacing appearance; legs red and bill dark [?]

..JDOUIN'S GULL (first winter): Recalls first-winter common gull ..t mantle usually marbled with dark feathers rather than uniformly ..ey; usually has cleaner-looking plumage than herring gull of similar ..e; bill looks robust even at a distance and has reddish base

..ERRING GULL (first winter): Seen from above, ..umage looks marbled grey-brown, darkest on ..maries, trailing edge of innerwing and on terminal ..nd on tail; appears palest on rump and usually ..ows pale wedge on inner primaries; ..ad looks grubby and bill dark

HERRING GULL (second winter): Compared to first-winter bird mantle is greyer, while inner primaries and rump are paler; bill dull pink and dark-tipped

..SSER BLACK-BACKED GULL (first winter): Similar to first-..nter herring gull; seen from above, usually appears ..re uniformly grey-..own and generally ..ker overall; in ..rticular, lacks that ..ecies' pale wedge ..inner primaries

LESSER BLACK-BACKED GULL (second winter): Although marbled with brown feathering, back and upperwings appear dark grey, much darker than on similarly aged herring gulls; bill often appears all dark; legs dull pink

..EATER BLACK-BACKED GULL (first winter): Seen from ..ove in flight appears mottled dark grey-brown; usually paler ..n same-age lesser black-backed gull and lacks herring gull's ..e wedge on inner primaries; head often looks pale; ..nd and bill always look large

GREAT BLACK-BACKED GULL (second winter): Can usually be identified by large size and proportionately massive head and bill alone; plumage appears paler overall than herring and lesser black-backed gulls' of similar age, head being particularly pale

Gull-billed Tern
Gelochelidon nilotica

Status: Summer visitor; local; **Voice:** Loud, deep, trisyllabic grating call; **Length:** 35–38cm; **Wingspan:** 100–115cm; **Habitat:** Lowland coasts and deltas; also lakes and marshes **Behaviour:** Sometimes hawks over agricultural land

Similar size to Sandwich tern but bulkier, with heavier more direct flight. Sexes similar. In breeding season has black crown reaching low down nape; hindneck, face and underparts white. Back, rump and tail ash grey. Upperwing pearl grey with duskier primaries towards tip. Underwing white except for dusky wedge near tip. Winter adult loses black cap but retains black mask. At all times in adult, bill black, thick and blunt, and legs and feet black. Juvenile darker than winter adult, with grey feathers of back and shoulders smudged brown; legs and feet red-brown.

Caspian Tern
Sterna caspia

Status: Rare summer visitor; local in winter; **Voice:** Utters loud, deep, barking notes; sharp alarm call; **Length:** 47–54cm; **Wingspan:** 130–145cm; **Habitat:** Sheltered coasts; **Behaviour:** Strong flier, often seen at higher altitudes than other terns

Huge gull-sized tern with massive bill, round body, blunt wings and short tail. Sexes similar. In breeding season, crown and shaggy nape black, and hindneck, face and underparts white. Back and upperwing silvery grey, darker towards wingtip. Underwing has large dusky patch at tip. Rump and tail whitish, sometimes with grey cast. In winter, cap more mottled, with black speckling extending on to face; wings become darker with wear. Bill bright coral red in summer, more orange in winter with dark tip. Legs and feet black at all times. Juvenile has mottled black cap extending on to face, and irregular brown flecking on back.

Sandwich Tern
Sterna sandvicensis

Status: Summer visitor; local; **Voice:** Distinct disyllabic 'keerr-ink'; shorter, sharp alarm note; **Length:** 36–41cm; **Wingspan:** 95–105cm; **Habitat:** Low-lying coasts with access to shallow water; **Behaviour:** Flies higher than most other seabirds

Large, pale tern with long bill and head. Tail short but deeply forked. Wings long and narrow. Sexes similar. In breeding season has jet black cap with shaggy crest to rear. Back and upperwing pale grey with silvery flight feathers. Rump and tail white. Underparts white. In winter, forehead white and cap mottled; shows dusky wedge on outerwing. At all times adult has black bill with yellow tip, and black legs and feet. Juvenile resembles winter adult, but has shorter and black bill and blackish flecking on upperwing and back.

Gull-billed tern

SUMMER

SUMMER

Caspian tern

Sandwich tern

JUVENILE

MER ADULT

Forster's Tern
Sterna forsteri

Status: Winter vagrant from North America; rare; **Voice:** Mainly silent in region; **Length:** 34–35cm; **Wingspan:** 75–80cm; **Habitat:** Vagrants favour sheltered coasts; **Behaviour:** As Sandwich tern

Medium-sized, elegant tern with long, forked tail. Mos likely to be seen in non-breeding plumage in Europe. Sexes similar. Breeding adult recalls common tern but large and with longer legs. Non-breeding adult extremely pale, an can look all white in flight except for conspicuous dark patc through eye, which gives panda-like appearance. Bill and le dark. First-winter bird similar to non-breeding adult but upperwings appear less uniformly pale.

Common Tern
Sterna hirundo

Status: Summer visitor; widespread; **Voice:** Utters harsh rasping and emphatic 'keey-yah' call; also short, sharp alarm **Length:** 31–35cm; **Wingspan:** 77–98cm; **Habitat:** Coasts and inland fresh waters, sometimes on artificial platforms; **Behaviour:** Has easy buoyant flight

Slightly shorter than black-headed gull, with which often seen, but slighter, with narrower, more pointed wings and long, forked tail. Similar to Arctic tern but with larger head, dark-tipped orange-red bill, stouter body, longe legs and shorter tail. Sexes similar. Summer adult has jet-black cap, pearl-grey upperparts with darker grey outer primaries and white rump and tail. Underparts white. Winte adult has white forehead and mottled black cap. Adult has red legs and feet at all times. Juvenile like winter adult but with ginger-brown mottling to back and forewing, and pale-orange bill with black tip.

Arctic Tern
Sterna paradisaea

Status: Summer visitor; locally common; **Voice:** Shrill, nasal grating notes and short, sharp alarm call; colonies very nois **Length:** 33–35cm; **Wingspan:** 75–85cm; **Habitat:** Inshore an offshore waters; nests on coasts; **Behaviour:** Performs longe migration of any bird, from Arctic to Antarctic

Difficult to separate from common tern. Arctic tern h shorter, uniformly coloured bill, longer tail and much shorter legs. Sexes similar. Summer adult pale blue-grey above and white below but with dusky grey wash on breast and belly. Rump and tail bright white. Jet-black cap, white cheeks and blood-red bill. White flight feathers, translucent from below, lack dark markings of common tern. Winter bird not seen in region, has crown speckled white. Legs and feet coral red in summer, darker in winter. Juvenile has white forehead and black cap; pale grey above, lacking brown tints of other juvenile sea terns.

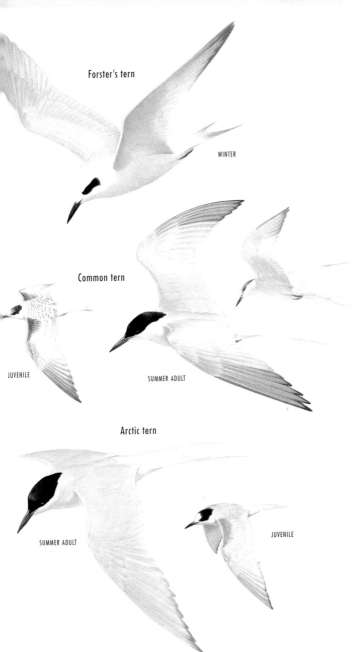

Forster's tern

WINTER

Common tern

JUVENILE

SUMMER ADULT

Arctic tern

SUMMER ADULT

JUVENILE

Roseate Tern
Sterna dougallii

Status: Summer visitor; rare; **Voice:** Calls include distinct rasping 'aakh' and whistled 'chewit'; **Length:** 33–38cm; **Wingspan:** 72–80cm; **Habitat:** Coasts with rocky islets, sand dunes; **Behaviour:** Buoyant flier

Medium-sized, pale sea tern with long, flowing tail streamers. Similar to common tern but with shorter wings and longer tail giving slimmer appearance. Sexes similar. In breeding season, adult has narrow, jet-black cap crown and nape. Lower face, rump and tail white. Upperpart have blue-grey wash, paler than in common tern. Underpart washed with strong pink. Flight feathers pale silvery grey a translucent from below. Winter adult loses rosy wash and forehead becomes white. Long, narrow, black bill with red base seen at all times in adults. Legs and feet coral red in summer, dull red in winter. Juvenile has heavy brown spotti on upperparts, reminiscent of young Sandwich tern.

Little Tern
Sterna albifrons

Status: Summer visitor; locally common; **Voice:** Rasping an churring 'kierr-ink' call; also shorter distinctive 'kik'; **Length** 22–24cm; **Wingspan:** 48–55cm; **Habitat:** Coasts and rivers with bare shingle; sand with shallow lagoons; **Behaviour:** plunge-dives for fish; has noisy courtship with fluttering flig

Smallest sea tern with larger head, longer bill and more sharply forked tail than marsh terns. Sexes similar. Summer adult has black crown, nape and line through eye to bill; forehead white. Back pale grey fading to white uppertail. Underparts pure white. Upperwing grey like back, with blackish outer primaries forming dark leading edge, and whiter trailing edge. Bill long and slender, yellow with black tip. Legs and feet orange-yellow. Non-breeding adult has darker bill and larger white forehead. Juvenile ha browner-grey feathers on back and upperwing.

Lesser Crested Tern
Sterna bengalensis

Status: Vagrant; rare; **Voice:** Calls include a harsh 'kier-rip'; **Length:** 34–36cm; **Wingspan:** 95–100cm; **Habitat:** Favours coastal waters; **Behaviour:** Solitary birds occasionally join nesting colonies of Sandwich terns well outside their tropic breeding range

Similar to Sandwich terns in size and structure but with robust, orange-yellow bill at all times. Sexes similar. Breeding adult has black cap and grey back and upperwing; otherwise white. Legs dark. Non-breeding adult and first-winter bird have black on head confined to patch from eye to nape and on rear of crown; plumage otherwise similar to breeding adult. Juvenile similar to non-breeding adult but back and upperwing mottled grey-brown.

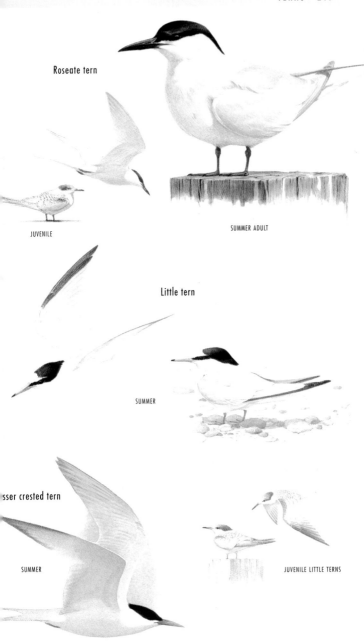

Roseate tern

JUVENILE

SUMMER ADULT

Little tern

SUMMER

sser crested tern

SUMMER

JUVENILE LITTLE TERNS

Whiskered Tern
Chlidonias hybridus

Status: Summer visitor; local; **Voice:** Loud croaking and cawing 'krrerch'; sharper alarm call; **Length:** 23–25cm; **Wingspan:** 74–78cm; **Habitat:** Clear water, lakes and marshes with floating vegetation; **Behaviour:** Buoyant flier

Largest marsh tern. Size invites confusion with a sea tern, but has shorter, less forked tail. Sexes similar. Summer adult has jet-black crown and nape, contrasting w white lower face. Neck and rest of upperparts uniform dark grey, including rump and uppertail. Below face underparts become dark slate grey. Vent and undertail coverts white. Upperwing grey, underwing coverts white. In winter, adult I grey upperparts and white underparts. Bill dark crimson-re in summer but black in winter and juvenile. Legs and feet r at all times. Juvenile resembles winter adult, but dark-brow back and pale-grey upperwing give saddle effect.

Black Tern
Chlidonias niger

Status: Summer visitor; locally common; **Voice:** Squeaky harsh 'kik-keek' call; growling 'krrr' when on nest; **Length:** 22–24cm; **Wingspan:** 64–68cm; **Habitat:** Continental fresh brackish waters, rich in floating and emergent vegetation; **Behaviour:** Foraging adults fly buoyantly over water, dippin to the surface to take prey

Smaller than all sea terns, with shorter, less forked tail. Sexes similar. Summer adult dark slate grey, wit head almost black and upperwing ash grey. Rump and uppertail grey. Underwing very pale grey; vent and undertai coverts white. In winter, grey upperparts and white underparts recall sea terns, but upperparts darker and with black smudge at shoulder. Can look blotchy during moult between summer and winter plumages. Juvenile as winter adult. At all times, bill black and fine; legs and feet red-brow

White-winged Black Tern
Chlidonias leucopterus

Status: Summer visitor; local; **Voice:** Call is a sharp churrin 'keer'; shorter alarm notes; **Length:** 20–23cm; **Wingspan:** 63–67cm; **Habitat:** Natural flooded grasslands and swamps **Behaviour:** Migrants often favour reservoirs and gravel pits

Small, compact marsh tern with striking summer plumage. Sexes similar. In breeding plumage has blac head, neck and body; upperwings greyer, showing bright silver-white wing coverts. Underwing shows black coverts a pale grey flight feathers. Rump, vent and tail white. In wint grey above and white below, with white collar and white rur contrasting with grey tail. Bill short and pointed, crimson when breeding, otherwise black. Legs and feet bright red in summer, darker in winter. Juvenile similar to winter adult t with darker, mottled brown back forming saddle.

JUVENILE

Whiskered tern

SUMMER ADULT

Black tern

JUVENILE

JUVENILE

SUMMER ADULT

WINTER ADULT

White-winged black tern

JUVENILE

SUMMER ADULT

Guillemot

Uria aalge

Status: Resident/summer visitor; common; **Voice:** Growling and guttural crowing calls; **Length:** 38–41cm; **Wingspan:** 64–70cm; **Habitat:** Breeds on rocky sea cliffs and stacks; overwinters at sea; **Behaviour:** Catches fish by diving underwater; strong flier but lacks agility

Longer-bodied and shorter-tailed than razorbill. In summer, head, neck and upperparts dark brown, underparts mainly white. Flanks streaked with brown. White line across closed wing formed by white tips to secondaries. Shows dark furrow behind eye; this is white and extends around eye in so-called bridled form, giving spectacled appearance. In winter, cheeks and neck white and upperparts greyer. At all times in adult birds, bill black, long and tapering, and legs and feet dark blue-grey. Juvenile resembles winter adult but has smaller bill.

Brünnich's Guillemot

Uria lomvia

Status: Scarce Arctic breeding species; vagrant further south; **Voice:** Utters growling and hoarse crowing calls; **Length:** 39–43cm; **Wingspan:** 65–73cm; **Habitat:** Breeds on Arctic sea cliffs; open Arctic waters in winter; **Behaviour:** As guillemot

Very similar to guillemot, but slightly larger and bulkier, with heavier bill and thicker head and neck. In summer, adult has darker brown-black upperparts than guillemot and white underparts; lacks brown flank streaks, and white breast meets brown-black throat in sharp point. In winter, upperparts retain blackish cast; white from throat extends on to face only below eye, not above as well, as seen in guillemot. At all times adult has black, deep and strong bill, with white lower edge to upper mandible extending from base to the mid-point. Legs and feet brown to front, black to rear. Juvenile smaller than winter adult; plumage similar except for mottled throat.

Razorbill

Alca torda

Status: Resident/summer visitor; common; **Voice:** Utters various growling calls; **Length:** 37–39cm; **Wingspan:** 63–68cm; **Habitat:** Breeds on sea cliffs and boulders of undercliff; overwinters inshore or on open sea; **Behaviour:** Noisy and quarrelsome at nesting colonies; lacks manoeuvrability in the air

Size of guillemot, with head, neck, back, upperwings and tail jet black in summer; underparts bright white. In winter, throat and upper-breast become dirty white and upperparts greyer. At all times, adult has deep, heavy black bill with neat white line across middle, and a white line connecting base of bill to eye. Legs and feet black. Juvenile smaller than adult, browner and with bulbous bill.

BRIDLED FORM

Guillemot

SUMMER

CHICK

WINTER

Brünnich's guillemot

WINTER

SUMMER

WINTER

SUMMER

Razorbill

CHICK

Black Guillemot
Cepphus grylle

Status: Resident/winter visitor; local; **Voice:** Thin, shrill whistle; **Length:** 30–32cm; **Wingspan:** 52–58cm; **Habitat:** Breeds on sea cliffs and maritime boulder slopes; overwinter in shallow coastal seas; **Behaviour:** Often seen around harbours and estuaries in winter

Medium-sized auk with round body, smallish head and oval-shaped wings. Sexes similar. Plumage strikingly different in summer and winter. Summer adult uniform dark chocolate brown except for large white oval patch on both upperwing and underwing coverts. In winter appears much whiter with back speckled grey and white; head, neck and underparts dirty white. Wing retains summer pattern. At all times adult has sharply pointed black bill with vivid orange gape, and bright red legs and feet. Juvenile resembles winter adult but upperparts and flanks more darkly mottled.

Little Auk
Alle alle

Status: Winter visitor; locally common; **Voice:** Twittering trills uttered at breeding colonies; whinnying alarm call in flight; **Length:** 18cm; **Wingspan:** 40–48cm; **Habitat:** Breeds on Arctic mountain and cliff scree slopes; cold open sea in winter; **Behaviour:** May be seen in winter gales flying with whirring wingbeats in long lines just above the waves

Size of starling. Sexes similar. Smart black and white plumage shows narrow white lines on shoulder and white tips to secondaries, visible when closed. Bill very small and black. Body short and stubby; has neckless appearance. Flies with very fast wingbeats. Summer adult has black head, neck and breast. In winter, throat and breast white. Rest of upperparts black, underparts white. Juvenile similar to adult but browner.

Puffin
Fratercula arctica

Status: Resident; locally common; **Voice:** Creaking, growling and grunting calls heard in breeding season only; **Length:** 27cm; **Wingspan:** 47–63cm; **Habitat:** Breeding colonies on sloping sea cliffs; overwinters at sea; **Behaviour:** Swims and dives expertly to catch fish

Smaller than guillemot and razorbill, with colourful, deep bill making head appear large. Sexes similar. Upperparts black and underparts white in all plumages, smartest in breeding adult, duller in juvenile. Summer adult has grey face, and triangular bill coloured bright red, blue-grey and yellow. Bill much less bright in winter. Red eye has surround of blue-grey horny appendages. Back, upperwing, rump and tail black. Underwing grey, rest of underparts white. Legs and feet bright orange. Juvenile has flesh-coloured feet and small, blackish bill, thinner than adult's.

Black guillemot

SUMMER

WINTER

NTER

NEWLY HATCHED CHICK

FOUR-WEEK-OLD CHICK

SIX-WEEK-OLD CHICK

FIRST WINTER

WINTER ADULT

SUMMER ADULT

Little auk

SUMMER

WINTER

Puffin

Black-bellied Sandgrouse
Pterocles orientalis

Status: Resident; rare; **Voice:** Musical cluckings and low bubbling notes, heard mostly in flight; **Length:** 33–35cm; **Wingspan:** 70–73cm; **Habitat:** Flat plains on sandy soils, grassland steppes; **Behaviour:** Most often seen flying in pair or small parties

Large, heavy-bodied, pigeon-like bird with short, pointed tail and broad, pointed, swept-back wings. Male has grey head, neck and breast with broad chestnut ar black half-collar on foreneck. Grey breast separated from black belly by narrow black and white bands. Back and upperwing ochre-yellow with blackish flecking. Flight feathers darker grey-black. Underwing distinctive with blac flight feathers and white coverts. Pointed tail barred yellow and black. Female similar to male but upperparts buff and spotted with black; breast buff with black spots. Juvenile similar to female. Bill and feet dark in all birds.

Pin-tailed Sandgrouse
Pterocles alchata

Status: Resident; rare; **Voice:** Noisy and distinctive repeate 'chata-chata' flight call; **Length:** 31–39cm; **Wingspan:** 54–65cm; **Habitat:** Warm arid Mediterranean steppes, dried-out marshes; **Behaviour:** Shy; most likely to be seen when flushed accidentally

Smaller and shorter-winged than black-bellied sandgrouse but with long, pointed tail streamers. Bot sexes have brown bill, white feathered legs and grey feet. Male has chestnut face, black throat, black margins to chestnut breast band and white underbody and underwings Back and upperwing have greenish marbling, white-edged maroon wing coverts and yellow rump barred black. Has da tail streamers. Female similar to male but with crown and nape streaked black; has more yellow, less chestnut and mc fine black barring on upperparts. Juvenile resembles femal but less bright and with short tail.

Black-bellied sandgrouse ♂ ♂ ♀

Pin-tailed sandgrouse ♀ ♂

Rock Dove
Columba livia

Status: Resident; common; **Voice:** Various moaning, cooing calls; **Length:** 31–34cm; **Wingspan:** 63–70cm; **Habitat:** Rock dove favours coasts and rocky areas; feral pigeon occurs in towns in towns; **Behaviour:** Wild rock doves are shy, fast-flying and wary; feral pigeons live alongside man

Much smaller than woodpigeon. Sexes similar. Adult medium-sized, blue-grey pigeon with two obvious black bars across rear half of innerwing; bright white underwing coverts and lower back seen in flight. Blue-grey plumage relieved on nape, neck and upper breast by green-purple gloss. Back, scapulars and innerwing paler ash grey, tail with broad brownish-black terminal band. Bill lead-coloured, off-white at base. Legs and feet dull to bright red. Juvenile like adult but duller, except for bright white on lower back.

Stock Dove
Columba oenas

Status: Resident; common; **Voice:** Disyllabic, warm, cooing 'oo-look'; also growling calls at nest; **Length:** 32–34cm; **Wingspan:** 63–69cm; **Habitat:** Woodland borders and open country; **Behaviour:** Unobtrusive; usually nests in tree-hole

Medium-sized, blue-grey pigeon. Resembles rock dove except that it lacks any white at all ages. Sexes similar. Adult plumage basically grey. Head and underbody bluer and sides of neck have glossy green sheen. Upper breast has warm pink wash. In flight, upperwing shows paler grey central panel and twin black bars on tertials. Grey tail has broad black terminal band. Bill grey-buff, off-white at base. Eye brown with grey orbital ring. Legs bright pinkish-red. Juvenile browner and duller than adult, lacking any green sheen.

Woodpigeon
Columba palumbus

Status: Resident; common; **Voice:** Multisyllabic cooing, with emphasis on second note; **Length:** 40–42cm; **Wingspan:** 75–80cm; **Habitat:** Woodland and scrub; agricultural fields next to woods in winter; **Behaviour:** Powerful flier with undulating, wing-clapping display

Largest pigeon in Europe. Sexes similar. Adult easily identified by blue-grey plumage with white neck patch, white wing crescents and black terminal band to longish, full tail. Sides and back of neck glossy green with purple sheen. Breast warm mauve-pink. In flight white wing crescents very obvious; also shows blackish primaries, with white outer web sometimes visible as pale panel. Bill reddish with yellow tip and off-white patch at base. Has pale-yellowish eye and mauve-pink legs. Juvenile much duller than adult and lacks white neck patch.

Rock dove

Stock dove

Woodpigeon

JUVENILE

ADULT

Collared Dove
Streptopelia decaocto

Status: Resident; common; **Voice:** Repeated, penetrating, unmusical cooing; **Length:** 31–33cm; **Wingspan:** 47–55cm; **Habitat:** Mixed habitats of gardens, farms, orchards and to avenues; **Behaviour:** Flies fast with clipped wingbeats; gathers in large feeding flocks in winter

Larger than turtle dove, with longer tail and uniform pale, sandy-grey plumage. Sexes similar. Adult has pale-grey crown. Face, neck and breast pinkish-buff, fading cream on belly and undertail coverts. Has narrow, white-edged black half-collar. Back, scapulars and smaller wing coverts sandy grey-brown. Greater coverts and secondaries show grey panel next to darker, dusky primaries. Underwing coverts white. Uppertail brown with whitish tips to outer feathers. Undertail has broad white terminal band. Bill black. Eye dark red with pale orbital ring. Legs and feet mauve-red. Juvenile duller than adult, lacking black half-collar.

Turtle Dove
Streptopelia turtur

Status: Summer visitor; widespread; **Voice:** Lazy, deep, purring 'coo'; **Length:** 26–28cm; **Wingspan:** 47–53cm; **Habitat:** Warm woodlands, open scrub, orchards and parks; **Behaviour:** Stays concealed in dense vegetation

Smaller and slighter than collared dove. Sexes similar. Adult has blue-grey crown with face, neck and breast warm pink. Patch of narrow black and white lines on neck. Back and rump brown with indistinct dark flecking. Closed wing has dappled pattern with black-centred, rich brown feathers. In flight shows blue-grey greater coverts and dusky flight feathers. Complicated tail pattern of white-tipped black feathers, except for central pair, which are wholly brown. Undertail black, rimmed white, contrasting with cream underparts. Dark bill with pale tip. Eye yellow with crimson orbital ring. Legs reddish. Juvenile duller than adult, lacking neck patch.

Collared Dove

Turtle Dove

Great Spotted Cuckoo
Clamator glandarius

Status: Summer visitor; locally common; **Voice:** Loud, harsh rasping calls and double 'kioc-kioc'; **Length:** 38–40cm; **Wingspan:** 58–61cm; **Habitat:** Warm Mediterranean scrub, open woodland; **Behaviour:** Lays eggs mainly in magpie nest

Much larger than cuckoo, with crest, broader wings and tail. Sexes similar. Adult has blue-grey crested crown; upper face and neck blackish-brown. Rest of upperparts dusky brown with prominent white tips to scapulars, underwing coverts and long, graduated tail. Chin, throat, foreneck and breast have warm orange-buff wash; rest of underparts off-white. Undertail coverts cream. Has long, stout, grey-black bill, red eyering and brown-grey legs and feet. Juvenile recalls bright adult but lacks crest; whole of crown dark brown. Light tips to feathers cream not white, and bright chestnut primaries conspicuous in flight.

Cuckoo
Cuculus canorus

Status: Summer visitor; common; **Voice:** Familiar male call 'cu-coo'; female makes repeated bubbling notes; **Length:** 32–34cm; **Wingspan:** 55–60cm; **Habitat:** Woodland, scrub, parkland and open uplands; **Behaviour:** Flight silhouette resembles small falcon or hawk but flight action weak

Similar size to collared dove but has longer tail. Male has slate-grey head, breast and upperparts. Underparts, from lower breast to undertail coverts, white with close, narrow blackish barring forming pattern of transverse lines across underbody. Upperwing darker grey-black, underwing paler. Darker tail feathers tipped and spotted white. Female similar to male but browner, with buff breast band. Occasional form has grey replaced with rufous, barred black. Decurved bill has yellow base with darker tip. Legs and feet yellow. Juvenile similar to rufous female but differs in having barred throat, white nape and white edges and tips to dark feathers.

Yellow-billed Cuckoo
Coccyzus americanus

Status: Autumn vagrant from North America; rare; **Voice:** Vagrants to Europe silent; **Length:** 28–30cm; **Wingspan:** 40–45cm; **Habitat:** Open woodland and scrub; **Behaviour:** Feeds on caterpillars; vagrants prone to starving in Europe in autumn

Sexes similar. Adult upperparts essentially grey-brown with chestnut on flight feathers, which is particularly striking in flight. Underparts whitish. Shows narrow yellow eyering. Underside of long tail black with large white spots at tips of tail feathers. Bill dark but base of lower mandible yellow. Legs greyish. Juvenile similar to adult but pattern on underside of tail more subdued and has less yellow on bill.

Great spotted cuckoo

JUVENILE

ADULT

ADULT ♂

JUVENILES

Cuckoo

CUCKOO CHICK

Yellow-billed cuckoo

Barn Owl
Tyto alba

Status: Resident; widespread; **Voice:** Screeching, whistling and snoring notes in breeding season; **Length:** 33–35cm; **Wingspan:** 85–93cm; **Habitat:** Open lowlands with small woods, hedges and fields; upland grasslands and heaths; **Behaviour:** Often nests in barns, old churches and farmhouses

Smaller than tawny owl but with longer, narrower wings. Unmistakable when seen well. Sexes similar. Adult from south and west European race has warm, vermiculated yellowish-brown upperparts contrasting with clear silver-white underparts. Crown, nape, back and rump warm yellowish-brown with soft grey mottling and rows of tiny blackish spotting. Coverts on closed wing similar; in flight, shows warm-buff flight and tail feathers with dark-brown barring. Shows complete heart-shaped white facial disc with dark rusty eye pits and black eyes. Underparts, including feathered legs, silky white. Feet grey-brown. Bill pinkish. Adult from central European race has buff body underparts and underwing coverts; similar in other respects to white-breasted race. Juvenile resembles adult as soon as down is lost.

Scops Owl
Otus scops

Status: Summer visitor; locally common; **Voice:** Repeated, short, human-like whistle reminiscent of slow time signal pips; **Length:** 19–20cm; **Wingspan:** 53–63cm; **Habitat:** Warm dry lowlands in open mixed woodland; parks with old hollow trees; **Behaviour:** Roosts in mature bushes and trees during the day

Small, large-headed owl with slender body and fairly long wings. Sexes similar. Adult has brown-grey or rufous upperparts with blackish streaks, bars and delicate pattern of vermiculations. Scapulars show as prominent line of black-tipped white feathers. Facial disc with incomplete blackish-brown border, mainly on sides. Shape accentuated by prominent streaked ear tufts, which are often flattened sideways. Underparts paler brown to buffish-white with dark brown streaks and vermiculations. Outer flight feathers broadly barred buff. Underwing paler buff. Bill blue-black. Eye yellow. Legs feathered, buff; feet grey. Juvenile inseparable from adult.

Barn owl

...E-BREASTED RACE

DARK-BREASTED RACE

BARN OWL CHICKS

Scops owl

GREY PHASE

NESTING BARN OWL

Eagle Owl
Bubo bubo

Status: Resident; rare; **Voice:** Deep, booming, far-carrying disyllabic hoot with sharp, croaking alarm call; **Length:** 60–75cm; **Wingspan:** 160–188cm; **Habitat:** Wilderness with rocky crags and mosaic of woods and open country; **Behaviour:** Flight action similar to buzzard's; nests in cave or large crevice

Largest European owl; barrel shaped with prominent ear tufts. Adult plumage usually warm brown, heavily marked on upperparts with thick black streaks and spots. Flight feathers barred black. Paler brown underparts have black droplets on breast; has narrower streaks and fine dark bars on belly and flanks. Head has laterally flattened black ear tufts and well-marked pale-grey facial disc with bright orange eyes. Chin and throat show furry whitish ruff. In flight dark leading edge to wing contrasts with yellowish flight feathers, barred blackish. Legs and feet feathered. Bill black. Juvenile paler and fluffier, lacking ear tufts, and has more completely barred underparts.

Snowy Owl
Nyctea scandiaca

Status: Resident; rare; **Voice:** Loud, booming double hoot and barking alarm; silent outside breeding season; **Length:** 53–66cm; **Wingspan:** 142–166cm; **Habitat:** Arctic tundra, from sea level into uplands; **Behaviour:** Adult does not tolerate disturbance and spends long periods watching over nest

Very large, essentially white owl, exceeded in size among European owls only by eagle owl. Has relatively small round head and long, rounded wings. Eyes golden yellow sunk in dusky pits. Bill black. Legs and feet densely feathered, white with black claws. Male almost entirely creamy white. Occasional small dark-brown spotting on underwing coverts hardly noticeable. Female ground colour white but heavily spotted and chevronned dark brown over whole of upperparts and most of underbody. Pure white face and centre of breast stand out. Juvenile has dark-grey head and body; rest of plumage like adult female.

Eagle owl

Snowy owl

♀

♂

Hawk Owl
Surnia ulula

Status: Resident; locally common; **Voice:** Trilling, hooting notes and screeching alarm call; **Length:** 36–39cm; **Wingspan:** 75–80cm; **Habitat:** Arboreal; pine and birch fore in tundra with clearings; **Behaviour:** Perches in clearings when watching for prey; aggressive defender of nest

Recalls sparrowhawk, with smaller head, slimmer bo and longer tail than other owls. Wings short and pointed. Sexes similar. Adult crown, nape and back blackis brown, spotted white. Has large whitish shoulder patch. Closed wing dark brown with few white spots. Flight feathe dark with whitish bars. Rump pale, barred blackish. Dark-brown tail narrowly barred pale grey. Face whitish with bro blackish curved borders to facial disc. Breast and belly very pale grey, narrowly barred blackish. Eyes striking pale yello Bill yellow-horn. Legs and feet feathered white. Juvenile paler and fluffier than adult, with more barring.

Pygmy Owl
Glaucidium passerinum

Status: Resident; local; **Voice:** Monotonous, fluty, repeated whistle; various hissing notes; **Length:** 16–17cm; **Wingspan** 34–35cm; **Habitat:** Taiga and montane coniferous forest; **Behaviour:** Fast, undulating flight similar to woodpecker's, tail often cocked when bird is perched

Tiny, small-headed owl. Sexes similar. Adult upperpa dark brown, spotted and barred with whitish-buff. Tw whitish curves back to back on nape. Crown brown, spotted buff. Rows of brown and buff spotting, white eyebrows and white sides to chin frame face. Throat and sides of breast brown, barred black. Rest of underparts white, streaked blackish. Tail brown with white barring. Shows white bars brown flight feathers. Eyes yellow. Legs and toes feathered white. Juvenile similar to adult but duskier.

Little Owl
Athene noctua

Status: Resident; widespread; **Voice:** Hollow, cat-like whist chattering warning call; **Length:** 21–23cm; **Wingspan:** 54–58cm; **Habitat:** Lowland agricultural habitats in west; arid rocky gorges and plains in east; **Behaviour:** Often perches in the open; most active around dawn and dusk

Sexes similar. Adult upperparts dark brown-grey, spotted with white. Crown and nape spotted white. Back dark brown with whitish fringes to lower neck feathe scapulars and coverts, creating pale lines. Tail has four pal bars. Facial disc buff-grey, with prominent pale eyebrows a yellow eyes. Underparts buff-grey with gorget of heavy stre on upper breast; finely streaked on belly and flanks. Bill gr brown. Longish legs feathered, buff-white; feet brown. Juvenile paler than adult, with more uniform plumage.

Hawk owl

Pygmy owl

Little owl

Tawny Owl
Strix aluco

Status: Resident; common; **Voice:** Classic melodious hoot 'huit-houuu'; common call 'ke-wick'; **Length:** 37–39cm; **Wingspan:** 95–100cm; **Habitat:** Deciduous/mixed woodlan and urban parks; **Behaviour:** Starts breeding early in the ye

 Medium-sized, broad-winged owl with large, rounded head and no ear tufts. Sexes similar. Adult has mottl barred and streaked plumage, varying from rufous-brown to grey-brown. Greyish facial disc is bordered blackish with white eyebrows, lores and sides to chin. Eyes large and blac Brown crown, neck and back streaked with black; line of white-spotted scapulars prominent. Flight feathers softly barred dark brown. Underwing buff-brown. Underparts usually paler, with uniform blackish streaks. Bill yellowish-grey. Legs and feet buff, feathered; claws grey. Juvenile similar to adult, but with shaggier feathers and finer barrin

Ural Owl
Strix uralensis

Status: Resident; declining; **Voice:** Deep hoot of three di- or trisyllabic notes; also harsh croaks; **Length:** 60–62cm; **Wingspan:** 125–135cm; **Habitat:** Temperate forests; sometimes overwinters in parks and around villages; **Behaviour:** Hunts along forest glades

Larger than tawny owl, with longer tail. Sexes simila Adult pale grey. Head, neck, back and underbody sho uniform pattern of dark-brown streaks. Pale facial disc outlined in dark brown. Eyes blackish-brown. Edges of scapulars white, forming rows of pale spots down back. Wir grey with warmer brown tones to broadly barred flight feathers. Underwings have whitish, black-tipped coverts an dark-brown-barred flight feathers. Tail grey with dark-brow bands. Bill yellow. Legs and feet feathered, buff-grey. Juver similar to adult but head whiter; underparts softly barred.

Great Grey Owl
Strix nebulosa

Status: Resident; local; **Voice:** Deep, muffled hoots with harsh alarm notes; **Length:** 65–70cm; **Wingspan:** 135–160c **Habitat:** Dense, mature forests; **Behaviour:** Aggressive towards intruders near nest

Huge owl with large, round head and long wings and tail. Sexes similar. Adult dark brown-black and white appearing grey at distance. Head, back, rump and tail pale grey, streaked and barred dark brown. Has dark blotching o back and indistinct rows of pale spots on scapulars and coverts. Closed wing brown, streaked and barred blackish. Facial disc shows concentric fine black and grey barring an white eyebrows, lores, moustache and chin. Eye and bill bright yellow. Underbody pale grey, streaked dark brown. Juvenile fluffier than adult and barred, not streaked.

Tawny owl

Ural owl

Great grey owl

Long-eared Owl

Asio otus

Status: Resident; widespread; **Voice:** Quiet, but far-carrying, repeated 'oo' notes; young like squeaking gate; **Length:** 35–37cm; **Wingspan:** 90–100cm; **Habitat:** Woodland, copse and scrub with open habitats for hunting; **Behaviour:** Roost communally in winter, often in thick shrub

Smaller than tawny owl, but appears tall and thin when alarmed. Sexes similar. Adult essentially rufous-brown. Most feathers fringed pale buff. Crown, neck and back streaked and barred with black. Closed wing shows white shoulder and white covert spots. Flight feathers rich orange barred blackish. Facial disc warm orange-buff divided by point of grey crown and white eyebrows. Prominent, blackish pale-fringed ear tufts. Eye bright orange. Bill grey. Underparts buff-brown with blackish arrowhead streaks. Belly and undertail unstreaked. Legs and feet feathered, buff; claws grey. Juvenile similar to adult but greyer, with more barring.

Short-eared Owl

Asio flammeus

Status: Resident/summer visitor; widespread; **Voice:** Low-pitched hollow 'hoo-hoo-hoo' series of notes; rasping calls at nest; **Length:** 37–39cm; **Wingspan:** 95–110cm; **Habitat:** Open country, moors, grassland and marshes; **Behaviour:** Hunts both by day and night

Long-winged owl. Sexes similar. Adult yellowish-buff heavily streaked with black. Head and neck buff with dark streaks. Back so heavily streaked it appears blackish. Rump paler with fewer streaks. Tail yellowish-buff, broadly barred dark brown. Facial disc surrounded by heavy black spotting; eyes yellow. Underbody warm buff with lighter streaks. In flight, wings shows dark carpal patch and dark tip. Bill grey. Legs and feet feathered, buff. Juvenile recalls adult but has greyer head and less heavily marked underparts.

Tengmalm's Owl

Aegolius funereus

Status: Resident; local; **Voice:** Soft, far-carrying, repeated short whistles; short, smacking yelp; **Length:** 24–26cm; **Wingspan:** 55–62cm; **Habitat:** Taiga; montane coniferous forests; **Behaviour:** Avid hunter of mammals and small birds

Smallish owl with large, square head and longish tail. Sexes similar. Adult upperparts dark brown with copious white spotting on crown, and fewer, larger spots on nape and back. Broad white edges to scapulars show as pale braces. Wing coverts and flight feathers dark brown, spotted with white. Tail dark brown with rows of tiny white spots. Facial disc outlined in black; eyes yellow. Underparts greyish-white, spotted with light brown. Bill yellowish-grey. Legs and feet feathered, white. Juvenile chocolate brown with white eyebrows and moustache, and white spotting on wings.

Long-eared owl

Short-eared owl

Tengmalm's owl

COMPARING OWLS

Given the nocturnal habits of most species, a fleeting a poorly illuminated view is often all that an observer c expect to see of a hunting owl. Nevertheless, in pa of their range some species are partly diurnal o least crepuscular for at least part of the ye Consequently, the prospect of being able to iden owls on some encounters is not as unlikely as it might seem at first.

EAGLE OWL: Massive, with extremely broad, rounded wings; wingbeats surprisingly rapid and shallow; strictly nocturnal

BARN OWL: Has pure white under and pale upperparts; flight buoyant and leis

GREAT GREY OWL: At least partly diurnal; plumage mostly grey-brown except for orange-brown flash near wingtips

TAWNY OWL: In car headlights underparts and underwings can look surprisingly pale; when flushed from daytime roost upperparts look rich brown; wings broad and rounded

SCOPS OWL: Entirely nocturnal; recalls little owl in flight but plumage more uniform and head shape rather angular

SHORT-EARED OWL: The most diurnal owl; underwings pale except for dark trailing edge and narrow barring near tips; upperwings tawny brown with dark carpal patches

SNOWY OWL: Large size and essentially white plumage distinctive; active in daytime and after dark

PYGMY OWL: At least partly diurnal; undulating flight; plumage rich brown above and pale but streaked below

URAL OWL: Mainly nocturnal; in daylight recalls buzzard with long, broad, rounded wings and relatively long tail, but size and head shape diagnostic

LITTLE OWL: At least partly diurnal and relatively easy to observe; round-headed and dumpy in flight; undulating, woodpecker-like flight

TENGMALM'S OWL: Entirely nocturnal; dumpy and large-headed in flight with broad, rounded wings; seen in fleeting glimpses

LONG-EARED OWL: Strictly nocturnal; darker brown than short-eared owl; head and body uniformly dark brown; upperwings show dark carpal patch; underwings pale

HAWK OWL: At least partly diurnal; in direct flight recalls sparrowhawk, with broad, pointed wings and long tail

Nightjar
Caprimulgus europaeus

Status: Summer visitor; widespread; **Voice:** Monotonous whirring 'churr'; disyllabic 'kwa-eek' note; **Length:** 26–28cm; **Wingspan:** 57–64cm; **Habitat:** Dry, open conifer woods, scrub, sandy heaths and semi-deserts; **Behaviour:** Hunts moths at night; roosts on the ground in daytime

Shape similar to small falcon or cuckoo. Adult dark grey and rufous-brown with heavy black barring and delicate vermiculations. Head, nape, back and rump grey, lightly streaked with black. Long grey tail barred black; outer feathers tipped white in male, buff in female. Scapulars and coverts edged silvery white, showing as pale lines. In flight rufous-brown flight feathers heavily barred black, showing white patch near wingtip in male, buff in female. Underparts brown, finely barred black; rufous towards undertail. White moustache. Very short bill black with wide gape. Juvenile resembles pale female, but lacks wing and tail spots.

Red-necked Nightjar
Caprimulgus ruficollis

Status: Summer visitor; locally common; **Voice:** Repetitive, low-pitched, double knocking 'cut-oc, cut-oc'; **Length:** 30–32cm; **Wingspan:** 65–68cm; **Habitat:** Stone pine woods; plantations with open sandy ground; **Behaviour:** Mainly nocturnal; best detected by song

Larger than nightjar, with longer wings and tail, and large head. Sexes similar. Adult mostly rufous-brown with complex variegated markings. Has greyish crown, brown back, and rump and tail variously streaked black. Pale-buff tips to scapulars and coverts create pale lines across closed wing. Warm rufous-pink collar and throat relieved by narrow white moustache and broad white spots to sides of chin. Underparts pale rufous-brown with narrow black bars and greyish band across breast. In flight both sexes show white wing spots and white patches on outertail feathers. Juvenile resembles dull adult with more buff plumage.

Common Nighthawk
Chordeiles minor

Status: Autumn vagrant; very rare; **Voice:** Vagrants to Europe silent; **Length:** 24–25cm; **Wingspan:** 60–65cm; **Habitat:** Vagrants favour open country; **Behaviour:** Not strictly nocturnal; often chases insects in afternoon

Similar to nightjar but has shorter, forked tail and longer wings. Male grey-brown but has pattern of barring and fine markings. Has distinctive white throat, white transverse patch across primaries and white subterminal band on tail; white in plumage most striking in flight. Female similar to male but lacks white on tail; throat patch buff not white. Juvenile similar to female but throat patch less distinct and plumage greyer.

Nightjar

♂

♀

Red-necked nightjar

Common nighthawk

♂

Swift

Apus apus

Status: Summer visitor; common; **Voice:** Shrill screaming whistle in breeding season; **Length:** 16–17cm; **Wingspan:** 42–48cm; **Habitat:** Aerial; usually in and around towns and villages; **Behaviour:** Spends whole life on the wing except when raising young

Medium-sized, all-brown swift, with small white throat patch. Mostly appears as all-dark blackish bird with long crescent-shaped wings and short, forked tail. Very similar in size and shape to pallid swift, but wings slightly narrower and tail more noticeably forked. Greyish forehead visible at extremely close range. In bright sunlight pale upper surface to flight feathers visible. Flight is powerful and rapid with winnowing wings. Parties make screaming calls as they fly together. Juvenile similar to adult.

Pallid Swift

Apus pallidus

Status: Summer visitor; common; **Voice:** Screaming whistle breeding season, deeper than swift's; **Length:** 16–17cm; **Wingspan:** 42–46cm; **Habitat:** Mediterranean zone, around towns, villages and coasts; **Behaviour:** Prefers dry rocky areas; will nest in old town buildings as well as on cliffs

Similar in size to swift but subtle differences in shape and colouring are important for identification. Slightly bulkier than swift overall, particularly noticeable in broader wings and shorter, more rounded tail forks. Plumage brown with pale margins to feathers creating sandy effect in good light. Forehead greyish-white. Slightly darker brown saddle on back contrasts with paler rump and upper surface to wings. Has prominent white throat patch. Underbody very pale sandy brown due to pale margins to most feathers. Juvenile inseparable from adult.

Swift

ADULTS

JUVENILE

Pallid swift

Alpine Swift
Apus melba

Status: Summer visitor; widespread; **Voice:** Loud, shrill, chattering call during breeding season; **Length:** 20–22cm; **Wingspan:** 54–60cm; **Habitat:** Aerial over southern Europe mountains, coasts and open country; **Behaviour:** Has powerful, fast flight and chattering call

Much larger than its European relatives, with bulky body and long, broad, crescent-shaped wings. Sexes similar. Upperparts warm sandy brown, appearing paler wh pale margins to fresh feathers evident. Black patch in front eye noticeable at close range. Chin and throat white. Shows broad, sandy-brown breast band. Lower breast, belly and flanks white. Underwing brown with darker brown flight feathers showing above and below wing. White chin hard to see but large white belly patch obvious. Juvenile shows mo prominent white tips to brown feathers than adult.

White-rumped Swift
Apus caffer

Status: Summer visitor; local; **Voice:** Whistle beginning as chatter, merging into trill; **Length:** 14cm; **Wingspan:** 34–36cm; **Habitat:** Rocky habitats; in vicinity of coastal towns in southern Spain; **Behaviour:** Lays its eggs in nest c red-rumped swallow; consorts with swifts and martins

Smallish, slim-bodied swift with long, deeply forked tail and dark plumage. Sexes similar. Adult has main blue-black colour to body and wings, with noticeable narrow bright white band across upper rump. Greyish crow and line over eye, small whitish chin and silvery sheen to underwing flight feathers visible at close range. Long, narrow wings give distinctive silhouette; very fluttery flight lacks power of larger relatives. Juvenile shows more whitis tips to body feathers than adult and less blue-black sheen t dull, dark plumage.

Little Swift
Apus affinis

Status: Possibly resident in Spain; vagrant elsewhere; rare; **Voice:** High-pitched screaming call uttered in flight; **Lengt** 12cm; **Wingspan:** 34–35cm; **Habitat:** Nests in buildings an on cliffs; otherwise entirely aerial; **Behaviour:** Intersperses glides with bouts of fluttering flight

Small compact swift. Recalls house martin in plumag details but easily recognised as a swift species by silhouette. Sexes similar. Adult has dark sooty-brown plumage except for square, white rump and white throat; forehead greyish. Tail relatively short and square-ended. Juvenile similar to adult but plumage not as dark.

Alpine swift

White-rumped swift

Little swift

Kingfisher
Alcedo atthis

Status: Resident; widespread; **Voice:** Song comprises starli
like bubbling whistles; also plaintive chattering whistle cal
Length: 16–17cm; **Wingspan:** 24–26cm; **Habitat:** Streams,
rivers and lakes with surrounding vegetation; **Behaviour:**
Perches above water before plunge-diving for fish

Small kingfisher with long bill and relatively large
head. Sexes similar. Adult has crown, nape, moustac
and all upperparts bright blue, tone varying with light and
viewing angle. Shows pale sheen on back. Crown and wing
coverts have pale blue spotting. Scapulars, flight feathers a
tip of tail darker blackish-blue. Face, underbody and
underwing coverts rich orange-chestnut, paler on throat ar
centre of belly. White spots present in front of eye, on sides
neck and under chin. Long dagger-shaped bill all black in
male; has reddish base in female. Legs and feet coral red.
Juvenile lacks brilliance of adult, and has greener upperpa
and bluish-grey breast. Legs dull orange.

White-breasted Kingfisher
Halcyon smyrnensis

Status: Resident/winter visitor; rare; **Voice:** Utters loud
rattling calls and shrill whistles; **Length:** 26–29cm;
Wingspan: 40–42cm; **Habitat:** Wetlands of all types; also
occasionally hunts over dry land; **Behaviour:** Prefers perch
1–3m above water, sheltered from direct sun

Distinctive and beautifully marked kingfisher. Sexes
similar. Adult has striking white throat and chest, ar
chestnut head, neck, breast and underparts. Back, tail and
wings iridescent blue except for black tips to primaries anc
black and chestnut wing coverts. Bill proportionately mass
and bright red; legs and feet bright red. Juvenile similar to
adult but colours duller.

Pied Kingfisher
Ceryle rudis

Status: Resident/winter visitor; rare; **Voice:** Loud, high-
pitched screaming call; **Length:** 25–26cm; **Wingspan:**
45–46cm; **Habitat:** Always found close to water; generally
fresh water but sometimes also coastal; **Behaviour:** Hovers
briefly in mid-air before diving after fish

Distinctive and well-marked kingfisher. Male has
striking black and white marbled upperparts.
Underparts essentially white except for two black breast
bands. Female similar to male but has only one black breas
band. Juvenile similar to female but has grey chest band, n
black. All birds have black bill and feet.

Kingfisher

♂

♀

Pied kingfisher

♂

ite-breasted kingfisher

Bee-eater
Merops apiaster

Status: Summer visitor; locally common; **Voice:** Liquid bubbling 'pruupp'; **Length:** 27–29cm; **Wingspan:** 44–49cm; **Habitat:** Warm open habitats with mixed agriculture; tree clumps, often near rivers; **Behaviour:** Pursues insects in fli

Has slim, elegant appearance and multicoloured plumage. Sexes similar. Adult has chestnut crown, nape and back shading to yellowish-brown on scapulars an rump. Uppertail dark shiny green, duller below with centra two feathers darker and elongated. Wing coverts chestnut, surrounded with bluish-green. Flight feathers shiny blue, dark-tipped. Forehead whitish with narrow pale-blue supercilium. Has black eye mask and black border to yello throat. Underparts pale turquoise-blue. Underwing orange with darker-tipped flight feathers. Long, slim, decurved bil black. Eyes reddish. Legs and feet brownish-black. Juvenil resembles dull adult but bluer on back and wings.

Blue-cheeked Bee-eater
Merops superciliosus

Status: Spring vagrant; rare; **Voice:** Bubbling, ringing disyllabic 'prr-ipp'; **Length:** 28–30cm; **Wingspan:** 46–48cm **Habitat:** Open, arid terrain, usually close to water; **Behaviour:** Perches on prominent branches

Attractively marked and aerobatic bee-eater. Sexes similar. Adult plumage essentially green although appears bluish on rump and lower back. Head markings distinctive: has black eyestripe and white forehead gradin; sky-blue supercilium; cheeks sky blue and throat yellow, grading to orange-red. Tail streamers extremely long, at le twice length of those of bee-eater. Juvenile similar to adul but plumage duller and tail streamers much shorter.

Roller
Coracias garrulus

Status: Summer visitor; locally common; **Voice:** Rasping, accelerating rattle. Harsh, short contact call; **Length:** 30–32cm; **Wingspan:** 66–73cm; **Habitat:** Warm lowlands, open forest, heaths and grasslands; **Behaviour:** Perches prominently along roadside wires

Large, crow-like bird, with very brightly coloured plumage. Adult has pale green-blue head, neck and underbody. Forehead and chin whitish, with narrow black mask. Back chestnut, rump purple-blue. Shoulder iridesce cobalt blue with pale green-blue coverts and blue-black fli feathers. Tail blue-black with pale-green outer webs and d tips to feathers. In flight, upperwing shows two-tone blue coverts and blackish flight feathers. Underwing shows pal blue coverts and blue, black-tipped flight feathers. Strong decurved and slightly hook-tipped bill black. Legs and fee black. Juvenile resembles dull adult.

Bee-eater

Blue-cheeked bee-eater

Roller

Hoopoe

Upupa epops

Status: Summer visitor; widespread; **Voice:** Song low, far-carrying mellow 'oo-oo-oo'; cawing contact calls; **Length:** 26–28cm; **Wingspan:** 42–46cm; **Habitat:** Warm, dry, varied open landscapes with some trees and bare ground; **Behaviour:** Nests in tree-hole, usually in orchard

Similar to jay in size and colour but slimmer when perched. Sexes similar. Adult head, neck, back and underbody pale brownish-pink, with warmer pinkish shade breast. Has long erectile crest of pink feathers, tipped with white and black, and white crescent on rump. At rest, transverse black and creamy-white barring crosses wings and shoulders, foremost bar being pale orange. Tail black with wavy white band near base. Undertail coverts whitish. In flight primaries black with single white crescent near tips. Long, slender, decurved bill black with pinkish base. Legs and feet black. Juvenile duller than adult, with dingy cream barring and shorter bill.

Wryneck

Jynx torquilla

Status: Summer visitor/resident; widespread; **Voice:** High-pitched, ringing 'pee-pee-pee', like small falcon; **Length:** 16–17cm; **Wingspan:** 25–27cm; **Habitat:** Lowland woodland fringes, orchards, parks and large gardens; **Behaviour:** Quiet and unobtrusive during breeding season; does not excavate nest like other woodpeckers

Similar in size to nightingale but longer and slimmer with plumage recalling nightjar. Sexes similar. At a distance adult appears mottled grey and brown; at close range very finely marked. Grey crown, sides to mantle and back bordered by black scapular stripe, which connects on side of neck with elongated black eyestripe. Wings brown with heavy dark barring and vermiculation. Long, full grey has transverse black bars. Throat and upper breast yellow with short black bars. Lower breast and belly creamy white with dark spots. Bill, legs and feet pale brown. Juvenile slightly paler than adult, with less barring.

Hoopoe

Wryneck

Grey-headed Woodpecker
Picus canus

Status: Resident; locally common; **Voice:** Repeated fluty whistles slowing and descending in pitch; **Length:** 25–26cm; **Wingspan:** 38–40cm; **Habitat:** Open deciduous woods; montane larch woods in central Europe; **Behaviour:** Excavates nest hole in mature tree

Smaller than green woodpecker, with less robust bill. Male has grey head marked only with red forecrown and narrow black moustache above whitish throat. Back, scapulars and wing coverts pale but intense green. Rump yellow. Breast and underbody pale grey. Tail greenish. Folded flight feathers brownish-black, barred with white. In flight upperwings green except for dark brown-grey primaries conspicuously barred white. Underwing dark grey, barred white. Bill dark grey, yellowish towards base. Female has no red on crown; otherwise similar to but duller than male. Legs and feet of both sexes grey. Juvenile browner and scruffier than adult.

Green Woodpecker
Picus viridis

Status: Resident; common; **Voice:** Ringing laugh known as yaffle; alarm call short 'kyack'; **Length:** 31–33cm; **Wingspan:** 40–42cm; **Habitat:** Open, broad-leaved lowland forest with clearings; parks, gardens and heaths; **Behaviour:** Feeds almost exclusively on ants

Large, bulky woodpecker. Male has red crown extending on to nape; has black face patch with red moustachial stripe. Upperparts bright green with bright yellow rump and brown-black primaries, barred cream. Tail dark greenish-grey with faint cream spotting. Rear of face, sides of neck and underparts pale clear yellow except for darker barring on flanks. Bill grey with yellowish lower mandible. Legs and feet grey. Female similar to male but has smaller black face patch, and lacks red moustache. Juvenile similar to adult but colours dulled by white spots and bars upperparts; has dark bars on underparts.

Black Woodpecker
Dryocopus martius

Status: Resident; locally common; **Voice:** Loud, far-carrying drumming; loud, melodious, repeated notes – often in flight; **Length:** 45–47cm; **Wingspan:** 64–68cm; **Habitat:** Mature northern taiga; southern montane deciduous forests; **Behaviour:** Noisy and showy; excavates living wood

Largest European woodpecker. Male glossy black with scarlet forehead and long crown. Female browner and lacks plumage gloss; red on crown restricted to small patch above nape. Has massive, grey-brown, chisel-like bill with darkish tip. Legs and feet dark grey. Juvenile resembles adult but with grey chin; red on crown less extensive or absent.

♂ Grey-headed woodpecker

Green woodpecker

♀

♀ Black woodpecker

♂

♂

Green woodpecker

♂

Great Spotted Woodpecker

Dendrocopos major

Status: Resident; common; **Voice:** Loud drumming; call is a sharp 'tchicc' and short rattle of similar notes; **Length:** 22–23cm; **Wingspan:** 34–39cm; **Habitat:** Adaptable to vario habitats with trees; prefers open, mature deciduous woods; **Behaviour:** Excavates new nest hole every year

Strong-billed pied woodpecker. Upperparts black, relieved by large white scapular patches, white spots across flight feathers and white barring on outertail feather Male has crimson nape patch, absent in female. Face and eyering mainly white with black moustache connecting wit black nape and with black extension bar on to sides of brea Shows white patches on sides of neck. Underparts creamy white with pinkish-red vent area and 'trousers'. Bill, legs an feet dark grey. Juvenile has red crown, dirty-white underpar and less distinct white barring on wings than adult.

Middle Spotted Woodpecker

Dendrocopos medius

Status: Resident; local; **Voice:** Drumming rare; far-carrying jay-like 'quah'; contact call soft; **Length:** 20–22cm; **Wingspa** 33–34cm; **Habitat:** Mixed deciduous woods; **Behaviour:** Needs dying timber for excavating nest sites and food

Smaller, less cleanly marked version of great spotted woodpecker. Male has red crown, which is shorter an duller in female. Remainder of upperparts black with white scapular patches, white barring on flight feathers and white outertail feathers, barred black. Face white with black moustachial border not connecting with black on nape. Downward extension of moustache on to sides of throat giv way to black streaking extending down flanks. Chin and throat white, shading to dirty yellowish on breast. Belly and vent pinkish. Bill, legs and feet grey. Juvenile similar to adu but duller, with less contrast and fewer flank streaks.

White-backed Woodpecker

Dendrocopos leucotos

Status: Resident; local; **Voice:** Long, loud accelerating drumming. Low quiet 'kjuck' and other hoarse squeaks; **Length:** 24–26cm; **Wingspan:** 38–40cm; **Habitat:** Extensive deciduous or mixed forests; **Behaviour:** Rather unobtrusive

Large pied woodpecker. Adult upperparts black with heavy white barring across wings, and white lower ba and rump. Black tail has barred white outer feathers. Male crown red; female crown black. Face white with black moustachial stripe turning up, but not connecting with, bla nape, and extending down to break into heavy black streaks covering sides of breast and flanks. Chin and throat white. Breast pale-buff; lower belly and vent pink-red. Bill, legs an feet grey. Juvenile similar to adult but has black streaks on red crown, greyish flanks and less red around vent.

♀

Great spotted
woodpecker

♂

Middle spotted
woodpecker

♂

White-backed
woodpecker

♂

Syrian Woodpecker
Dendrocopos syriacus

Status: Resident; locally common; **Voice:** Long, loud drumming; call soft, short 'chjuck'; **Length:** 22–23cm; **Wingspan:** 34–39cm; **Habitat:** Warm, open landscapes with scattered trees; orchards and parks; **Behaviour:** Favours more open terrain than other woodpeckers

Similar to great spotted woodpecker. Adult has generally black upperparts and white underparts. Black moustachial line turns up and back, but does not join with black of neck, giving more open-looking white face than on great spotted woodpecker. Male has red nape. Has bolder white barring on wings, but white bars on outertail feathers almost absent. Vent pale pink. Bill, legs and feet dark grey. Juvenile similar to adult but has red crown and flank streak.

Lesser Spotted Woodpecker
Dendrocopos minor

Status: Resident; widespread; **Voice:** Quiet, high-pitched drumming; soft whistling 'pee-pee-pee', repeated up to 20 times; **Length:** 14–15cm; **Wingspan:** 25–27cm; **Habitat:** Open, broad-leaved woodland; riverine alders; **Behaviour:** Has fluttery, buoyant flight; often found in highest branches

Smallest pied woodpecker, about size of nuthatch. Adult upperparts predominantly black with heavy white barring across back and wings; tail black with outer feathers barred white. Male has short red crown; white in female. Rear of crown black. Buff-white face above black moustache curving upwards around ear coverts, with downward extending bar. Underparts buffish-white, streaked black on flanks, with black spots on undertail coverts. No red around vent. Bill, legs and feet grey. Juvenile similar to adult but with browner and more streaked and spotted underparts.

Three-toed Woodpecker
Picoides tridactylus

Status: Resident; local; **Voice:** Long, rattling drumming; contact call soft, longish 'gjug'; **Length:** 21–22cm; **Wingspan:** 32–35cm; **Habitat:** Northern conifer forests; central montane spruce forests; **Behaviour:** Tame but unobtrusive

Medium-sized black and white woodpecker lacking red in plumage. Northern race adult has black nape, face and moustache with white rear supercilium and white strip under ear coverts. Back and rump white with ragged black border. Wing and tail black with narrow white barring on flight feathers and outertail feathers. Underparts buff-white with grey barring on sides of breast and flanks, and black spotted undertail coverts. Male has yellow crown; black with white flecks in female. Alpine race darker, with less white on back and heavier markings on underparts. Bill, legs and feet grey. Crown mottled yellow. Juveniles of both races greyer on underparts than respective adults.

Syrian woodpecker

♂

♀

Three-toed woodpecker

♂

Lesser spotted
woodpecker

♂

COMPARING WOODPECKERS IN FLIGHT

Most European species of woodpecker are, on the whole, rat[...] retiring birds and often the best views are had of birds in fli[...] Such observations are generally brief and so it is important t[...] observers familiarise themselves with key aspects of plum[...] and behaviour to make positive identification possible. All [...] birds shown here are in adult male pluma[...]

BLACK WOODPECKER: Unmistakable when seen well. Recalls crow in flight with exaggerated and slow wingbeats; flight direct, not undulating

GREY-HEA[...] WOODPECKER: Superfic[...] similar to green woodpe[...] with essentially greenish upperp[...] and yellow rump; smaller than that spe[...] however, and proportionately less bulky. H[...] looks paler than that of green woodpecker [...] to absence of mask-like mark[...]

MIDDLE SPOTTED WOODPECKER: Upperwing pattern similar to great spotted and Syrian woodpeckers; largely black with interrupted white barring on flight feathers and white shoulder patches. Note the mainly pale head with red on nape

GREEN WOODPECK[...] Low, undulating fl[...] invariably accompanied by [...] yaffling alarm calls. In good l[...] rump looks strikingly yellow, and red on [...] and nape often visible; plumage otherwise greenish [...] upperparts and grubby grey on underp[...]

SYRIAN WOODPECKER: Similar to great spotted woodpecker with mainly black upperwings showing interrupted white barring on flight feathers and white shoulder patches. Close scrutiny of facial markings will reveal that black moustachial stripe does not link to black on nape or shoulder

[GR]EAT SPOTTED [WO]ODPECKER: Seen in [fligh]t, superficially similar to [Syri]an woodpecker. Look closely at [faci]al markings to see whether black [mo]ustache links to black on nape and shoulders

LESSER SPOTTED WOODPECKER: Easily recognised by small size and extensive interrupted white barring on otherwise black upperwings

[WH]ITE-BACKED [WO]ODPECKER: [upp]erwings largely black [with] interrupted white barring [on f]light feathers; white shoulder [pat]ches absent. Shows conspicuous [and] diagnostic white rump and lower back

THREE-TOED WOODPECKER: Upperwings look more uniformly black than other medium-sized woodpeckers'. Extensive white band along entire length of back is diagnostic

Skylark
Alauda arvensis

Status: Resident; common; **Voice:** Loud, melodious warblin, flight song; call is a liquid rippling 'chirropp'; **Length:** 18–19cm; **Wingspan:** 30–36cm; **Habitat:** Grasslands in lowlands and uplands; cultivated fields; **Behaviour**: Deliver pleasant, warbling song while fluttering high in the sky

Most familiar European lark. Sexes similar. Adult upperparts buff, streaked blackish-brown. Crown wel streaked, with short crest prominent only when erect. Show pale-buff supercilium and surround to buff cheeks. Closed wing shows blackish buff-edged coverts forming wingbars. Tail blackish-brown with white edges. In flight, wings show clear white trailing edge. Underparts buff-white with heavy streaking across breast and flanks. Bill grey-brown. Legs an feet pale brown. Juvenile recalls adult but has speckled wh upperparts with black drop-shaped streaks on breast.

Woodlark
Lullula arborea

Status: Resident; widespread; **Voice:** Flight-song is beautifu descending series of rich, mellow, fluty whistles; **Length:** 15cm; **Wingspan:** 27–30cm; **Habitat:** Warm, dry, sandy lowlands with heathland vegetation and scattered trees; **Behaviour:** Forages for seeds in flocks in winter

Smaller and slighter than skylark. Sexes similar. Upperparts buff, heavily streaked blackish. Sexes similar. Adult face has white supercilia meeting on nape, ar dark-brown surround to warm buff cheeks. Hind-neck and rump whitish-buff. Has small crest at rear of crown. Closed wing shows black and white bar at wing bend. Tail short an dark. Underparts buff-white with necklace of prominent black streaks. Fine bill, dark grey-brown with paler base. Le and feet pink. Juvenile similar to adult but less well marke

Dupont's Lark
Chersophilus duponti

Status: Resident; local; **Voice:** Song beautiful mixture of flu notes and finch-like twittering; **Length:** 18cm; **Wingspan:** 26–31cm; **Habitat:** Dry, open, Mediterranean steppes with sparse vegetation; cereal fields in winter; **Behaviour:** Prefe to run rather than fly when startled

Smaller than skylark with long bill and no crest. Sexe similar. Adult upperparts brown, heavily streaked wit blackish-brown. Face well marked with long buff-white supercilium and eyering forming spectacle; pale-grey half-collar surrounds brown cheeks. Mantle, scapular and wing feathers neatly edged with buff, giving scaly effect. Tail brown, edged with white. Underparts white with heavy blac spotting across chest and streaking down flanks. Long, decurved bill grey-brown. Long legs brownish-white. Juveni similar to adult but upperparts less streaked and more scaly

Skylark

Woodlark

Dupont's lark

Calandra Lark

Melanocorypha
calandra

Status: Resident; local; **Voice:** Loud, rich, fluty song interspersed with grating notes; shrill buzzing contact cal▐ **Length:** 18–19cm; **Wingspan:** 34–42cm; **Habitat:** Grassla▐ steppes and cultivated fields; **Behaviour:** Runs on ground perches prominently on bushes

Larger than skylark with broader wings, short tail a▐ heavy bill. Sexes similar. Adult crown, nape, back a▐ wings buff-brown with blackish feather centres forming streaks. Face warm brown with creamy supercilium and narrow eyering. Tail dark brown with white outer feathers Underparts cream with blackish patches on sides of breas▐ and warm yellowish wash, spotted black, extending down to flanks. In flight shows white trailing edge to wings and black underwing. Bill grey-brown with dark tip. Legs and ▐ pale brown. Juvenile similar to adult but more speckled o▐ upperparts and throat; lacks clear black patches on breas▐

Short-toed Lark

Calandrella
brachydactyla

Status: Summer visitor; widespread; **Voice:** Song jingling melodious with swallow-like twittering; **Length:** 13–14cm▐ **Wingspan:** 25–30cm; **Habitat:** Dry, open steppes and cultivated fields; **Behaviour:** Feeds unobtrusively on grou▐

Smaller and paler than skylark, with compact body, neat, finch-like bill and no crest. Sexes similar. Adu▐ upperparts sandy buff, lightly streaked dull brown. Crown rufous-brown. Off-white supercilium contrasts with brown▐ cheeks. Closed wing shows blackish-centred coverts with ▐ margins. Rump pale buff; tail blackish with white edges. Underparts white with sandy wash across breast and brow▐ patches on breast sides. Bill grey-brown with yellow base. Legs and feet brown. Juvenile upperparts more speckled t▐ adult's, with gorget of dark streaks on upper breast.

Lesser Short-toed Lark

Calandrella rufescens

Status: Resident/summer visitor; local; **Voice:** Continuous melodious song in flight; loud, rippling alarm call; **Length** 13–14cm; **Wingspan:** 24–32cm; **Habitat:** Steppes and sem▐ desert with low shrubs; **Behaviour:** Has low, circular song-fl▐

Similar to short-toed lark but with heavier streakin▐ long wing point and tiny bill. Sexes similar. Adult upperparts rufous-brown with strongly marked blackish feather centres. Pale-cream supercilia frame brown face a▐ meet across pale forehead. Underparts buff-white with bre▐ wash across chest; black streaks form gorget. Streaks exte▐ on to flanks. Wings brown with pale feather edging; three primaries project into point when at rest. Bill pale grey-br▐ with darker tip. Legs and feet yellowish. Juvenile similar t▐ adult but more speckled.

Calandra lark

Short-toed lark

Lesser short-toed lark

Crested Lark
Galerida cristata

Status: Resident; common; **Voice:** Song loud with fluty whistles and mimicry; **Length:** 17cm; **Wingspan:** 29–38cm; **Habitat:** Open, dry plains and habitats such as waste grou[n] **Behaviour:** Characteristically runs from danger

Bulky, skylark-sized bird with long bill, spiky crest, deep chest and upright stance. In flight looks comp[act] with broad wings and short tail. Sexes similar. Adult sandy buff on upperparts and underparts. Shows blackish streak[s] on crown, including crest, and back, chest and flanks. Fac[e] has cream supercilium and eyering forming spectacle; als[o] neat black moustachial and malar stripes. Tail dark with b[uff] outer feathers. Underwing coverts orange-buff. Longish bi[ll] grey-brown. Legs and feet flesh-coloured. Juvenile crest shorter than adult's; upperparts darker with white speckli[ng]

Thekla Lark
Galerida theklae

Status: Resident; local; **Voice:** Loud, fluty song with whistl[es] and mimicry; alarm-call is repeated fluting whistle; **Lengt[h]** 17cm; **Wingspan:** 28–32cm; **Habitat:** Mediterranean habit[at] including scrub and cultivated plains; **Behaviour:** Often perches on bushes

Same size as crested lark but slighter in build, with shorter bill and fuller fan-shaped crest. Sexes simila[r] Adult upperparts greyish-brown; underparts show grey che[st] and white belly. Shows distinct blackish streaks on crown, whole of neck and back. Rump rufous. Throat finely streak[ed] Heavy black spotting on chest extends to flanks. In flight, underwing appears dull grey-brown. Bill grey-brown with paler base. Legs and feet flesh-coloured. Juvenile almost inseparable from juvenile crested lark.

Shore Lark
Eremophila alpestris

Status: Resident; local; **Voice:** Subdued twittering song of thin musical notes; **Length:** 14–17cm; **Wingspan:** 30–35cm **Habitat:** Tundra or montane plains; coasts in winter; **Behaviour:** Difficult to spot on the ground; flight powerfu[l] with bounding action

Smaller and slimmer than skylark, with crouched appearance. Male has pale-yellow face and throat w[ith] black forecrown and black mask curving down below eye. black gorget across upper breast. Rear crown and nape reddish-brown; tufted black feathers on sides of crown for 'horns'. Rest of upperparts mottled brown. Tail dark with white outer feathers. Lower breast and belly white with pinkish-brown wash and faint black streaking on flanks. Female duller and more heavily streaked than male. In bo[th] sexes bill grey, and legs and feet black. Juvenile recalls ad[ult] but is speckled and lacks face pattern.

Crested lark

Thekla lark

Shore lark

SUMMER

WINTER

Sand Martin
Riparia riparia

Status: Summer visitor; widespread; **Voice:** Harsh, twitter quiet song; harsh, grating, single-syllable contact call; **Length:** 12cm; **Wingspan:** 27–29cm; **Habitat:** Aerial, in vicinity of sandy banks and near to water; **Behaviour:** Ofte gathers in large flocks before winter migration

Smallest hirundine in Europe, with short, slightly forked tail. Sexes similar. Adult upperparts, includi flight and tail feathers, dark greyish-brown with sandy ton Brown extends down on to cheeks and broad band across breast, with light-brown smudges on flanks. Rest of underparts white. Underwing dusky brown. Throat often speckled brown. Bill, legs and feet black. Juvenile similar adult but upperparts show pale fringes to feathers.

Crag Martin
Ptyonoprogne rupestris

Status: Summer visitor/resident; locally common; **Voice:** Quiet, but persistent, guttural twittering song. Short, sing note contact call; **Length:** 14cm; **Wingspan:** 32–34cm; **Habitat:** Mountainous regions and river valleys and gorge with exposed rock faces; coasts in winter; **Behaviour:** Glic frequently like swift; quarters same sheltered crag repeate

More bulky than sand martin, with broad wings, aln unforked tail and uniform dusky plumage. Sexes similar. Adult upperparts dusky brown-grey. Underparts da buff with smoky tone. Underwing coverts blackish. At close range buff throat speckled with dark brown. Lateral tail coverts show pale chevrons. In flight white spots visible towards tips of tail feathers. Bill black. Legs and feet dark brown. Juvenile has warmer plumage tones than adult.

Red-rumped Swallow
Hirundo daurica

Status: Summer visitor; common; **Voice:** Quiet, twittering chattering song; short, descending, whistling alarm note; **Length:** 16–17cm; **Wingspan:** 32–34cm; **Habitat:** Aerial ov meadows and pasture, open water and villages; in warm latitudes; **Behaviour:** Nests in natural crevices; less dependent on humans than other hirundines

Similar in size to swallow but bulkier, with blunter streamers turned inwards. Sexes similar. Adult crow mantle, scapulars and upperwing coverts blue-black, not a shiny as swallow's. Wings and tail brown-black, including undertail coverts, which gives effect of whole tail having b dipped in black paint. Has broad pale-chestnut band acros nape, and chestnut lower back shades to buff rump. Foreh and cheeks speckled rufous-buff. Underparts buff, faintly streaked black. Underwing coverts buff, contrasting with blackish flight feathers. Bill black. Legs and feet dark. Juvenile duller than adult, with shorter tail streamers.

Sand martin

Crag martin

Red-rumped swallow

Swallow
Hirundo rustica

Status: Summer visitor; common; **Voice:** Song pleasant warble with some rattling notes; alarm call loud, short 'chit'; **Length:** 17–19cm; **Wingspan:** 32–35cm; **Habitat:** Aerial above pasture, open water, villages and farms; **Behaviour:** Often found near villages nesting in old buildings

Classic swallow shape with small bill and long, forked tail streamers. Sexes similar. Adult upperparts and breast band shiny blue-black. Forehead, chin and most of throat above breast band rich rufous-red. Underparts, including underwing coverts and long undertail coverts buff white, with black under-surfaces of flight feathers and black underside to tail. When spread, tail shows white spots towards tips of all but outermost feathers, which are elongated into streamers. Female has shorter streamers than male. Bill and feet black. Juvenile similar to adult but has less shiny plumage, paler head, mottled breast band and no real tail streamers.

House Martin
Delichon urbica

Status: Summer visitor; common; **Voice:** Soft, sweet twittering song; long, trilling alarm call; **Length:** 12.5cm; **Wingspan:** 26–29cm; **Habitat:** Usually in high air space above towns, villages and occasionally coastal cliffs; **Behaviour:** Often nests in urban buildings; feeds on insects high in the sky

Short and stubby hirundine with large head and noticeably forked short tail. Summer adult has dark blue-black upperparts except for prominent white rump. Underbody from chin to vent clear white in male, slightly dirty white in female. Dull-grey underwing coverts and dusky grey under-surfaces to flight and tail feathers. Winter adult has white underparts mottled or smudged with brownish-black, and is less smart. Bill black. Legs feathered white, and feet flesh-pink. Juvenile duller greyish-black on upperparts than adult, with some white mottling on nape.

ADULT ♂

JUVENILE

Swallow

House martin

Tawny Pipit
Anthus campestris

Status: Resident; widespread; **Voice:** Monotonous song of metallic repeated phrases; alarm call like house sparrow 'cherrup'; **Length:** 16.5cm; **Wingspan:** 25–28cm; **Habitat:** D sandy ground with scant vegetation; **Behaviour:** Needs area of bare ground to run along in search of insects

Long, slim pipit, size of yellow wagtail. Sexes similar. Adult crown, mantle, scapulars and rump sandy ochre mottled with dark brown on all but rump. Closed wing dark sandy brown with line of dark spots formed by blackish coverts with pale tips. Tail brown with cream edges. Face pa with long, cream supercilium and narrow, black lores and moustachial stripe. Chest and flanks sandy buff, usually unstreaked; rest of underbody whiter. Has longish, fine bill, brown with buff-pink base. Spindly legs and feet yellowish with long hind-claw. Juvenile more streaked than adult.

Tree Pipit
Anthus trivialis

Status: Summer visitor; common; **Voice:** Loud, rich song starting with rattle, ending in descending piping notes; loud 'tseeep' call; **Length:** 15cm; **Wingspan:** 25–27cm; **Habitat:** Mosaic of grassland or heath and woodland edge or forestry plantations; **Behaviour:** Feeds and nests on ground but requires trees for look-outs and song-posts

Well-marked pipit. Sexes similar. Adult head, nape, back and wings buff-brown with black streaks on bac. Face has yellowish supercilium and eyering and brown eyestripe. Cream margins and tips to dark wing feathers giv closed wing striking pattern. Rump unstreaked. Tail dark brown with white edges. Chin and throat buffish-white; brea and flanks warmer with dark spotting. Belly and undertail coverts buff-white. Bill dark grey-brown with pinkish base. Legs and feet flesh-pink. Juvenile similar to adult.

Meadow Pipit
Anthus pratensis

Status: Resident; common; **Voice:** Flight song comprises th whistling calls ending in descending scale; call thin quiet 'tsip'; **Length:** 14.5cm; **Wingspan:** 22–25cm; **Habitat:** Grasslands, bogs and tundra; **Behaviour:** Sings in flight; cal note uttered when escaping from danger

Medium-sized pipit lacking distinctive features. Sexe similar. Adult head, nape, back and wings variable, greenish-olive to dark buff-brown, with blackish streaks on crown and back. Shows thin off-white supercilium. Rump usually olive-brown, unstreaked. Tail dark brown with white edges. Underparts greyish-white to olive with chest band of narrow blackish spots and streaks extending on to flanks. B grey-brown. Legs pinkish-buff. Juvenile has heavier streakir on upperparts than adult and pale margins to wing feathers

Tawny pipit

Tree pipit

Meadow pipit

Richard's Pipit
Anthus novaeseelandiae

Status: Autumn vagrant; rare; **Voice:** Flight call loud, sparrow-like 'chrreep'; **Length:** 18cm; **Wingspan:** 30–32cm; **Habitat:** Grassland; **Behaviour:** Lurks in lush grassland me of the time; occasionally ventures into the open

Large, long-legged, long-tailed pipit, with diagnostic extremely long hind-claw. Sexes similar. Adult has brown upperparts with dark streaks. Underparts very pale buff with warm wash and dark streaks on breast. Head has streaked crown, buff lores and broad supercilium. Bill long and stout; upper mandible dark, lower mandible pink. Legs and feet pink. Juvenile similar to adult but back darker wit paler feather margins giving scaly appearance. Dark streak on breast prominent. First-autumn birds (most likely to be seen in Europe) intermediate between juvenile and adult.

Olive-backed Pipit
Anthus hodgsoni

Status: Autumn vagrant; rare; **Voice:** Call thin 'tseep'; **Length:** 14–15cm; **Wingspan:** 25–26cm; **Habitat:** Breeds in taiga forest and boggy woodland; otherwise favours damp, grassy areas; **Behaviour:** Habitually pumps tail up and dow and (uniquely for pipit) will feed in tree branches

Small, well-marked bird, recalling tree pipit. Sexes similar. Adult upperparts dull olive-green with little streaking on mantle and back compared to other pipits; ru unstreaked. Underparts marked with lines of black spots o breast and flanks; belly and undertail white. Broad supercili buff in front of eye and white behind eye. Black and white marks on ear coverts distinctive. Legs pink and bill buffish-pink. Juvenile resembles adult but upperparts browner.

Red-throated Pipit
Anthus cervinus

Status: Summer visitor; rare; **Voice:** Loud twittering and whistling song with bubbling trill; call loud, thin buzzing n **Length:** 15cm; **Wingspan:** 25–27cm; **Habitat:** Arctic and su Arctic tundra and swamps; muddy pastures on migration; **Behaviour:** Creeps slowly through vegetation; hard to flush

Smallish, short-tailed, stripy pipit with markedly different summer and winter plumages. Sexes simila Breeding adult upperparts dark-brown, heavily streaked wi black. Mantle often shows pale-buff braces. Yellowish-buff margins to blackish wing coverts show as double wingbars. Buff margins to tertials contrast with dark, heavily streake rump. Tail dark with white edges. Face and chin plain pinkish-buff. Breast and flanks warm reddish-buff; streake black on flanks. Rest of underbody paler buff. Winter adult and juvenile more black and white than summer adult, wit heavy streaking on chest. Bill dark grey-brown with pinkis base, and legs and feet yellowish-buff at all times.

Richard's pipit

Olive-backed pipit

WINTER

Red-throated pipit

SUMMER

Rock Pipit

Anthus petrosus

Status: Resident; common; **Voice:** Song accelerating serie loud, full, rattling notes; alarm call loud, metallic 'tsup'; **Length:** 16–17cm; **Wingspan:** 22–27cm; **Habitat:** Rocky s cliffs and crags along coasts; also saltmarshes and beache winter; **Behaviour:** Very bold and noisy

Larger and darker than meadow pipit, with strong and legs. Sexes similar. Adult upperparts dark oliv grey with blackish mottled streaking. Pale-buff superciliu and pale-grey wingbars and tertial edging relieve drab appearance. Dark-brown tail has dirty-buff edges. Under creamy buff to darkish olive, with variable amounts of streaking on breast and flanks. Northwestern races so he streaked on underbody they appear uniform on upperpar and underparts. In winter paler birds become much dark with more blackish streaking. Bill dark grey-brown. Legs brown-grey. Juvenile similar to adult but more mottled.

Water Pipit

Anthus spinoletta

Status: Resident; common; **Voice:** Melodious, twinkling s contact call full, almost grating 'tseep'; **Length:** 17–18cm **Wingspan:** 23–28cm; **Habitat:** Montane short grasslands heaths; lowland wetlands in winter; **Behaviour:** May form small flocks in winter

Medium-sized pipit, less streaked in summer than other pipits. Sexes similar. Summer adult upperpa grey-brown, brownest on back and closed wing. Prominer double wingbar formed by pale-grey margins and tips to v coverts, and panel caused by pale edgings to tertials give strong pattern to closed wing. Tail brown-black with oute edges white. Underbody dull white with pinkish wash on breast. Winter adult loses grey cast to upperparts, and pi wash from breast becomes browner with streaked under Bill dark grey-brown. Legs and feet dark brown-grey. Juv similar to winter adult but with cleaner appearance.

Buff-bellied Pipit

Anthus rubescens

Status: Autumn vagrant; very rare; **Voice:** Flight call sha 'pipit'; **Length:** 17cm; **Wingspan:** 24–26cm; **Habitat:** Grassland; **Behaviour:** As meadow pipit

Large, well-marked pipit. Similar to water pipit; formerly classified as North American race of this species. At all times has buff wash to underparts. Sexes similar. Breeding adult has grey-brown upperparts, strea except on nape and rump. Underparts buffish with limit dark streaking on breast and flanks. Autumn birds of all similar to breeding adult but upperparts warmer brown; underparts more intensely buff and with heavier streaki All birds have dark legs and dark bill, pinkish at base.

Rock pipit

Water pipit

SUMMER

WINTER

Buff-bellied pipit

Yellow Wagtail
Motacilla flava

Status: Summer visitor; widespread; **Length:** 17cm; **Wingspan:** 23–27cm; **Habitat:** Lowland wetlands, particularly water meadows, saltmarshes and dune slacks; **Behaviour:** Wags tail less then other wagtails

Species with many geographical races, which are mainly separable in adult male plumages, where head colour and pattern are important. Smallest, most compact European wagtail with pipit-like silhouette. Adult males of all races have greenish-yellow mantle, greyish-gre wings with whitish-yellow fringes to coverts and tertials, and dark greyish tail with white outer feathers. Underbody bright lemon yellow. Bill and legs black. Blue-headed wagt (*M. f. flava*) has blue-grey head with strong white supercilium, white chin and blackish cheeks; grey-headed wagtail (*M. f. thunbergi*) has slate-grey head with broken white supercilium, yellow chin and black cheeks; Spanish wagtail (*M. f. iberiae*) is small with slate-blue crown, narrow white supercilium and dark-green mantle; black-headed wagtail (*M. f. feldegg*) is large with velvet black he and long bill; ash-headed wagtail (*M. f. cinereocapilla*) lac white supercilium on ash-grey head; yellow wagtail (*M. f. flavissima*) has yellow head. Female and juvenile bir are less brightly yellow than males, with more uniform oliv buff plumage tones.

Citrine Wagtail
Motacilla citreola

Status: Autumn vagrant/rarely seen in spring; rare; **Voice:** Flight call a sharp 'srreep'; **Length:** 17–18cm; **Wingspan:** 24–25cm; **Habitat:** Damp grassland and freshwater margin **Behaviour:** Feeds among partly submerged vegetation or a the very edge of the water

Adult male unmistakable but female and juvenile bi potentially confusable with corresponding plumages white and yellow wagtails. Male in breeding plumage has lemon-yellow head and underparts and black collar. Back grey and wings dark but with two prominent white wingbar Tail black with white outer feathers. Non-breeding male ar breeding female have dull-yellow face and underparts, and grey-brown crown, nape and back. White wingbars less conspicuous than on breeding male. First-winter birds have pale-grey upperparts with white supercilium and border to ear coverts and two white wingbars; underparts white. Bill and legs dark in all birds.

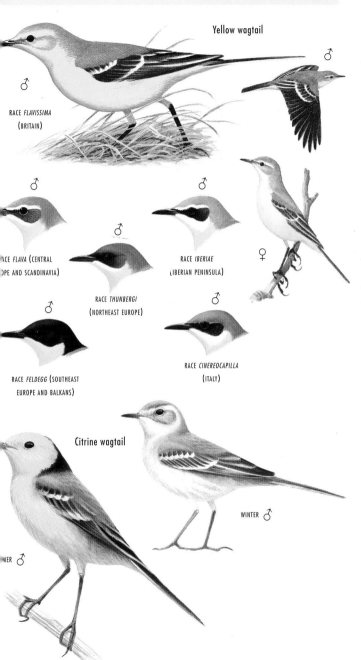

Yellow wagtail

♂

RACE *FLAVISSIMA*
(BRITAIN)

♂

RACE *FLAVA* (CENTRAL
EUROPE AND SCANDINAVIA)

♂

RACE *THUNBERGI*
(NORTHEAST EUROPE)

♂

RACE *IBERIAE*
(IBERIAN PENINSULA)

♀

♂

RACE *CINEREOCAPILLA*
(ITALY)

♂

RACE *FELDEGG* (SOUTHEAST
EUROPE AND BALKANS)

Citrine wagtail

WINTER ♂

SUMMER ♂

Grey Wagtail
Motacilla cinerea

Status: Resident/summer visitor; local; **Voice:** Song series shrill elements, getting louder; usual contact call shrill 'tchee'; **Length:** 18–19cm; **Wingspan:** 25–27cm; **Habitat:** Running fresh water, particularly upland streams; **Behaviour** Darts above streams in short sallies for insects

Long, slim wagtail with very long tail. Male has slaty-grey upperparts with olive-yellow rump. White supercilium connects white surround to cheek, contrasting with black bib. Closed wing shows yellowish-white fringes t tertials and inner secondaries, with main flight feathers blackish. In flight, upperwing shows white bar; underwing greyish with white centre. Tail black with white outer feathers. Underbody lemon yellow with greyish flanks. Fem and non-breeding adults of both sexes lack black bib and have buffer underparts. Legs and feet flesh-coloured. Bill greyish-black. Juvenile resembles non-breeding adult but with prominent buff fringes to wing feathers.

Pied Wagtail
Motacilla alba yarrellii

Status: Resident; common; **Voice:** Song hurried warbling twitter; main contact call loud 'chissik'; **Length:** 18cm; **Wingspan:** 25–30cm; **Habitat:** Waterside habitats and grassland; **Behaviour:** Like slim black and white pipit with fast running action and wagging tail

Male crown, nape, chin to upper breast, wing and mc of tail black. Mantle, scapulars and rump black. Forehead, cheeks, underbody and underwing white. Fringe and tips of wing feathers and outertail feathers also white. Female more mottled and less contrasting than male. Non-breeding adults lack black throat, leaving narrow black bre band. Bill and legs black in all plumages. Juvenile recalls non-breeding female but has dusky-brown tinge to plumage

White Wagtail
Motacilla alba alba

Status: Resident; common; **Voice:** Song twittering warble; shrill 'tchissick'; **Length:** 18cm; **Wingspan:** 25–30cm; **Habitat:** Farmland, wetlands, open country; **Behaviour:** As pied wagtail

Superficially similar to pied wagtail in all plumages rump grey, not black, at all times. Breeding male has black cap and nape and black throat and upper breast. Bac and rump grey. Underparts white, and blackish wings show two white wingbars. Tail long and black with white outer feathers. On non-breeding male black on underparts confir to band on upper breast; plumage somewhat grubby. Breed female markings less well defined than on male. In winter loses black cap, and face looks grubby. Juvenile similar to non-breeding female. Bill and legs black in all plumages.

Grey wagtail

SUMMER ♂

Pied wagtail

SUMMER ♂

SUMMER ♀

White wagtail

SUMMER ♂

Waxwing

Bombycilla garrulus

Status: Resident; local; **Voice:** Weak wheezing and twitteri song; call thin shrill whistle; **Length:** 18cm; **Wingspan:** 32–36cm; **Habitat:** Northern spruce and pine forests; in winter irruptive into towns and gardens; **Behaviour:** Often very confiding in winter when feeding on berries

Size and proportions of starling. Sexes similar. Adult plumage basically warm pinkish-buff brown with sma areas of black and striking colours. Head has fluffy, backward-pointing crest. Brown shades into chestnut arou face, and pinkish on neck, breast and flanks. Narrow black eyestripe and wide black bib. Grey rump. Blackish tail has broad yellow tip. Belly yellowish, contrasting with orange-brown vent. Closed wing shows remarkable pattern of whit tips to primary coverts and secondaries with waxy red appendages. Dark primaries have white and yellow margin Bill and legs black. Juvenile duller than adult, without rich plumage tones or wing decoration.

Dipper

Cinclus cinclus

Status: Resident; local; **Voice:** Song pleasing rippling warb of mellow whistles; call sharp 'tzit'; **Length:** 18cm; **Wingspa** 26–30cm; **Habitat:** Fast-flowing, rocky streams and rivers, usually in mountains; lower altitude in winter; **Behaviour:** Often seen bobbing perched on rocks in middle of stream

Recalls small rotund thrush with short, rounded win and cocked tail. Sexes similar. Adult has dark-brown head and neck. Rest of upperparts, wings and tail very dark slate with feathers margined blackish, giving mottled effec Chin, throat and breast bright white. Rear underparts dark blackish-brown; British race shows chestnut on anterior margin of dark underparts. Underwing black-brown. Juven upperparts all dark slate, mottled by black feather margins Underparts white, heavily mottled, spotted and barred with dusky feather tips. All ages show striking white eyelid whe bird blinks and black-brown bill and legs.

JUVENILE

Waxwing

ADULTS

Dipper

MAINLAND EUROPEAN RACE

BRITISH RACE

Wren
Troglodytes troglodytes

Status: Resident; common; **Voice:** Shrill, trilling song; tick
alarm call; **Length:** 9–10cm; **Wingspan:** 13–17cm; **Habitat:**
Wide variety of habitats which offer some cover; **Behaviour**
Feeds in thick cover; aggressive; roosts communally in wint

Tiny, round, restless bird. Adult has rufous-brown
upperparts with paler buff-brown underparts, barred
all over. Supercilium narrow and creamy and throat pale bu
Closed wing shows white barring on short, dark primaries.
Undertail coverts and flanks also show some buff-white
barring. In flight, appears as brown, round, whirring bee-lik
bird. Bill long, thin and slightly decurved, dark grey-brown
with yellowish lower mandible. Legs light brown. Juvenile
similar to adult, but warmer brown.

Dunnock
Prunella modularis

Status: Resident; common; **Voice:** Song a weak truncated
warble; call a sharp 'tzchik'; **Length:** 14.5cm; **Wingspan:**
19–21cm; **Habitat:** Scrub in mountainous coniferous forest
secondary scrub in west Europe; **Behaviour:** Creeps close t
ground, twitching wings and tail

Size of house sparrow, but slimmer. Greyish-brown
appearing dull at distance. Adult head, neck, throat
and breast slate grey with brown streaks on crown, greyish-
white streaks on face. Mantle, scapulars and wing coverts
rich brown, streaked with black. Closed wing dark with buf
fringes forming wingbar. Rump unstreaked dull brown, tail
blackish-brown. Slate grey of breast shades into brown on
flanks and to whitish-grey on belly. Eye noticeably red-brow
Short, fine bill blackish with pale-brown base. Legs pinkish
brown. Juvenile similar to adult but browner, with more
streaks on underparts and striking wingbar.

Alpine Accentor
Prunella collaris

Status: Resident; local; **Voice:** Chattering warble; rippling,
ventriloquial call; **Length:** 18cm; **Wingspan:** 30–33cm;
Habitat: Montane above tree-line; rocky alpine grassland;
Behaviour: Sings on boulders; feeds and nests on ground

Bulky passerine recalling small lark. Adult head, brea
and belly ash-grey with brownish tinge in some lights
Chin whitish with neat black speckling. Mantle grey-brown
with black-brown streaking. Rump grey and uppertail cover
rufous, streaked black. Tail dark brown, tipped white. Close
wing shows black, white-tipped coverts forming panel again
rufous-edged secondaries and dark primaries. Underwing
mottled rufous and grey. Flanks streaked, blotched chestnu
Undertail coverts have black and white arrowhead barring.
Bill black with yellow base. Legs red-brown. Juvenile duller
than adult with scaly appearance.

Wren

Dunnock

JUVENILE

ADULT DUNNOCK

Alpine accentor

Rufous Bush Robin
Cercotrichas galactotes

Status: Summer visitor; local; **Voice:** Song jerky robin-like warble; contact and alarm calls short 'tsip' notes; **Length:** 15cm; **Wingspan:** 22–27cm; **Habitat:** Steppes with planted scrub; also parks, orange groves and gardens; **Behaviour:** Flight dashing; when perched, cocks tail and bobs head

Size of large warbler but with long, graduated tail. Adult Iberian race has rufous-brown upperparts and wings with brighter rump and bright reddish-chestnut tail, tipped black and white. Head shows long cream supercilium and eyering, brown eyestripe and paler cheeks. Closed wing shows two pale wingbars. Chin and throat whitish, with rest of underbody and underwing sandy-pink, brightest on breast and flanks. Southeast European race greyer. Bill grey-brown with pale base. Legs and feet brown. Juvenile similar to adult but has lightly speckled throat and breast.

Robin
Erithacus rubecula

Status: Resident; common; **Voice:** Both sexes sing series of mellow whistled warbles; call a sharp 'tic'; **Length:** 14cm; **Wingspan:** 20–22cm; **Habitat:** Shady, undisturbed woodland also gardens and town parks; **Behaviour:** Uses song to advertise territory throughout year

Small, round chat with large head. Adult has olive-brown upperparts. Rump grey-brown with warmer brown uppertail coverts and tail. Often shows short, narrow wingbar formed by buff tips to greater coverts. Orange-red forehead, surround to eye, forecheeks, chin, throat and breast. Brown upperparts separated from orange face and chest by band of soft blue-grey. Flanks warm buff; belly and undertail coverts white. Bill dark brown and legs brown. Juvenile has brown upperparts and buff underparts, all copiously spotted with pale buff.

Siberian Rubythroat
Luscinia calliope

Status: Autumn vagrant; very rare; **Voice:** Calls include a low whistle and harsh 'tchak'; song rich and melodious; **Length:** 14cm; **Wingspan:** 23–25cm; **Habitat:** Open taiga forest and damp woodland; **Behaviour:** Shy and skulking

Size and shape similar to bluethroat. Male unmistakable with essentially grey-brown plumage, palest on underparts. Head well marked with pale supercilium, dark lores, white submoustachial stripe and ruby-red throat, narrowly outlined in black. Plumages brightest in late spring. Female lacks male's red throat but plumage otherwise similar. Juvenile recalls juvenile robin. First-year plumage similar to adult's (male and female differences apparent) but usually retains juvenile's pale tips to greater wing coverts. Bill dark and legs pinkish in all birds.

Rufous bush robin

JVENILE

Robin

Siberian rubythroat

SUMMER MALE

Thrush Nightingale
Luscinia luscinia

Status: Summer visitor; common; **Voice:** Beautiful, long an᷈ varied warble with deep 'tchock' notes and rattles; **Length** 16.5cm; **Wingspan:** 24–27cm; **Habitat:** Open woodland an᷈ thicket scrub, often along rivers; also orchards and parks; **Behaviour:** Likes proximity to water; nests in deep cover

Very difficult to separate from nightingale on sight alone. Adult has dark olivaceous-brown upperparts with warmer brown uppertail coverts and dull rufous-brow᷈ tail. Underparts dull whitish-grey with clean throat border by brown malar stripe and breast. Chest and flanks mottle᷈ dusky-brown. Bill dark grey-brown with pale base to lower mandible. Legs brown. Juvenile darker, with contrasting pa᷈ spots on tips of tertials and wing coverts. Legs pale flesh.

Nightingale
Luscinia megarhynchos

Status: Summer visitor; common; **Voice:** Mellow, musical a᷈ varied song, with pure whistles and rattles; **Length:** 16.5cr᷈ **Wingspan:** 23–26cm; **Habitat:** Scrub in woodland; **Behaviour:** Less tied to water than thrush nightingale

Resembles small thrush. Adult has uniform russet-brown upperparts with warmer tone to rump and uppertail coverts, and bright chestnut-brown tail with dar᷈ central feathers. Face uniform brown with buff eyering. Closed wing shows darker brown-centred flight feathers. Underparts dull cream-white with brownish suffusion acro᷈ breast and down flanks. Vent and undertail coverts bright᷈ cream-buff. Bill dark with pale base. Legs pale brown or fl᷈ Juvenile speckled but soon moults to resemble adult with buff tips to wing coverts and tertials.

Bluethroat
Luscinia svecica

Status: Local summer visitor; scarce in winter and on passage; **Voice:** Song mimics other species in loud, short, warbling phrases; contact call 'chuck'; **Length:** 14cm; **Wingspan:** 20–23cm; **Habitat:** Moist, wooded tundra; scru᷈ near water; **Behaviour:** Skulking behaviour characteristic

Adults of both sexes have face with buffish supercil᷈ bordered above by black and below by brownish che᷈ Tail dark brown with orange-chestnut bases to outer feath᷈ Breeding male has metallic blue throat and upper breast v᷈ reddish-chestnut or white central spot, depending on race᷈ spot absent in some races. Blue throat is bordered below b᷈ narrow black, white and chestnut bands. Underparts off-white with greyish flanks. Non-breeding male has pale thr᷈ Female usually lacks male's throat pattern and has black moustache joining brown-black necklace. Grey-brown bill᷈ ochre-brown legs seen in both sexes. Juvenile spotted wit᷈ pale buff; resembles female in autumn.

Thrush nightinggale

Nightingale

Nightingale

JUVENILE

♀

Bluethroat

♂

Red-flanked Bluetail
Tarsiger cyanurus

Status: Summer visitor/rare vagrant to northwest Europe;
Voice: Calls include soft 'hueet'; high-pitched, whistling so◼
recalls that of redstart; **Length:** 14cm; **Wingspan:** 22–24cm
Habitat: Breeds in taiga forest and upland mixed forests;
Behaviour: Bobs up and down, spreading or flicking tail

Attractive but shy songbird. Unmistakable male has
dark-blue upperparts including tail and pale
underparts, pure white only on throat; flanks washed with
orange-red. Female has blue tail but otherwise brown
upperparts. Underparts pale; whitest on throat and with
orange-red wash to flanks. Eye has white eyering. Juvenile
similar to female but with pale spots on upperparts and da◼
bars on underparts. First-autumn male and female similar
female. Legs dark and bill dark and stubby in all birds.

Black Redstart
Phoenicurus ochruros

Status: Resident; common; **Voice:** Song a quick, scratchy
warble; contact call 'sit'; **Length:** 14.5cm; **Wingspan:**
23–26cm; **Habitat:** Open, rocky and stony habitats in
mountains; also coasts and wasteland in cities; **Behaviour:**
Feeds on insects; uses regular perches for foraging sorties

Spring male has dusky slate head, back, wing coverts
and underparts; blackest on head, back and breast.
Wings brown-black with off-white panel. Centre of belly
greyish-white, vent and undertail coverts orange. Rump an◼
tail chestnut with central tail feathers and tips dark brown
After autumn moult plumage colours muted by pale feather
edging. Female body dull grey-brown with orange areas less
bright than male; has buff wing panel. Bill and legs black in
both sexes. Juvenile resembles speckled female.

Redstart
Phoenicurus phoenicurus

Status: Summer visitor; common; **Voice:** Melancholy song
with sweet and rattling phrases; contact call soft 'tchuk';
Length: 14cm; **Wingspan:** 20–24cm; **Habitat:** Open, broad-
leaved woodland, parkland or wooded heaths; **Behaviour:**
Uses regular perches for fly-catching or foraging sorties

Slimmer than robin, with longer wings and tail. Male
has white forehead and supercilium. Crown and back
blue-grey. Wings blackish-brown with buffish fringes and ti◼
to feathers. Rump, uppertail coverts and tail bright chestn◼
with dark-brown central feathers. Face, throat and upper
breast black, contrasting with orange-buff lower breast and
flanks. Belly white and undertail coverts orange. Underwin◼
coverts pale chestnut. Female plumage greyish-brown, dar◼
on upperparts than underbody. White throat and eyering;
chestnut tail. Bill and legs black in both species. Juvenile ◼
tail like adult but rest of plumage speckled buff and brown.

Red-flanked bluetail

Black redstart

♂

♀

Redstart

♀

♂

Whinchat

Saxicola rubetra

Status: Summer visitor; widespread but declining; **Voice:** Song a long series of short, fluty and scratchy phrases; call harsh 'tzec'; **Length:** 12.5cm; **Wingspan:** 21–24cm; **Habitat:** Open grassland and scrub, particularly hay meadows and bracken on hills; **Behaviour:** Often perches on fence wire

Smaller than robin. In flight, looks long-winged and very short-tailed. Adult male has black-brown head with long, broad white supercilium reaching nape, and similar white border to cheek, upturned at rear. Back dark brown with heavy blackish streaking. Rump paler with rufous tinge. Wing coverts black with bold white bar extending on tertials. Flight feathers brown-black with white bases to outer primaries. Tail black with white sides to base. Underbody warm orange. Female similar but duller. Bill and legs black both sexes. Juvenile recalls dull female with black-brown upperparts, buff underparts and no clear pattern to face.

Stonechat

Saxicola torquata

Status: Resident; widespread but declining; **Voice:** Song a series of scratchy and whistled phrases; call a harsh 'tchac'; **Length:** 12.5cm; **Wingspan:** 18–21cm; **Habitat:** Dry, scrub areas, particularly heaths and sand dunes; **Behaviour:** Perches upright on gorse bushes, singing or calling

Smaller than robin, with shorter, more rounded wings than whinchat. Male has dark brown-black head and throat, with isolated white patches on sides of neck. Mantle and scapulars evenly dark brown. White rump streaked blackish. Closed wing shows white panel on coverts. Breast and flanks warm orange, shading to greyish-white on centre of belly and undertail coverts. Underwing dark. Female less smart, with upperparts overall mottled brownish, and white areas replaced by buff. Juvenile greyer and heavily spotted, resembling bright but uniform buffish female by first autumn.

Siberian Stonechat

Saxicola maura (formerly comprised Saxicola torquata maura, S. t. variegata and S. t. armenica)

Status: Late autumn vagrant, rare; **Voice:** Calls include hard 'tchack'; **Length:** 12.5cm; **Wingspan:** 18–20cm; **Habitat:** Vagrants usually on rough ground; **Behaviour:** As stonechat

Very similar to stonechat and still considered by some authorities to be a race (or races) of this species. Male has black head and upperparts except for pure white unstreaked rump and white wing panel. Underparts white, extending as half collar on to sides of neck (more extensive than in stonechat); shows orange-red flush to breast. Plumage brightest during breeding season. Female and immature birds very similar to corresponding plumages of stonechat but much paler. Rump very pale and has pale supercilium, white wingbar and white panel on secondaries.

Whinchat

♀

♂

♂

Stonechat

♀

Siberian stonechat

Isabelline Wheatear
Oenanthe isabellina

Status: Summer visitor; rare; **Voice:** Song is loud and mimetic, unlike other wheatears; call is 'tchok', 'click' and 'dweet'; **Length:** 16.5cm; **Wingspan:** 27–31cm; **Habitat:** Bar hillsides, and dry plains, all with sparse vegetation; **Behaviour:** Nests in rodent burrows or bee-eater holes; fee by making quick dashes along ground after invertebrate pr

 Largest and palest wheatear in the region, with upri stance. Sexes similar. Less contrast between upperparts and underparts than in other wheatears. Generally pale sandy-brown above and buffish-white below with brown wings showing broad creamy fringes to coverts and secondaries. Dirty-white supercilium, black lores and eyes. Tail white with broad, black terminal band and less noticeable vertical bar. Bill and legs long, strong and black Hard to distinguish from females of some other wheatears. Juvenile paler than, but otherwise similar to, adult.

Northern Wheatear
Oenanthe oenanthe

Status: Summer visitor; widespread; **Voice:** Song is an energetic, short, pleasing warble; call is 'chak'; alarm call i 'weet-chak, chak'; **Length:** 14.5–15.5cm; **Wingspan:** 26–32c **Habitat:** Open, very diverse habitats; Arctic tundra, sand dunes, cliff-tops, moors, mountains; **Behaviour:** Solitary or breeding grounds but forms small flocks at coastal stop-ove on migration

Male easily identified. Females and first-winter bird lack diagnostic features and are similar to other wheatear species; identification is best done by noting tail pattern and length, face pattern, colour tones of body plumage, and remembering it is the only wheatear breedin in north and northwest Europe. Male has diagnostic grey crown and back, white supercilium, black mask through ey and widening over cheek, and black wings; chin to breast pink-buff, rest of underparts white. Rump, uppertail covert and tail white, the last with tip marked by broad, black upside-down 'T'. Female similarly patterned but wings, cro cheek patch and back all brown-toned. Underparts usually buffer. Juvenile has dark upperparts with 'scaly' appearanc and pale underparts with darker crescent-shaped marking

NORTHERN WHEATEAR,
GREENLAND RACE

Isabelline wheatear

BREEDING FEMALE

BREEDING MALE

Northern wheatear

ADULT MALE, AUTUMN

JUVENILE

Desert Wheatear
Oenanthe deserti

Status: Vagrant, mainly to southeast Europe; regular; **Voice** Alarm call a sharp 'chek'; **Length:** 14–15cm; **Wingspan:** 25–27cm; **Habitat:** Arid steppe and semi-desert; **Behaviour** Active feeder; uses low perches from which to scan for inse

Male superficially similar to male black-throated rac of black-eared wheatear. All-black tail diagnostic in a birds. Male has black face and throat continuous with black wings. Plumage otherwise pale sandy brown except for whit rump and hint of pale supercilium. First-winter male simila to adult male but pale feather margins make contrast between pale and dark areas of plumage less striking. Adul female essentially sandy brown, palest on throat and belly, warmest on breast and with hint of pale supercilium. Rump white and tail black as in male. Juveniles and immatures resemble adult female. Bill and legs black in all birds.

Black-eared Wheatear
Oenanthe hispanica

Status: Summer visitor; widespread; **Voice:** Song a rich warble interspersed with scratchy, buzzing phrases; **Length** 14.5cm; **Wingspan:** 25–27cm; **Habitat:** Warm Mediterranea habitats with stony ground; **Behaviour:** Has dashing flight

Slim wheatear with relatively long tail. Adult male se as black-throated and pale-throated forms. Both form have uniform sandy-buff crown, nape, mantle and underbod Face and wings black. Rump white. Tail white with black inverted 'T' marking. Forehead and supercilium creamy white. Throat either black or sandy as underbody. In autum buff feather margins reduce contrast in plumage. Females o both races recall male but lack strong head pattern. Bill an legs black in both sexes. Juvenile resembles female but has buff-spotted upperparts and scaly brown breast.

Black Wheatear
Oenanthe leucura

Status: Resident; local; **Voice:** Call a distinctive 'pee-pee-pe song a quiet mixture of warbles and chatter; **Length:** 18cm; **Wingspan:** 26–29cm; **Habitat:** Gorges and rock-strewn places, quarries and screes; **Behaviour:** Less solitary than most wheatears, three to five usually feeding together; more approachable in breeding season

Distinctive, large wheatear. Male black except for white rump and tail coverts, white tail with end marked by an upside-down 'T', the end bar being narrower than on northern wheatear. Black underwings contrast with greyish-white in fringes of flight feathers. Female separable at close range, more sooty brown than black, especially on face and underparts when feathers are worn. Bill and legs black in both sexes. Juvenile similar to female.

Desert wheatear

BLACK-THROATED RACE

Black-eared wheatear

PALE-THROATED RACE

Black wheatear

Cyprus Pied Wheatear
Oenanthe cypriaca

Status: Summer visitor; range restricted to Cyprus; **Voice:** Song a continuous series of buzzing notes; various clicking calls; **Length:** 14cm; **Wingspan:** 23–25cm; **Habitat:** Open, stony, arid areas and fallow fields; **Behaviour:** Usually feed close to nest, which is in hole or rock crevice

 Smallest European wheatear. Male has white crown and nape. Face, chin to upper breast, neck, back an wings black. Rump and uppertail coverts white. Tail white with black central feathers; all feathers black-tipped. Underparts from lower breast to undertail coverts pale cinnamon. Underwing coverts black and flight feathers du After autumn moult plumage is browner with little contra breeding plumage acquired by wear. Female resembles du male with dark olive-brown crown contrasting with pale-b supercilium and nape. Bill and legs of both sexes black. Juvenile dark with pale-spotted upperparts.

Pied Wheatear
Oenanthe pleschanka

Status: Summer visitor; rare; **Voice:** Calls include a sharp 'tchek'; song includes rattling, buzzing and warbling phras **Length:** 14–15cm; **Wingspan:** 26–27cm; **Habitat:** Stony hillsides and broken ground; **Behaviour:** Often perches on boulders and bushes and drops on to prey on the ground

Superficially similar to black-throated form of black eared wheatear. Tail pattern also similar to black-ea wheatear's: white with black central feathers and trailing edge. Male has black face and throat linked by black feathering to black wings. Crown, nape and underparts essentially white. Males in autumn and winter have pale-brown feather edges, so white elements of plumage look bu and black elements look greyish. Female has dark grey-bro head, throat and upperparts; underparts grubby white. During winter, pale feather margins reduce contrast in plumage. First-winter male has plumage between that of adult male and adult female. First-winter female similar to adult female in winter. Bill and legs dark in all birds.

Cyprus pied wheatear

Pied wheatear

COMPARING IMMATURE WHEATEARS While adult wheatears in spring usually present few problems to the observer, the identification of immature wheatears in autumn is fraught with difficulties. Migrant birds are often seen out of range and normal habitat and so close attention must be paid to subtle plumage differences and the pattern of markings on the tail and rump.

NORTHERN WHEATEAR (first-autumn): Plumage generally sandy ʋn, palest on underparts showing orange-buff ᵢ to throat and upper st; tail and p markings as t – white rump and upper tail with k terminal band and central ꜧers forming inverted 'T'

NORTHERN WHEATEAR (female): Similar to juvenile but plumage generally greyer on upperparts; shows more striking eyestripe and supercilium

ABELLINE WHEATEAR (first-winter bird): Always difficult to distinguish from immature northern wheatear but is larger and longer-legged with more upright posture, and contrast between sandy body plumage and darker wings never as striking; lacks that species' warm-toned flush to throat and upper breast; broader black terminal band on tail

DESERT WHEATEAR (first-winter bird): Plumage looks rather sandy grey except for suggestion of adult male's black plumage pattern on throat and pale supercilium; despite pale feather tips wings appear dark; pattern of white rump and entirely black tail diagnostic and identical to that of adult

K-EARED WHEATEAR -autumn bird): Overall age colour is sandy ᵢn but shows facial k, and wings ys appear dark well-defined; pattern on and tail as adult – dark terminal band on ᵢuch narrower than on northern wheatear

PIED WHEATEAR (first-winter bird): Upperparts and throat look dark olive-brown while underparts are warm orange-buff; shows buffish supercilium and tail and rump pattern as adult – 'T'-shaped black marking on otherwise white tail – but terminal band not as broad as on northern wheatear

Rock Thrush
Monticola saxatilis

Status: Summer visitor; widespread; **Voice:** Song mellow, flute-like warble; call 'chack, chack'; **Length:** 18.5cm; **Wingspan:** 33–37cm; **Habitat:** Sunny, dry stony terraces w scattered trees; **Behaviour:** Feeds by darting from a perch to prey on the ground; male's song includes much mimicry

Like large wheatear, with erect posture and characteristically wagging tail. Breeding male unmistakable with slate-blue head and throat, blue rump a brownish-black wings. Uppertail coverts, tail, underparts a underwing orange and back white, giving dazzling effect th is most pronounced in flight. Female lack's male's blue in plumage. Head, throat and back mottled brown and buff. Lacks male's white patch on back and has pale-fringed wir feathers. Underparts buff with brown crescent-shaped markings. Tail orange. Bill and legs of both sexes dark brov Juvenile similar to female but even more strongly marked.

Blue Rock Thrush
Monticola solitarius

Status: Resident/summer visitor; widespread; **Voice:** Song loud and melodious, of simple phrases; call and alarm deep 'tak, tak'; **Length:** 20cm; **Wingspan:** 33–37cm; **Habitat:** Ro coastlines, rocky mountain valleys; **Behaviour:** Territoria and shy; best observed when male is singing in spring

Larger than any wheatear and nearly as big as a redwing, but stockily built. Male is only all-blue songbird in the region. Plumage mostly dull slate blue but with black tone on wings and tail. Whole bird looks black i poor light. Female dark grey-brown, with no blue tone; side of head and throat spotted brown, rest of underparts cover with scaly buff markings. Bill dark grey-brown and legs bla in both sexes. Juvenile similar to female.

Swainson's Thrush
Catharus ustulatus

Status: Autumn vagrant from North America; very rare; **Voice:** Call soft 'kwik'; **Length:** 18cm; **Wingspan:** 28–30cm; **Habitat:** Woodland; **Behaviour:** As song thrush

Small, compact thrush. Like other *Catharus* thrushe has proportionately large head and short tail compar to most European thrushes. Conspicuous buffish-yellow eyering good diagnostic feature in all birds. Sexes similar. Adult upperparts and tail olive-brown. Underparts greyish-white but sides of neck and breast buffish-yellow; shows conspicuous black spots on neck, these fading in intensity. First-winter bird (plumage most likely to be encountered i Europe) similar to adult but overall tone of upperparts warmer brown, sometimes showing pale spots. All birds hav dark bill with buffish base to lower mandible, and pink legs

Rock thrush

♀

♂

Blue rock thrush

♀

Swainson's thrush

FIRST WINTER

Gray-cheeked Thrush
Catharus minimus

Status: Autumn vagrant from North America; rare; **Voice:** C thin 'wee-arr'; **Length:** 18cm; **Wingspan:** 29–31cm; **Habitat** Woodland; **Behaviour:** Unobtrusive, generally keeping to thick cover

Small, dainty thrush. Superficially similar to Swainson's thrush but always lacks that species' buff eyering. Sexes similar. Adult has essentially grey-brown upperparts and tail. Underparts, ear coverts and sides of ne greyish-white; has dark spots on breast and sides of neck, these fading in intensity towards belly. First-winter bird (plumage most likely to be encountered in Europe) similar adult but often has buffish margins to wing coverts and ter feathers. Some birds may show faint eyering but this is alw greyish-white. All birds have pink legs and dark bill with pinkish-grey base to lower mandible.

Veery
Catharus fuscescens

Status: Autumn vagrant from North America; very rare; **Voice:** Call a soft 'phee-uw'; **Length:** 17cm; **Wingspan:** 29–30cm; **Habitat:** Woodland; **Behaviour:** Shy and retiring

Compact, unobtrusive thrush. Has large-headed proportions typical of all *Catharus* thrushes, but plumage recalls nightingale. Sexes similar. Adult and first-winter birds have warm brown upperparts and tail. Underparts mostly greyish-white. Throat, sides of neck and upper breast have pale-buffish wash and faint grey-brown spotting. All birds have pink legs and dark bill with buffish base to lower mandible.

Hermit Thrush
Catharus guttatus

Status: Autumn vagrant from North America; very rare; **Voice:** Calls include soft 'chok'; **Length:** 17cm; **Wingspan:** 26–28cm; **Habitat:** Woodland; **Behaviour:** Habitually cocks tail and then slowly lowers it

Small, dumpy thrush. Plumage recalls that of thrush nightingale. Sexes similar. Adult has olive-brown hea and back but reddish-brown lower rump and tail. Underpar greyish-white with faint buffish wash to flanks and sides of neck. Shows narrow white eyering and dark spots on throa and upper breast. Margins of primary feathers reddish-brow producing effect of warm-toned wing panel. First-winter bi similar to adult. All birds have dark bill with pale-buff base lower mandible, and dull-pink legs.

Gray-cheeked thrush

FIRST WINTER

Veery

FIRST WINTER

Hermit thrush

FIRST WINTER

White's Thrush
Zoothera dauma

Status: Autumn vagrant from Siberia; very rare; **Voice:** Call thin 'zee'; **Length:** 27cm; **Wingspan:** 45–46cm; **Habitat:** Woodland and forest; **Behaviour:** Shy and retiring

Large and distinctive thrush. Plumage recalls that of immature mistle thrush but markings much bolder and contrasting, and overall appearance scaly. Sexes similar. Adult has essentially pale-buff upperparts and breast and white underparts, but all elements of plumage, except wing, tail and undertail feathers, covered with conspicuous black crescent markings. Buff-brown wings have pale feather margins and primaries with dark bases and tips. Juvenile similar to adult but dark markings more rounded than crescent-shaped. All birds have dark bill with pale-buff base to lower mandible, pinkish legs and striking black and white bands on underwing.

Siberian Thrush
Zoothera sibirica

Status: Autumn vagrant from Siberia; very rare; **Voice:** Call thin 'tzit'; **Length:** 22cm; **Wingspan:** 34–35cm; **Habitat:** Woodland and farmland; **Behaviour:** Usually seen with migrating redwings and fieldfares

Distinctive medium-sized thrush. Male has essentially blue-black plumage with prominent white supercilium. Flanks paler than upperparts and show dark crescent-shaped markings; belly white. First-winter male similar to adult male but dark elements of plumage less intense. Has pale supercilium and throat, both with buffish wash. Female (all ages) has similar plumage pattern to first-winter male but dark elements of plumage replaced by warm brown. Underparts rather pale with brown crescent-shaped markings. All birds have black and white bands on underwing, pale tips to outer feathers, dark bill with yellow base to lower mandible and dull-orange legs.

American Robin
Turdus migratorius

Status: Autumn and winter vagrant from America; very rare; **Voice:** Calls include staccato 'tuk-tuk-tuk'; **Length:** 25cm; **Wingspan:** 36–38cm; **Habitat:** woodland, farmland and gardens; **Behaviour:** Eats insects, and berries in autumn

Attractive, well-marked thrush. Male has sooty-grey upperparts, darkest on tail and head. Shows conspicuous white 'eyelid' markings and white throat with dark streaking. Breast and belly brick red and undertail white. Female similar to male but red elements of plumage much less intense. First-winter bird similar to female but plumage colours even duller, appearing browner on upperparts. All birds have yellowish bill and legs.

White's thrush

Siberian thrush

♂

American robin

♂

Black-throated Thrush
Turdus ruficollis

Status: Autumn and winter vagrant from central Asia; very rare; **Voice:** Calls thin 'tzip' and sharp 'chak-chak'; **Length:** 25cm; **Wingspan:** 38–40cm; **Habitat:** Woodland, farmland and gardens; **Behaviour:** Associates with common migrating thrushes

Distinctive thrush. Occurs as two distinct races. Male of race *atrogularis* has pale grey-brown upperparts a tail, striking black throat and upper breast, and white belly and undertail. Female (all ages) and first-winter male have pale grey-brown upperparts. Underparts pale but throat an breast have distinct black spotting. Male of race *ruficollis* (referred to as red-throated thrush) has pale grey-brown upperparts, striking brick-red throat, upper breast and oute tail and white belly and undertail. Female (all ages) and first-winter male have pale grey-brown upperparts and mos white underparts. Show black spotting on throat, buffish wash to upper breast and sides of neck, and buffish supercilium. All birds have dark bill with yellow base to low mandible, yellow legs and reddish underwing coverts.

Eye-browed Thrush
Turdus obscurus

Status: Autumn vagrant from Siberia; very rare; **Voice:** Call thin 'tsee'; **Length:** 23cm; **Wingspan:** 36–38cm; **Habitat:** Woodland, farmland and gardens; **Behaviour:** Feeds on open ground

Attractive, medium-sized thrush. Male has dark-grey head with white supercilium, dark lores and white at base of bill. Back and wings brown. Breast and flanks orange red but underparts otherwise white. Female (all ages) and first-winter male have similar plumage pattern to adult ma but colours much less intense. All birds have dark bill with yellowish base to lower mandible and dull-orange legs.

Ring Ouzel
Turdus torquatus

Status: Resident/summer visitor; locally common; **Voice:** Song rich and fluty; chattering alarm call; **Length:** 24cm; **Wingspan:** 38–42cm; **Habitat:** Mountains and moorland; winters on Mediterranean slopes; **Behaviour:** Undisturbed males sit on rocks to sing, but skulk when alarmed

Size and shape of blackbird. Male has blackish plumage with pale fringes to feathers on wings and underparts. Conspicuous white crescent on breast diagnost Legs dark flesh in colour; bill yellow with black tip. Female has brownish plumage, with more noticeable pale fringes t feathering giving scaly appearance. Pale crescent band of female has dark feather edging. Juvenile similar to female but crescent band usually faint. In flight, wings of both sex show pale upperwing panel.

ck-throated thrush

RACE *ATROGULARIS* ♂

Eye-browed thrush

♂

Ring ouzel

♀

♂

Blackbird
Turdus merula

Status: Resident; common; **Voice:** Call sounds like 'see'; ala shrill chatter; song variety of flute-like, musical phrases; **Length:** 24–25cm; **Wingspan:** 34–38.5cm; **Habitat:** In most places where trees are present, but also on moors and in towns; **Behaviour:** Hunts for invertebrates in leaf litter or forages in meadows and lawns for worms

Male should not be confused with any other bird. Th only all-black bird in Europe with bright golden-yell bill and long, broad tail. Black coloration is glossy but not iridescent. Orange-yellow 'eyelids' form eyering. Legs dark brown. Immature male's bill dark grey-brown, turning gold through first winter, and plumage dull black. Female head and body dark brown. Underparts often have rufous tone a dark thrush-like mottling on breast, some birds being more marked than others. Legs dark brown, and in parts of the northwest, including Britain, bill dark but yellow at base o lower mandible. Juvenile like female but more rufous and more spotted below.

Fieldfare
Turdus pilaris

Status: Resident; common; **Voice:** Call 'tchak, tchak'; song weak warble with some wheezes and chuckles; **Length:** 25.5cm; **Wingspan:** 39–42cm; **Habitat:** Open woodland, and beyond tree-line, gardens and parks; overwinters on open grounds or fruiting hedgerows; **Behaviour:** Noisy and aggressive at colonial nest site and in defence of winter food source

Large thrush with unmistakable plumage pattern. Adults of both sexes have slate-grey head, nape and rump contrasting with chestnut back and black tail. Throa and breast golden-brown, streaked black. Rest of underpar white, flanks streaked black. Combination of white underwing, grey rump and black tail diagnostic. Bill yellow breeding male; has dusky tip and culmen in winter male, females in all plumages and juveniles. Juvenile plumage recalls mistle thrush but shows pale streaks on back.

♀

JUVENILE

Blackbird

♂

Fieldfare

Song Thrush
Turdus philomelos

Status: Resident; common; **Voice:** Call 'tsip'; alarm rattle ' tic-tic'; song loud, repetitive, musical; **Length:** 23cm; **Wingspan:** 33–36cm; **Habitat:** Parks, woods, hedges and gardens; **Behaviour:** Beats snails on stone to break shell

Medium-sized thrush. Sexes similar. Adult has warr brown upperparts. Rump and uppertail coverts mor olive, crown and tail with rufous tone. Indistinctly marke face has whitish eyering, pale-cream moustachial stripe a blackish-brown streak from base of bill, which contrasts w white throat. Underparts white with golden-brown wash o sides of breast and flanks; breast marked with blackish-br spots that fade out on belly; spots arranged more in streak than random spots of mistle thrush. Underwing coverts ar axillaries golden buff. Bill blackish-brown; legs pale flesh. Juvenile similar to adult but with pale streaks on back.

Redwing
Turdus iliacus

Status: Resident; common; **Voice:** Call far-carrying 'see-ip song variable, 4–6 fluty notes plus warbling; **Length:** 21cm **Wingspan:** 33–34.5cm; **Habitat:** Open woods, thickets, bir scrub; overwinters on grassland and open woodland; **Behaviour:** In winter roosts in large flocks

Small thrush, most like song thrush. Sexes alike. A has long, deep creamy-white supercilium contrastin with dark-brown cheeks and brown crown. Dark-brown st runs from base of bill. All upperparts dark warm brown, darker on flight feathers. Breast yellowish-buff on sides, c brown streaks forming gorget. Undertail coverts white. Be white, streaked with lighter brown on sides. Flanks and underwing chestnut red (song thrush's underwing buff). blackish-brown. Legs yellowish or flesh-brown. Juvenile h patterning of adult but heavily streaked with buffish wash face and flanks. In flight, silhouette rather like starling's.

Mistle Thrush
Turdus viscivorus

Status: Resident; common; **Voice:** Call harsh, distinctive rattle; song loud, short, fluty phrases; **Length:** 27cm; **Wingspan:** 42–47.5cm; **Habitat:** Woods, farmland, parks a gardens; **Behaviour:** Sings even in wild weather in midwi

Largest thrush. Sexes similar. Adult recalls song th but is larger, with whitish underparts covered with large, wedge-shaped black spots; flanks and breast marke with buff. Upperparts and wings greyish-brown with conspicuous greyish-white fringes to tertials and wing coverts. Tail grey-brown with diagnostic white tips to oute feathers. White underwing striking in powerful, direct flig bird closes wings after each burst of wingbeats. Juvenile similar to adult but spotted white on upperparts.

JUVENILE

Song thrush

ADULT

Redwing

Mistle thrush

ADULT

JUVENILE

Grasshopper Warbler
Locustella naevia

Status: Summer visitor; widespread; **Voice:** Short quiet 'p call; song high-pitched, monotonous trill; **Length:** 12.5cm; **Wingspan:** 15–19cm; **Habitat:** Undergrowth in marshes, t hedges, heathland, new plantations; **Behaviour:** Singing b can sometimes be approached to within a metre

Small, uniformly coloured warbler. Sexes similar. A upperparts olive-brown, spotted and streaked with dark brown from crown to rump. Wings darker brown with buff to reddish fringes to feathers, visible at close range. Streaks on rump fade out on reddish-brown uppertail cov Tail reddish-brown, softly barred darker. Underparts most buff, but almost white on chin, throat and centre of breas and belly. Undertail coverts streaked with brown. Bill blackish-brown with bright yellow base. Legs pale yellowi brown to pink. Juvenile very similar to adult.

River Warbler
Locustella fluviatilis

Status: Summer visitor; locally common; rare vagrant to northwest Europe; **Voice:** Sharp 'tsick' call; song curious, rhythmic, 'chuffing' sound; **Length:** 13cm; **Wingspan:** 19–22cm; **Habitat:** Dense vegetation in backwaters, bogs, carrs, flooded woods; **Behaviour:** Runs about in dense cover to feed

Unstreaked, small- to medium-sized warbler. Upperparts, wings and tail olive-brown, darker on uppertail coverts and tail, slightly greyer on head and bac Underparts dull white with olive-brown wash on flanks ar sides of breast. Undertail coverts long, to tip of tail, buff-brown with broad white tips. Bill dark brown with pale ba Legs flesh to brown. Sexes similar but female greyer abov Juvenile similar to adult.

Savi's Warbler
Locustella luscinioides

Status: Summer visitor; local; **Voice:** Call 'pit'; alarm shar rattle; song accelerating ticking sound; **Length:** 14cm; **Wingspan:** 18–21cm; **Habitat:** Reedy swamps and fens, overgrown fringes of lakes; **Behaviour:** Regularly climbs prominent perch to sing, often through the night

Medium-sized warbler, resembling large reed warbl Similar to other plainly coloured warblers. Sexes similar. Adult distinguished by dark, unstreaked, reddish-brown head and upperparts, with faint buff supercilium fading out behind eye. Underparts brownish-white with rufous-brown along sides of breast and flanks to undertai coverts. Wings and tail uniform reddish-brown like upperparts. Tail broad and graduated towards tip. Bill da grey-brown. Legs pale brown. Juvenile similar to adult.

Grasshopper warbler

River warbler

Savi's warbler

♂

Cetti's Warbler
Cettia cetti

Status: Resident; widespread; **Voice:** Call sharp 'chip'; son
very distinctive, loud and abrupt; **Length:** 13.5cm; **Wingsp**
15–19cm; **Habitat:** Bushy places giving thick shelter by
watersides, swamps, marshes; **Behaviour:** Males often
polygynous and take little part in rearing young

Medium-sized warbler with short, rounded wings, a
relatively long, broad, graduated tail. Sexes similar
appearance but males 10 per cent larger and 30 per cent
heavier than females. Adult upperparts and wings uniform
chestnut brown. Face broken only by off-white eyering and
short, grey supercilium. Chin and central underparts off-
white, rest grey-brown or darker brown, especially on flan
and undertail coverts; dull-white tips of undertail coverts
especially obvious when bird cocks its tail in excitement.
dark brown. Legs brown-flesh. Juvenile similar to adult.

Fan-tailed Warbler
Cisticola juncidis

Status: Resident; widespread; **Voice:** Call is persistent 'zip
Song is high-pitched, sharp 'tsip-tsip- …' or 'zit-zit- …';
Length: 10cm; **Wingspan:** 12–14.5cm; **Habitat:** Rough, gra
plains, grain fields, marshes, rice fields; **Behaviour:** Skulk
but inquisitive; may be seen perching on grass stems

Tiny, short-winged, buff-coloured bird with short fa
tail. Adult has warm buff upperparts streaked black
brown on crown, mantle and wings. Nape, rump and uppe
coverts almost unstreaked. Pale face has short creamy
supercilium and pale circle around eye. Breast and flanks
buff. Chin, throat, belly and undertail coverts white. Tail
brown with underside marked with black sub-terminal ba
and white tip. Bill brown above, grey below, with dark tip
breeding male and flesh-pink tip on other males and fema
Juvenile similar to female.

Moustached Warbler
*Acrocephalus
melanopogon*

Status: Resident; widespread; **Voice:** Call soft 't-rrrt'; alar
'churr'; song distinctive musical medley; **Length:** 12–13cm
Wingspan: 15–16.5cm; **Habitat:** Swamps and reedbeds;
Behaviour: Skulking; when nervous, cocks tail like wren

Similar to aquatic and sedge warblers, but separab
with care; note especially head pattern, upperparts
duller wings, behaviour and diagnostic song. Sexes simila
Adult nape and mantle rufous brown; nape unmarked but
mantle streaked black. Unstreaked rump almost same col
as dark-brown tail. Wings olive-brown with paler feathers.
Underparts whitish with rusty flanks, vent and sides to
breast. Head has distinctive pattern of black crown and bl
white supercilium – square-ended behind eye – highlighte
by dusky lore and eyestripe. Juvenile similar to adult.

Cetti's warbler

Fan-tailed warbler

Moustached warbler

Aquatic Warbler

Acrocephalus paludicola

Status: Summer visitor; local; rare passage migrant to northwest Europe in autumn; **Voice:** Call harsh 'churr'; son[g] incorporates short rattles, with some fluty notes; **Length:** 13cm; **Wingspan:** 16.5–19.5cm; **Habitat:** Marshes of sedge and iris; **Behaviour:** Stays in low, dense cover but can be drawn into open by imitating its call

Similar to sedge and moustached warblers. Sexes similar. Adult upperparts sandier than sedge warble[r] with long dark-brown streaks highlighted by paler stripes. Rump rusty, streaked with brown. Underparts creamy buff, becoming white with wear, with fine brown streaks on side[s] breast and on flanks. Head pattern diagnostic: long, pale-b[rown] crown stripe and supercilium, separated by dark-brown str[ipe] at side of crown; supercilium highlighted by brown eyestri[pe] from behind eye. Tail dull black with tawny fringes and feathers pointed. Bill dark brown and legs orange-yellow. Juvenile brighter than adult; recalls juvenile sedge warble[r].

Sedge Warbler

Acrocephalus schoenobaenus

Status: Summer visitor; common; **Voice:** Call 'tuc'; alarm 'churr'; song loud and varied mix of harsh and musical note[s] **Length:** 13cm; **Wingspan:** 17–21cm; **Habitat:** Reedbeds an[d] other lush vegetation near water; **Behaviour:** Sometimes sings from exposed perch

Resembles moustached and aquatic warblers. Sexes similar. Adult upperparts and head strongly marked. Nape, mantle and scapulars olive-brown with dark streaks. Unstreaked rump tawny; tail dark brown. Wings buff-brown with lighter edges to tertials and greater coverts. Underpar[ts] off-white, whitest on throat and belly, more rufous on flank[s]. Head has black-streaked crown and long creamy superciliu[m] above dusky-olive lores. Bill blackish, paler at base; legs greyish. Juvenile has creamier supercilium than adult, yellower underparts and distinct brown spots across breast[?].

Paddyfield Warbler

Acrocephalus agricola

Status: Summer visitor to Bulgaria and Romania; local; rar[e] vagrant to northwest Europe; **Voice:** Call soft 'chak'; song musical, varied and mimetic; **Length:** 13cm; **Wingspan:** 16–17cm; **Habitat:** Dry reedbed margins; **Behaviour:** Skulk[s]

Similar to reed warbler but with more contrast in plumage. Sexes similar. Adult upperparts warm brow[n] appearing greyish on head. Underparts whitish. Head show[s] broad, pale supercilium, emphasised by dark border above and below. Adult plumage in late summer often dull. Juven[ile] similar to adult but plumage shows less contrast. All birds have dark bill with yellowish base to lower mandible; legs variable but often pinkish-grey to pinkish-brown.

Aquatic warbler

Sedge warbler

Paddyfield warbler

Reed Warbler
Acrocephalus scirpaceus

Status: Summer visitor; common; **Voice:** Call 'churr-churr'; alarm harsher; song low guttural churring, with long phrase **Length:** 13cm; **Wingspan:** 17–21cm; **Habitat:** Edges of reedbeds and nearby vegetation; **Behaviour:** Inquisitive or singing birds will climb reed stems

Medium-sized warbler. Sexes similar. Adult upperpar uniform olive-brown, with often noticeably more rufo rump and uppertail coverts, and darker brown primaries ar tertials. Underparts white with buff undertail coverts and sides of breast. In late summer, plumage drabber and greye above and paler below. Indistinct supercilium dull cream. B dark grey or greyish-brown with pale base. Legs usually greyish. Juvenile brighter and rustier than adult, but face pattern less distinct; similar to juvenile marsh warbler.

Blyth's Reed Warbler
Acrocephalus dumetorum

Status: Summer visitor to Sweden and Finland; local; very rare autumn vagrant to northwest Europe; **Voice:** Call soft 'chek'; song series of whistling phrases, each repeated seve times, in manner of song thrush; **Length:** 13cm; **Wingspan:** 18–19cm; **Habitat:** Waterside scrub; **Behaviour:** Generally sings at night

Medium-sized, slim warbler, similar to both reed and marsh warblers. Sexes similar. Adult has uniformly pa grey-brown upperparts, including wing and tail. Underparts whitish with hint of grey-buff wash on flanks and sides of neck. Head has dark lores, pale eyering and pale superciliu this most prominent in front of eye and above lores. Wings relatively short compared to other similar *Acrocephalus* warblers. Bill rather long, needle-like and dark, and legs da grey. Juvenile similar to adult but upperparts warmer brow Bill as adult but legs normally pinkish-grey.

Great Reed Warbler
Acrocephalus arundinaceus

Status: Summer visitor; local; **Voice:** Call 'chak'; alarm hars chatter; song very loud, harsh 'churrs' and rattles; **Length:** 19–20cm; **Wingspan:** 25–29cm; **Habitat:** Mostly aquatic vegetation, especially dense reedbeds; **Behaviour:** Male sin throughout day when attracting a mate

Similar to reed warbler but clearly larger with longer stouter bill. Female tends to be brighter above and le white below than male. Sexes otherwise similar. Adult upperparts warm olive-brown, with darker crown, fawnier rump and wing coverts edged rufous. Shows creamy supercilium, dusky eyestripe and pale-cream eyering. Underparts mainly creamy buff, but more buff on flanks; ch and throat off-white. Bill grey-brown, with pinkish base to lower mandible. Legs pale brown. Juvenile similar to adult.

Reed warbler

Blyth's reed warbler

♂

Great reed warbler

Marsh Warbler
Acrocephalus palustris

Status: Summer visitor; common; **Voice:** Call 'tchuc'; alarm 'chirrr'; prolonged, very musical song; **Length:** 13cm; **Wingspan:** 18–21cm; **Habitat:** Dense low vegetation, osier beds, other rank vegetation; **Behaviour:** Sings in upright posture, often raising and fanning wings

Medium-sized warbler, very hard to separate from re and Blyth's reed warblers. Sexes similar. Adult upperparts more olive-brown than on reed warbler, and lacl rufous rump. Has short, wide-based bill, round-headed appearance, long wings showing eight to nine primary tips, pear-shaped or pot-bellied appearance and long undertail coverts. Less agile than reed warbler. Has astonishing mimetic song. Juvenile similar to adult.

Olivaceous Warbler
Hippolais pallida

Status: Summer visitor; locally common; **Voice:** Call 'tack'; alarm repeated ticking; song high-pitched, rapid, scratchy warble; **Length:** 12–13.5cm; **Wingspan:** 18–21cm; **Habitat:** Shrubs, orchards, gardens, palm groves, lowlands and bush hills; **Behaviour:** Males very vocal in breeding season; tend form neighbourhood groups

Medium- to large-sized warbler. Sexes similar. Pluma recalls garden warbler; dull brown above, creamy-wh below with pale-buff wash on sides of breast and flanks; yellowish wash in spring. Has dull-white supercilium. Face dominated by flat crown, rather long, prominent bill and da eye with whitish eyering. Rump washed buff, faintly distinc from tail. Wings short relative to body size. Legs very variak brownish to bluish-grey. Juvenile similar to adult.

Booted Warbler
Hippolais caligata

Status: Summer visitor to Estonia; local; rare autumn vagr to northwest Europe; **Voice:** Call sharp 'tchak'; **Length:** 12c **Wingspan:** 18–20cm; **Habitat:** Areas of scrub and watersid vegetation; **Behaviour:** Builds cup-shaped nest in low shru

Small, pale *Hippolais* warbler, superficially similar t *Phylloscopus* warbler. On close inspection, however, always appears more stocky, has more robust and broader-based bill and pale lores. Sexes similar. Adult has pale sanc brown upperparts. Underparts whitish but with buffish was to flanks. Head has pale but rather indistinct supercilium. Juvenile similar to adult but with slightly darker upperpart and flanks. All birds have dark bill with pale base to lower mandible and pinkish-grey or blue-grey legs.

Marsh warbler

Olivaceous warbler

Booted warbler

Olive-tree Warbler
Hippolais olivetorum

Status: Summer visitor; locally common; **Voice:** Call 'tuc'; song lower pitched and slower than its relatives; **Length:** 15cm; **Wingspan:** 24–26cm; **Habitat:** Open-canopy woods, groves and orchards; **Behaviour:** Keeps mostly to tree cano

Large greyish warbler, with long wings and dagger-lik bill. Sexes similar. Adult upperparts and wings brownish-grey, with whitish edges to greater coverts, secondaries and tertials forming wing panel. Has buff-whit supercilium and whitish eyering. Bill's size accentuated by long, flat crown. Tail grey with white edges. Underparts dir white with grey wash on breast, flanks and neck. Feather wear by late summer makes bird look duller and wing pane obscure. Legs greyish-olive. Juvenile as autumn adult but upperparts more olive and wing panel more extensive.

Icterine Warbler
Hippolais icterina

Status: Summer visitor; widespread; **Voice:** Call 'tec' and, i spring, diagnostic 'deeteroo'; song loud with long warble; **Length:** 13.5cm; **Wingspan:** 20.5–24cm; **Habitat:** Sunny wooded lowlands, cultivated lands and gardens; **Behaviour** Male defends breeding territory vigorously; shy on passage

Medium-sized warbler, with long bill accentuated by rather flat crown, long wings reaching at least to end uppertail coverts. Sexes similar. Adult basically green abov and yellow below. Area between bill and below eye yellow, giving pale-faced effect. Wings have distinct pale panel formed by yellow edges to dark-olive tertials and secondari Legs bright blue-grey. Late-summer adults in worn plumag browner above and whiter below. Care needed to separate from other *Hippolais* warblers, in particular melodious warbler. Juveniles usually flushed with yellow.

Melodious Warbler
Hippolais polyglotta

Status: Summer visitor; widespread; **Voice:** Call 'hooeet'; alarm harsh 'tchurrrr'; song sustained, varied and musical; **Length:** 13cm; **Wingspan:** 17.5–20cm; **Habitat:** Principally wooded lowlands, often near water; **Behaviour:** Feeds restlessly in shrubs and trees, using fluttering action

Medium-sized, long-billed warbler. Difficult to separ from icterine warbler, but smaller, with shorter, rounded wings that do not reach tips of uppertail coverts. Sexes similar. Adult upperparts brownish-green (duller tha icterine warbler's), underparts rich yellow. Wings and tail olive-brown; wings lack pale wing panel. Head brownish-green with yellow supercilium from bill to behind eye, whic has yellow eyering. Late-summer adult in worn plumage appears dun-coloured above and whitish below. Juvenile in fresh plumage sometimes bright yellow or yellowish-green.

Olive-tree warbler

JUVENILE

Icterine warbler

ADULT

Melodious warbler

Dartford Warbler
Sylvia undata

Status: Resident; local; **Voice:** Call 'tuc' and grating alarm 'tchirrr'; song musical chatter, some liquid notes; **Length:** 12.5cm; **Wingspan:** 13–18.5cm; **Habitat:** Low, dense cover coastal scrub, heathland or maquis; **Behaviour:** Best seen fine, sunny morning, when male will sing perched on a bus

Slim, small-bodied warbler with long tail. Male dark slaty-brown above with greyer head, and wine-red below. Wings almost uniformly brownish-black. Tail grey-black with narrow white edges. Throat white-spotted in fresh plumage but spots wear off by June or July. Bill dark brown. Legs brownish-yellow. Eye and eyering orange to re Female and juvenile resemble male, but browner on upperparts and paler below. In poor light all ages and sexe look uniformly dark.

Marmora's Warbler
Sylvia sarda

Status: Summer visitor/resident; local; **Voice:** Call explosi 'crrip' or 'tsig'; song weak, high-pitched warble; **Length:** 12 **Wingspan:** 13–17.5cm; **Habitat:** Heath and low scrub on d hillsides and coastal slopes; **Behaviour:** Generally skulkin spends more time on ground than other warblers

Darkest warbler in region, very like Dartford warble build and actions but tail slightly shorter. Male dull blue-grey above and below. Wings and tail dull black, latte with dusky white edges, often not noticeable. Legs yellow-brown. Female plumage drabber and browner than male's Eye and eyering of both sexes orange to red. Juvenile ever browner than female, with dull-yellow eyes.

Spectacled Warbler
Sylvia conspicillata

Status: Summer visitor; local; **Voice:** Call high 'tseet'; song short, sweet, rapid, variable warble; **Length:** 12.5cm; **Wingspan:** 13.5–17cm; **Habitat:** In low scrub and rough ground beside cultivation; also in glasswort in wet lowland with salt-laden soils; **Behaviour:** Shy and skulking; scolds intruders from a prominent perch while cocking tail

Recalls small whitethroat or subalpine warbler with moustache. Male grey to sandy brown above with striking orange edges to wing feathers forming glowing pa Black tail clearly edged white. Underparts pink except for white chin, grey throat and buffish-grey head, which in sor lights appears black between bill and below eye. Eye ochr orange in white eyering. Female browner on head and upperparts than male, with no black on face; underparts le pink, more buff. Chin white. Female looks more like whitethroat than male does. Juvenile similar to female bu with buffish suffusion to plumage.

Dartford warbler

♂

Marmora's warbler

♂

Spectacled warbler

♂

Subalpine Warbler
Sylvia cantillans

Status: Summer visitor; widespread; rare spring visitor to northwest Europe; **Voice:** Call 'tec'; alarm oft-repeated 'tec'; song like whitethroat, but more musical; **Length:** 12cm; **Wingspan:** 15–19cm; **Habitat:** Thickets, woodland glades, stream banks; **Behaviour:** Male usually sings from cover, but sometimes from a perch in the open

Small, elegant warbler, similar to Dartford warbler in proportions. Male has pale blue-grey upperparts, dark pink-chestnut breast and unmarked throat, and white 'moustache'. Rest of underparts and belly white; undertail coverts buff. Wings and tail dark grey-brown with pale-grey fringes to wing feathers, and white outertail feathers. Bill blackish-brown, legs yellowish-brown. Eye red in red eyering. Female pale grey-brown above, with duller moustache, and pinkish-buff below; white more extensive than on male and wings browner. Hard to tell from spectacled warbler in autumn. Juvenile washed out but has hint of moustache.

Sardinian Warbler
Sylvia melanocephala

Status: Resident/summer visitor; widespread; **Voice:** Harsh alarm rattle; 'treek, treek' call; song rapid medley, harsh and musical; **Length:** 13.5cm; **Wingspan:** 15–18cm; **Habitat:** Scrub and open woodland; **Behaviour:** Perky behaviour reminiscent of whitethroat

Male needs care at first to separate from other black headed warblers. Distinguished by black hood extending well below eye to lores and ear coverts; sharply divided from pure white chin and upper throat. Has steep forehead, red eye and red eyering. Rest of upperparts grey; underparts off-white, grading to grey on flanks. Bill buffish brown with black tip. Legs reddish. Wings blackish with grey edged feathers. Tail black, edged white. Female has same head pattern as male but black replaced by dusky grey, still with red eye and eyering. Upperparts dirty brown; flanks dirty brown but underparts otherwise white. Wings and tail dark brown with pale edges as on male. Juvenile similar to female.

Desert Warbler
Sylvia nana

Status: Vagrant to northwest Europe from Asia and north Africa; very rare; **Voice:** Call harsh chatter; **Length:** 11.5cm; **Wingspan:** 15–17cm; **Habitat:** Arid, stony ground and semi desert; **Behaviour:** Generally skulking

Small, extremely pale warbler. Sexes similar. Adult has pale sandy-brown upperparts; tail appears warmer brown than rest of upperparts in Asiatic birds. Underparts pale whitish-buff. Eye has yellow iris. Legs yellow and bill has dark upper mandible and mostly yellow lower mandible. Juvenile like adult.

♂

Subalpine warbler

♀

♂

Sardinian warbler

♀

Desert warbler

Cyprus Warbler
Sylvia melanothorax

Status: Resident/summer visitor; locally common in Cypru only; **Voice:** Call grating 'tchek'; song vigorous rattle of hig and low notes; **Length:** 13.5cm; **Wingspan:** 15–18cm; **Hab** Maquis scrub and forest edge; **Behaviour:** Shy and skulki

Male has black and white mottled underparts, from chin to undertail coverts, and pale fringes to innerv feathers. White 'moustache' pronounced. Black tail with white edges contrasts with grey mantle, back and rump. H yellow to chestnut eye in yellowish to red eyering. Female male but duller and browner; moustachial stripe dull whit Eye and eyering duller than on male. In both sexes bill buffish-yellow with black tip, and legs variable, flesh-yello reddish-brown. Juvenile similar to female but markings le pronounced; similar to juvenile Sardinian warbler.

Rüppell's Warbler
Sylvia rueppellii

Status: Summer visitor; local; **Voice:** Hard 'tak, tak'; song rapid, chattering, with some call notes and pure tones; **Length:** 14cm; **Wingspan:** 18–21cm; **Habitat:** Thorny scru maquis, on rocky slopes and in gulleys; **Behaviour:** Sings f conspicuous perch or in song-flight

Male has black head and upper breast, relieved only red eye and eyering, and conspicuous white 'moustache'. Rest of upperparts grey. Rest of underparts greyish-white. Tail black with white outer feathers. Wings mainly black with striking whitish fringes and tips to terti Bill quite long, blackish with paler, yellowish base to lower mandible. Legs reddish-brown. Female and juvenile duller and browner than male, most showing faint impression of male's head markings. Bill and leg colouring similar to ma

Barred Warbler
Sylvia nisoria

Status: Summer visitor; widespread; annual autumn vagra to northwest Europe; **Voice:** Call harsh 'charr'; song short warble with harsh call notes mixed in; **Length:** 15.5cm; **Wingspan:** 23–27cm; **Habitat:** Scrub, riverine woodland o orchards; **Behaviour:** Displaying male perches conspicuou jerking and fanning tail

Bulky, robust warbler with pale wingbars, pale-edge tertials and white-tipped tail. Bill grey-brown with base, and proportionately large legs greyish or brownish a times. Male has grey head, face and upperparts. Eye pale yellow. Underparts dull white from chin to undertail cover barred with dark grey-brown crescents, emphasised by wh tips. Tail long and broad, dark brown with white edges. Female like male but duller and browner above, with barr less clear below and paler eye. Juvenile recalls garden warbler, being unbarred and dark-eyed.

Cyprus warbler

♂

Rüppell's warbler

♂

JUVENILE

Barred warbler

ADULT ♂

Orphean Warbler
Sylvia hortensis

Status: Summer visitor; widespread; vagrant to northwest Europe; **Voice:** Call 'tac, tac' or 'trrrr' alarm; song pleasant thrush-like warble; **Length:** 15cm; **Wingspan:** 20–25cm; **Habitat:** Stunted forest and scrub on hillsides, olive groves and gardens; **Behaviour:** Forages in upper foliage

Robust warbler resembling large blackcap but easily separated by white outertail feathers and pale yellow white eyes of adults. Male has dark cap extending to lores and ear coverts. Nape and upperparts grey-brown; wings an tail dusky brown. Has pale-grey fringes to tertials and large coverts. Underparts white but with pinkish flush on breast breeding season. Bill long, blackish. Legs grey or grey-brow Female similar to male but duller, with greyer upperparts. Juvenile browner than female and lacks dark head.

Lesser Whitethroat
Sylvia curruca

Status: Summer visitor; widespread; **Voice:** Hard 'tack' or 'churr'; song loud rattle often preceded by quiet warble; **Length:** 12.5–13.5cm; **Wingspan:** 16.5–20.5cm; **Habitat:** Woodland edge, thick hedges, shrubberies with thick dark cover; **Behaviour:** Active but skulking bird

Small to medium-sized, slim warbler. Adult greyer above and whiter below than whitethroat and lacks contrasting rufous wing panel, so upperparts look dull grey brown and underparts dull white. Shows dark face mask, formed by black lores and ear coverts against slate grey of rest of head. Primaries and tail browner and darker than re of upperparts. Tail has white outertail feathers. Sexes simil but, seen side by side, male sometimes has blacker mask an paler pink flush on breast than female. Juvenile similar to female but browner.

Whitethroat
Sylvia communis

Status: Summer visitor; widespread; **Voice:** Scolding 'charr sharp 'tac'; song short, rapid, chattery warble; **Length:** 14cr **Wingspan:** 18.5–23cm; **Habitat:** Open habitats with thicke and shrubs; **Behaviour:** Often scolds observer from bush

Similar in size to blackcap but with proportionately longer tail giving slimmer appearance. Male has grey cap extending to below eye, whitish eyering and brown eye Chin and throat pure white. Breast pale pinkish-buff and re of underparts white. Upperparts dull brown, suffused with grey in spring plumage. Very distinctive panel on wing form by rufous edges to wing coverts, secondaries and tertials. T dark brown with white outer feathers. Bill buffish-brown w dark tip; legs pale flesh to brown. Female and juvenile have same tail and wing patterns as male but throats duller and rest of plumage browner. Bill and leg colour as male.

Orphean warbler ♂

Lesser whitethroat

JUVENILE

ADULTS

Whitethroat

♀

Garden Warbler
Sylvia borin

Status: Summer visitor; widespread; **Voice:** Call loud, hard 'tac, tac'; song rich, sustained, flowing warble; **Length:** 14c▮ **Wingspan:** 20–24.5cm; **Habitat:** Open deciduous or mixed woodland with thick undergrowth; **Behaviour:** Often sings from thick cover; song similar to blackcap's

Plainest of the *Sylvia* warblers and medium- to large-sized. Sexes similar. Adult has plain brown plumage on upperparts, darker brown wings and pale-buff underparts (latter feature separating it from *Phylloscopus* warbler); belly and undertail coverts white. Eyering pale. Rounded head and stubby bill help distinguish it from *Hippolais* warblers. Juvenile more strongly marked buff below and tawny above.

Blackcap
Sylvia atricapilla

Status: Summer visitor/resident; common; **Voice:** Call lou▮ repeated 'tac'; song loud, rich warble, rising in pitch; **Leng▮** 13cm; **Wingspan:** 20–23cm; **Habitat:** Open woodland and copses with thick undergrowth, even in towns; **Behaviour▮** Forages and sings in treetops

Largish warbler, easily identified if seen clearly. Ma▮ has diagnostic black forehead and crown (cap) abo▮ ash-grey nape and face. Upperparts ashy brown, darker on tail and primaries (although wing coverts and tertials edg▮ paler). Chin, breast and flanks grey, the first two silvery w▮ plumage is fresh; belly and undertail coverts white. Bill d▮ black, legs slate. Female similar to male but cap bright re▮ brown and upperparts browner. Juvenile very like female ▮ cap much duller brown.

Garden warbler

Blackcap

♂

♀

Arctic Warbler
Phylloscopus borealis

Status: Summer visitor; locally common; **Voice:** Calls 'tzic' and 'tseep'; song loud, energetic but monotonous trill; **Length:** 10.5–11.5cm; **Wingspan:** 16.5–22cm; **Habitat:** Taiga forest, willow and birch forest, often near water or damp ground; **Behaviour:** Keeps mostly to upper branches to feed and sing

Superficially similar to several other members of the genus *Phylloscopus* (especially willow and greenish warblers, and chiffchaff) but bulkier in the body. Adult largely greenish above and off-white below. Best features are obvious creamy wingbar, and yellowish-white supercilium from bill to nape, often upturned at hind end. Shows dark eyestripe. Brown bill noticeably pointed; legs pale yellowish-brown. Juvenile similar to adult but with brighter colours.

Greenish Warbler
Phylloscopus trochiloides

Status: Summer visitor; widespread; **Voice:** Call distinctive 'chee-wee', the second note lower; song wren-like medley; **Length:** 10cm; **Wingspan:** 15–21cm; **Habitat:** Open woodland (coniferous or broad-leaved) copses, overgrown orchards; **Behaviour:** Active mainly in the forest canopy

Small and superficially similar to willow warbler. Plumage pale greyish-olive above, dull white below. Has long yellowish-white supercilium reaching nearly to the nape (often upturned at the end), dark eyestripe, pale wingbar (in fresh plumage). Bill has pale lower mandible; legs variable shade of brown, distinguishing bird from Arctic warbler. Juvenile in first-winter plumage similar to adult but sometimes shows faint second wingbar.

Wood Warbler
Phylloscopus sibilatrix

Status: Summer visitor; widespread; **Voice:** Usual call plaintive 'pew, pew'; song in two phases, mainly a trill; **Length:** 12cm; **Wingspan:** 19.5–24cm; **Habitat:** Prefers hilly terrain, and woodland with good canopy (beech and oak especially); **Behaviour:** Forages in tree canopy; hovers well

The most distinctive *Phylloscopus* warbler; larger than others, with relatively longer wings and shorter tail. Sexes similar. Adult appears to be three-colour bird: yellowish-green upperparts; bright yellow supercilium, throat and breast; pure white belly and undertail coverts. Tail, flight feathers and tertials brown, outer edges of first two edged yellowish-green, but tertials edged white or yellowish-white. Bill has dark-brown upper mandible, pale-flesh lower mandible. Legs pale yellowish-brown. Juveniles similar to brightly coloured adult.

Arctic warbler

Greenish warbler

Wood warbler

Bonelli's Warbler

Phylloscopus bonelli

Status: Summer visitor; locally common; **Voice:** Call 'hu-ee (western race), 'chirp' (eastern race); song trill on one nc **Length:** 11.5cm; **Wingspan:** 16–20cm; **Habitat:** Woods, including cork oak and pine, usually 700m–2,000m above sea level; **Behaviour:** Feeds actively in upper canopy of woodlands

Small, highly active warbler. Sexes similar. Adult generally pale, with light grey-brown upperparts, washed with pale olive-green. Head and nape often appear particularly pale. Has silky white underparts and pale yellowish rump (often seen only when it hovers). Upper mandible of bill brown, lower mandible flesh-coloured. Legs dull brown. Juvenile similar to adult but duller.

Chiffchaff

Phylloscopus collybita

Status: Summer visitor/resident; common; **Voice:** Call monosyllabic 'hweet, hweet'; song diagnostic 'chiff-chaff-chiff'; **Length:** 10–11cm; **Wingspan:** 15–21cm; **Habitat:** Woodland, but not deep forest or coniferous plantations; a copses, hedgerows; **Behaviour:** Flicks wings and tail with distinctive sideways movement

Very like willow warbler. Sexes similar. Adult dull brownish-olive above and dull pale yellow below, shading to buff flanks. Browner above and more buff below than willow warbler, with much less yellow tint (although is more noticeable on autumn juveniles). Eastern forms noticeably greyer above and whiter below than western for with whitish wingbar. Iberian birds have warm brown upperparts and yellowish underparts; considered by some authorities to be a separate species: Iberian chiffchaff. All forms show pale-yellow supercilium, pale eyering, contrast dark eyes and dark legs. Juvenile and first-winter birds ha warm brown upperparts and underparts suffused with yell

Radde's Warbler

Phylloscopus schwarzi

Status: Autumn vagrant from Siberia; rare; **Voice:** Call a tongue-clicking 'chek'; **Length:** 12cm; **Wingspan:** 16–18cm **Habitat:** Scrub and dense woodland; **Behaviour:** Movemer slow and deliberate; vagrants often feed on ground

Rather large, plump *Phylloscopus* warbler with shor thick bill and proportionately large head. Sexes sim Adult has dark olive-brown upperparts and dirty yellowish buff underparts. Head shows dark eyestripe, speckled ear coverts and long, yellowish supercilium, brightest behind e Juvenile similar to adult but upperparts have yellowish ton All birds have bill with brown upper mandible and pinkish lower mandible; legs dull pink.

Bonelli's warbler

Iberian chiffchaff

Chiffchaff

Radde's warbler

Dusky Warbler
Phylloscopus fuscatus

Status: Autumn vagrant to northwest Europe from Siberia; rare; **Voice:** Call a sharp 'chek'; **Length:** 11cm; **Wingspan:** 15–18cm; **Habitat:** Scrub and damp woodland; **Behaviour:** Typically active warbler

Superficially similar to chiffchaff but legs pink, not blackish, and plumage darker (similar to that of Radde's warbler); facial markings rather striking. Sexes similar. Adult has dark-brown upperparts and pale grey-brown underparts. Head shows dark but diffuse eyestripe and long, pale supercilium, usually appearing brightest in front of eye or equally bright along entire length (supercilium on Radde's warbler is brightest behind eye). Juvenile similar to adult. All birds have narrow bill, more needle-like than that of Radde's warbler.

Willow Warbler
Phylloscopus trochilus

Status: Summer visitor; common; **Voice:** Call plaintive, disyllabic 'hoo-eet'; song lovely cascade of pure notes; **Length** 10.5–11.5cm; **Wingspan:** 16.5–22cm; **Habitat:** Woods, forest mostly coppices, scrub, anywhere with a few trees; **Behaviour:** Male aggressively establishes territory; chases female during courtship

Delicate little warbler, size of a blue tit but slimmer. Sexes similar. Adult olive-green above, yellowish-white below; colours cleaner than on very similar chiffchaff. Has pale yellow supercilium, brown bill and orange-brown legs (the latter reliably distinguish it from chiffchaff). Adults become browner above and whiter below during summer from feather abrasion. Juvenile in autumn has much yellower supercilium, throat and breast than adult.

Pallas's Warbler
Phylloscopus proregulus

Status: Late-autumn vagrant from Siberia; rare; **Voice:** Call a thin 'hueet'; **Length:** 9cm; **Wingspan:** 13–15cm; **Habitat:** Woodland; **Behaviour:** Extremely active

Superficially similar to yellow-browed warbler but even smaller and more strikingly marked. Sexes similar. Adult has greenish upperparts and pale greyish-white underparts. Most conspicuous features are long, yellowish supercilium, yellowish crown stripe and yellowish double wingbar; pale-yellow rump most conspicuous on hovering bird. Juvenile similar to adult but upperparts browner. First-winter bird effectively indistinguishable from adult in the field.

Dusky warbler

JUVENILE

Willow warbler

SOUTHERN BIRD

NORTHERN BIRD

Pallas's warbler

Yellow-browed Warbler
Phylloscopus inornatus

Status: Late-autumn vagrant from Siberia; rare; **Voice:** Call include thin 'tsu-eet', often sounding disyllabic; **Length:** 10cm; **Wingspan:** 15–18cm; **Habitat:** Woodland; **Behaviour** Very active feeder

Intermediate in size between goldcrest and chiffchaf Sexes similar. Adult has olive-brown to greenish-brow upperparts and dirty-white underparts. Most striking featu are long, pale-yellow supercilium and double pale-yellow wingbar. Wing feathers, especially tertials, are pale-tipped. Juvenile and first-winter birds similar to adult but upperpa generally duller and browner. All birds have dark brown bill and legs.

Goldcrest
Regulus regulus

Status: Resident; widespread; **Voice:** Calls frequently; song repeated double note and trill; all very high pitched; **Lengt** 9cm; **Wingspan:** 13.5–15.5cm; **Habitat:** Coniferous woods f breeding; wanders widely in winter; **Behaviour:** Restless; ca be very tame and approachable

Europe's smallest bird. Sexes similar. Adult has dull-greenish upperparts and pale olive-green underparts darker on the flanks. Wing coverts greenish with two white wingbars. Appears to be large-eyed, black on a whitish face Forehead whitish; crown of male orange-yellow, lined each side with black (often not noticeable in the field); in display male raises crest to reveal startling orange centre. Crown centre of female yellow. Juvenile lacks crown colours and markings.

Firecrest
Regulus ignicapillus

Status: Resident; local; **Voice:** Very high pitched; 'zit, zit,' c lower than goldcrest; song rapid string of calls; **Length:** 9cr **Wingspan:** 13–16cm; **Habitat:** Less restricted to conifers than goldcrest; gardens, scrub, tree heath; **Behaviour:** Mor active than goldcrest, and goes after larger prey; defends territory with loud, penetrating song

Adult more brightly coloured than goldcrest. Most striking feature is striped head: male has golden-orange crown stripe, lined each side with black; crown stri of female yellow. In display, male raises crown feathers to reveal astonishing orange 'fire-crest'. Adults of both sexes otherwise similar. Both show white supercilium underlined black eyestripe. Mantle to uppertail coverts bright olive-green, tail darker and browner; all underparts white. Striki bronze-coloured patch on side of neck. Bill black, legs brow Juvenile plumage similar to adult but lacks yellow or orang crown. Immature birds on autumn migration have invariab acquired adult-like plumage.

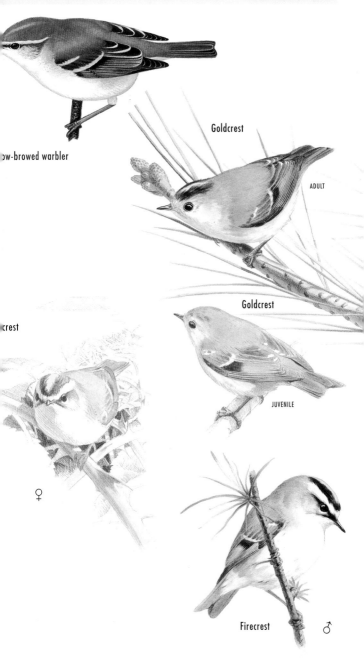

ow-browed warbler

Goldcrest

ADULT

Goldcrest

JUVENILE

crest

♀

Firecrest ♂

**COMPARING IMMATURE
PHYLLOSCOPUS
WARBLERS**

Adult *Phylloscopus* warblers in spring are comparativ
easy to identify, not least because males often sing distinc
and diagnostic songs. In autumn, however, it is a differ
matter. Birds are generally silent, apart from uttering
occasional call, and the plumage of immature birds of
differs in subtle ways from that which characterises the ad
of the same species.

BONELLI'S WARB

Considerably duller than adult but
degree of contrast between greyish h
and neck, white underparts and greenish-ye
upperparts; yellowish rump and flash on w
usually visible; frenetic feeding activity often useful

CHIFFCHAFF: Plum
generally warmer-toned t
adult's, with upperparts olive-bro
and underparts paler and flushed w
yellow; never as yellow as immat
willow warbler, and legs always bl

WOOD WARBL

Plumage duller than spr
adult but still shows contr
between greenish-bro
upperparts and white underpa
yellowish wash to face and to bro
conspicuous pale supercili

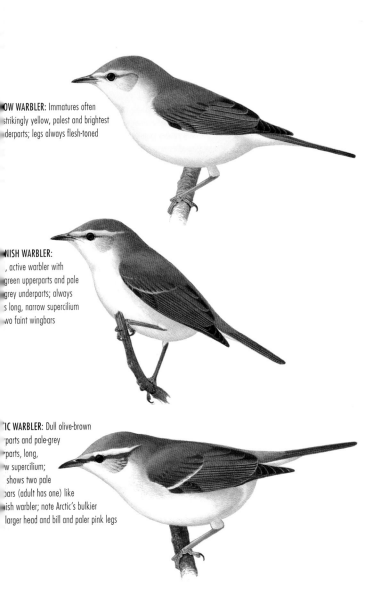

OW WARBLER: Immatures often strikingly yellow, palest and brightest derparts; legs always flesh-toned

NISH WARBLER:
, active warbler with green upperparts and pale grey underparts; always s long, narrow supercilium wo faint wingbars

IC WARBLER: Dull olive-brown parts and pale-grey parts, long, w supercilium; shows two pale bars (adult has one) like ish warbler; note Arctic's bulkier larger head and bill and paler pink legs

Pied Flycatcher

Ficedula hypoleuca

Status: Summer visitor; widespread; **Voice:** Call loud 'whit' 'wee-tic'; alarm 'phweet'; song a rapid sequence of high and low notes; **Length:** 13cm; **Wingspan:** 21.5–24cm; **Habitat:** Deciduous and mixed open woodland; also orchards; **Behaviour:** Becomes very secretive after breeding

Breeding male black above and plain white below, but black relieved by white forehead, often divided into t spots, white-edged tertials that meet white bar on greater wing covert, and white basal half of outertail feathers. Male east of central Europe increasingly grey-brown not black. After breeding, male moults: black elements of plumage replaced by brown or grey, so white wing panel not so strik Female resembles non-breeding male but tail and rump no as black. Bill and legs black. Juvenile resembles non-breed adult with buff-spotted crown, mantle and breast.

Collared Flycatcher

Ficedula albicollis

Status: Summer visitor; common; vagrant to northwest Europe; **Voice:** Call 'seep'; song like pied flycatcher's; **Lengt** 13cm; **Wingspan:** 22.5–24.5cm; **Habitat:** Deciduous woodland, parks, orchards; **Behaviour:** As pied flycatcher

Breeding male unmistakable but other plumages probably not separable from semi-collared and pied flycatcher. Breeding male black above, white below. Black relieved by white forehead and four diagnostic features: broad, striking white collar round neck, separating cap fro mantle; white wing panel from tertials to flight feathers; whitish patch on lower back and rump; black (or only mott white) outertail feathers. Female, immature and non-breeding male hard to separate from one another and from semi-collared and pied flycatchers in similar plumages; female more grey-toned above and paler than other species

Semi-collared Flycatcher

Ficedula semitorquata

Status: Summer visitor; rare; **Voice:** Calls include loud 'whi song rapid sequence of high and low notes; **Length:** 13cm; **Wingspan:** 23.5–24cm; **Habitat:** Deciduous forest up to 2,000m and riverine forest; **Behaviour:** As pied flycatcher

Breeding male black above and white below; black broken by white patch on forehead. White on neck extends into half-collar up to nape. Large wing panel forme by white outer halves to tertials meeting white-tipped grea coverts and bases to flight feathers; short, distinct white ba on median coverts and greyish band across lower back and rump. Outertail white, has more white throughout than on pied or collared flycatchers. Non-breeding male, female and juvenile similar to one another and to equivalent plumages pied and collared flycatchers. Bill and legs black at all time

Pied flycatcher

♀

♂

♀

Collared flycatcher

♂

♂

ni-collared
catcher

Red-breasted Flycatcher
Ficedula parva

Status: Summer visitor; widespread in breeding range; annual autumn passage migrant to northwest Europe; **Voi[ce]** Call short, harsh 'zit'; song cadence, descending in pitch; **Length:** 11.5cm; **Wingspan:** 18.5–21cm; **Habitat:** Mixed an[d] deciduous forest with much undergrowth; **Behaviour:** Agil[e] on the wing; flicks and cocks its tail frequently

Smallest European flycatcher. Adults of both sexes ashy brown above, flanks washed with buff. Wings a[nd] tail dark brown. Tail has diagnostic long white patches ea[ch] side at the base, noticeable in flight and when bird flicks [its] tail. Male has orange-red chin, throat and upper breast. Female has buff throat and breast. Juvenile spotted, but retains white tail patches. First-winter plumage similar to female. In all plumages note dark eye and white eyering.

Spotted Flycatcher
Muscicapa striata

Status: Summer visitor; common; **Voice:** Call 'tzee-zuk-zu[k]' song quiet, short, squeaky; **Length:** 14.5cm; **Wingspan:** 23–25.5cm; **Habitat:** Woodland edge, glades, parks, garde[ns] **Behaviour:** Catches insects in sallies from perch

Largest flycatcher in the region, and the only one w[ith] streaked underparts. Sexes similar. Adult upperpar[ts,] wings and tail grey-brown, appearing unmarked at long ra[nge.] Forehead and crown streaked black, outlined in white. Underparts white, washed with brown on sides of breast a[nd] flanks. At close range throat, sides of breast and flanks sh[ow] dull-brown streaks. Bill dull grey-brown. Legs brown or bl[ack.] Juvenile superficially similar to adult but upperparts buff[on] head, back, rump, lesser and median coverts show pale, round, buff-white spots; underparts spotted not streaked.

Bearded Tit
Panurus biarmicus

Status: Resident; local; **Voice:** Call explosive, metallic 'pir[g]' song quiet and easy to miss; **Length:** 12.5cm; **Wingspan:** 16–18cm; **Habitat:** Large reedbeds; **Behaviour:** Flies low [over] reeds, with whirring wings and trailing tail

Short-winged, very long-tailed, unmistakable bird w[ith] predominantly tawny-russet plumage at all times. Male has grey head and striking black 'moustaches' of loo[se] feathers highlighted by white chin and throat. Tail gradua[ted] with white tips to feathers forming ladder effect. Underta[il] coverts black. Closed wing appears banded: white on oute[r] flight feathers, rufous centre panel, black and white terti[als.] Has stubby yellow bill, orange eye and black legs. Female lacks male's head pattern, is duller and less russet; under[tail] coverts buff; otherwise similar to male. Juvenile resemble[s] female but has obvious black back and wing coverts.

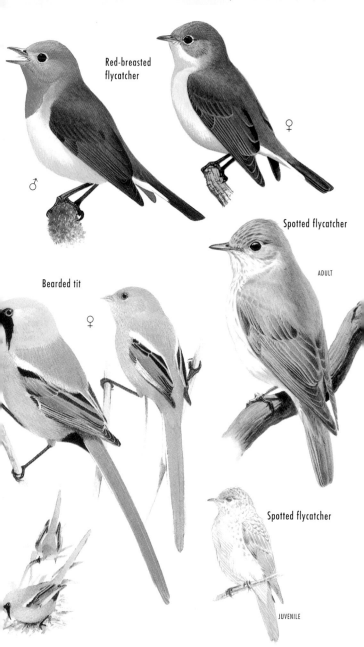

Red-breasted flycatcher

♂

♀

Spotted flycatcher

ADULT

Bearded tit

♀

Spotted flycatcher

JUVENILE

Long-tailed Tit

Aegithalos caudatus

Status: Resident; widespread; **Voice:** Call low, repeated 'tsupp'; alarm trilled 'tsirrrrup'; song rapid repetition of cal **Length:** 14cm; **Wingspan:** 16–19cm; **Habitat:** Deciduous woodland; for nesting, thick scrub like gorse, bramble or briar; **Behaviour:** Pairs build unique oval nest

Tiny-bodied, long-tailed bird. Sexes similar. Adults from most of Europe have head and underparts whitish, washed with dusky pink on nape, and from belly t undertail coverts; black bands extend from bill, above eyes mantle. Upperparts, wings and tail dull black, with pink scapulars and rump, and white tips and edges to graduate tail feathers. Pink tones wear off. Adults from north and e Europe have pure white head and noticeably white-edged tertials and secondaries; southern birds have grey backs, darker faces, and little or no pink. Eyering red in all birds. Juvenile shorter and darker than adult, with little pink.

Sombre Tit

Parus lugubris

Status: Resident; rare; **Voice:** Call loud 'churrrr'; song unmusical repetition of a single note; **Length:** 14cm; **Wingspan:** 21.5–23cm; **Habitat:** Open forest, orchards, scr **Behaviour:** Retiring and elusive

Dull plumage pattern similar to marsh tit. Sexes similar. Adult has sooty-black, long cap. Sooty-black chin and throat appear as large bib. Cheeks, ear coverts a sides of neck white. Upperparts, wings and tail ashy brown with distinct greyish-white fringes to tertials and inner secondaries. Underparts dull creamy white with ashy-brow wash on the sides. Bill strong, black. Legs grey. Female similar to male but with less contrasting cap. Juvenile sim to adult female, but cheeks look grubby.

Siberian Tit

Parus cinctus

Status: Resident; local; **Voice:** Call 'sip' and 'tchay' similar willow tit; song unmusical repetition of calls; **Length:** 13.5 **Wingspan:** 19.5–21cm; **Habitat:** Coniferous taiga, tree-lin river banks; **Behaviour:** Very confiding, and will allow clos approach even at nest site

Rather large, often fluffy-looking tit, a little smaller than great tit. Sexes alike. Adult has sooty-brown ca and nape, with darker line through eye. White face. Large sooty-black bib with broken edge. Upperparts warm brown Wings dark brown and all flight feathers clearly edged wit greyish-white, making biggest contrast between wings and back of all black-capped tits. Tail grey-black with dull whi outer feathers. Underparts two-toned: dull-white breast a belly; rusty-red sides of breast and flanks. Bill black. Legs grey. Juvenile similar to adult.

WESTERN AND SOUTHERN EUROPEAN BIRD

Long-tailed tit

NORTHERN AND EASTERN EUROPEAN BIRD

Long-tailed tit

ombre tit

Siberian tit

Marsh Tit

Parus palustris

Status: Resident; widespread; **Voice:** Calls 'pitchoo' and na[...]
'ter-char-char-char'; song repetition on one note; **Length:**
11.5cm; **Wingspan:** 18–19.5cm; **Habitat:** Deciduous
woodland, especially oak and beech, not marshes; **Behavio[...]
Pairs for life and spends the whole year in same territory

In Europe, one of four dark-capped tits with similar
plumage pattern (see also willow, Siberian and som[...]
tits). Sexes similar. Adult has glossy black cap. Wings, tail
and upperparts greyish-brown, with dark brown centres to
tail feathers. Small black chin and centre of throat, rest of
face white. Wings, tail and upperparts greyish-brown, with
dark-brown centres to tail feathers. Underparts dull white[...]
with pale-buff tinge on flanks and undertail coverts. Bill sh[...]
and black. Legs dark blue-grey. Juvenile similar to adult bu[...]
cap not glossy. Acquires adult plumage by September.

Willow Tit

Parus montanus

Status: Resident; widespread; **Voice:** Calls 'eez-eez-eez' an[...]
characteristic, nasal 'tchay, tchay'; warbling song; **Length:**
11.5cm; **Wingspan:** 17–20.5cm; **Habitat:** Montane, conifer[...]
forest; trees on damp ground; mixed woodland; **Behaviour:**
Excavates own nest hole, low in a very rotten stump

Very similar in size and appearance to marsh tit, but
looks less smart than that species. Sexes similar. Ad[...]
has black cap extending down to mantle. Black bib quite
extensive, with poorly defined borders. Tail is slightly roun[...]
ended, not square or slightly forked. Best plumage differer[...]
is this species' light patch on secondaries in closed wing ([...]
always conspicuous, however). Scandinavian and central
European birds greyer on back and whiter on face than
British birds, which are similar to marsh tit. Juvenile simi[...]
to adult of any given race. Call notes as well as plumage
details important in separating this species from marsh tit[...]

Crested Tit

Parus cristatus

Status: Resident; local; **Voice:** Call low-pitched purring tri[...]
song makes repeated use of calls; **Length:** 11.5cm; **Wingsp[...]
17–20cm; **Habitat:** Pine forest in the north; mixed woods;
also in beech or cork oak woods in south; **Behaviour:** New
nest hole excavated each year in rotten wood

Small tit with backward-pointing black crest, with t[...]
feathers tipped white. Sexes similar. Adult has very
distinctive face pattern of black line on a white face, runn[...]
behind eye and around rear of ear coverts; another black l[...]
starts at end of crest and runs down sides of neck to join
black bib. Upperparts buff-brown, wings and tail grey-brow[...]
Bill black, quite long for a small tit. Legs olive-grey. Juven[...]
has shorter crest than adult but otherwise similar.

Marsh tit

Willow tit

Willow tit

Crested tit

Blue Tit
Parus caeruleus

Status: Resident; common; **Voice:** Call 'tsee-tsee'; alarm 'ch r r'; song tremolo 'tsee-tsee-tsee-tsuhuhuhu'; **Length:** 11.5c **Wingspan:** 17.5–20cm; **Habitat:** Anywhere with trees, even inner-city parks and gardens; **Behaviour:** Feeds high up in broad-leaved trees; visits garden birdtables in winter

Adult is the only European tit with bright blue crown bordered with white. Sexes similar. Has dark lines fr bill through eye, around back of head and around otherwise white cheeks. Upperparts yellowish-green, underparts sulphur-yellow, with small blackish central streak. Wings dark blue with white wingbar. Tail dark grey-blue. Bill shor black. Legs dusky blue. Juvenile washed yellow and lacks blue in plumage but similar to adult in other respects.

Azure Tit
Parus cyanus

Status: Resident; local within breeding range; rare vagrant to eastern Europe; **Voice:** Utters a trilling song; calls includ nasal 'tzee-tzee'; **Length:** 13cm; **Wingspan:** 19–20cm; **Habitat:** Mainly broad-leaved woodland; **Behaviour:** Retiri searches twigs and buds for food; visits reedbeds in winter

Attractive tit, unmistakable when seen well. Sexes similar. Adult has largely white plumage. Head show narrow black stripe running back from eye to join black na band. Back pale blue-grey and wing blue with white wingba and white tips to secondary feathers. Tail proportionately long; blue with white feather tips. Bill stubby and dark and legs dark. Juvenile similar to adult.

Azure tit

Blue tit

ADULT

JUVENILE

Coal Tit
Parus ater

Status: Resident; common; **Voice:** Call piping 'tsee'; song loud and clear 'teechu, teechu, teechu'; **Length:** 11.5cm; **Wingspan:** 17–21cm; **Habitat:** Typically coniferous forest and woodland, but now anywhere with firs, including cemeteries and parks; **Behaviour:** Agile when foraging in foliage; readily visits birdtables in winter

Adult has glossy black cap and white cheeks; large white patch on nape is diagnostic. Cap extends down to level of eye; chin, throat and upper breast black, joined to cap by black collar. Underparts buff, paler towards the centre. Upperparts, wings and tail olive-grey. Median and greater wing coverts have white tips, forming two wingbars. Slightly smaller and shorter-tailed than blue tit. Black bill rather fine. Legs lead-blue. Sexes similar but female has less extensive bib. Juvenile similar to adult but markings less distinctive.

Great Tit
Parus major

Status: Resident; common; **Voice:** Call loud 'tink, tink, tink'; song far-carrying 'teacher, teacher, teacher'; **Length:** 14cm; **Wingspan:** 22.5–25.5cm; **Habitat:** Almost anywhere with trees, except coniferous forest; even in cities; **Behaviour:** Spends more time on the ground than other tits; visits birdtables in winter

The largest common tit, with quite a long tail. Sexes similar. Adult basically yellow-green above and yellow below. Wings have black flight feathers, blue-grey coverts and black tertials tipped white. Shows white wingbar and white outertail feathers. Distinctive head pattern comprises glossy blue-black cap with white triangular cheek patch. Black on chin and throat extends into bold black stripe down centre of underparts, forming wide black patch between legs on male, much narrower patch on female. Bill strong, black. Legs blue-grey. Juvenile similar to adult but has sooty crown, browner back, cheeks washed yellow and underparts duller yellow.

Coal tit

JUVENILE

Great tit

ADULT ♂

Corsican Nuthatch
Sitta whiteheadi

Status: Resident; rare; **Voice:** Call quiet 'yip'; song trill of short notes, ascending in pitch; **Length:** 12cm; **Wingspan:** 21–22cm; **Habitat:** Tall, old and undisturbed pine forest at 1,000–1,500m above sea-level; **Behaviour:** Not shy; feeds and moves like nuthatch

Noticeably small nuthatch. Finest bill, longest-looking head and shortest tail of the European nuthatches. Adult essentially grey-blue above, dull white below. Male has dramatic head pattern of jet-black crown and long white supercilium, underlined with long black eyestripe. Female has black crown replaced by dusky blue. Both sexes show dark primaries. Outertail feathers black with white tips. Bill black, greyish at base. Legs lead-grey. Juvenile similar to adult female but with buff wash to all underparts except throat.

Nuthatch
Sitta europaea

Status: Resident; widespread; **Voice:** Call loud 'chwit-chwit', song rapid 'chu-chu-chu', slow 'pee, pee, pee'; **Length:** 14cm; **Wingspan:** 22.5–27cm; **Habitat:** Broad-leaved and mixed woods, open parkland, avenues of older trees; **Behaviour:** Moves head first down tree-trunk in search for food

Easily recognised by plump body, short tail, long head and woodpecker-like bill. Sexes similar. Adult upperparts all blue-grey. Cheeks and throat white. Rest of underparts orange-buff merging into orange in birds from central, southern and western Europe but much paler in Scandinavian race. Has chestnut markings on flanks and white-centred chestnut undertail coverts. Shows broad black eyestripe. Outertail feathers black with white sub-terminal spots. Bill long, pointed, greyish-black. Legs yellowish-brown. Juvenile similar to adult but duller below.

Rock Nuthatch
Sitta neumayer

Status: Resident; local; **Voice:** Call excited trill; song a loud trill, variable in tempo; **Length:** 13.5–14.5cm; **Wingspan:** 23–25cm; **Habitat:** Sunny, rocky slopes with poor shrub vegetation up to 1,000m; **Behaviour:** Lively, calling frequently; hunts on ground and in rock crevices

Similar in appearance to nuthatch but much paler. Sexes similar. Adult basically blue-grey above from forehead to tail, and dirty white below. Underparts change from white on face and throat, to buff belly; darkest on undertail coverts. Long, broad black eyestripe separates grey crown and white face. Grey tail is unmarked. Bill black with paler base to lower mandible. Legs dark grey. Juvenile similar to adult but duller and with less distinct eyestripe.

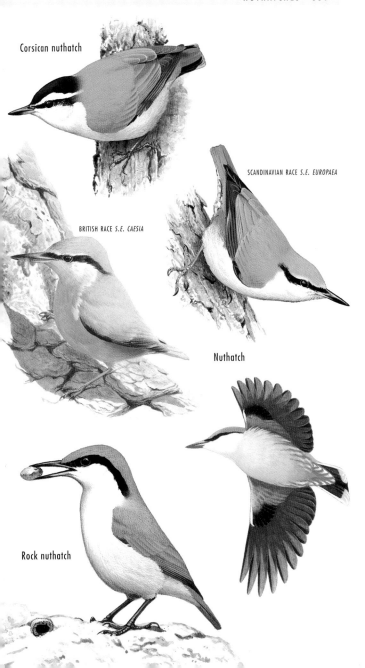

Corsican nuthatch

SCANDINAVIAN RACE *S.E. EUROPAEA*

BRITISH RACE *S.E. CAESIA*

Nuthatch

Rock nuthatch

Wallcreeper
Tichodroma muraria

Status: Resident; local; **Voice:** Call short chirp; song clear whistles in crescendo, rising in pitch; **Length:** 16.5cm; **Wingspan:** 27–32cm; **Habitat:** Rocky, broken, precipitous mountain terrain, 1,000–2,000m; **Behaviour:** Moves in sho flights like jumps or hops supported by wings; fairly confid

Unmistakable. Breeding male upperparts grey from forehead to uppertail coverts. Lower face, throat an upper breast black, shading to dusky grey on rest of underparts. Undertail coverts white-spotted. Large butter like wings. Wing coverts crimson. Flight feathers sooty bla with crimson bases. Outer four primaries have grey tips wi two white spots behind. Tail black, tipped grey, with white spot on outertail feathers. In non-breeding male tail and flight feathers look blacker but face and upper breast, become pale. Legs black. Bill black, needle-like, long and decurved. Female and juvenile similar to non-breeding ma

Treecreeper
Certhia familiaris

Status: Resident; widespread; **Voice:** Call thin 'tsiew'; song high-pitched cadence lasting 2.5–3 seconds; **Length:** 12.5c **Wingspan:** 17.5–21cm; **Habitat:** Mainly broad-leaved tree also conifers; **Behaviour:** Spirals up and around tree-trun

Sexes similar. Adult is brown above and silky white below. At close range shows rufous rump, long white supercilium and white mottled and streaked back. Wings show two pale-buff wingbars on coverts, buff band across secondaries and primaries, and white-spotted tertials. Tai long and brown, with dark shafts; feathers stiff and pointe Bill long, gently decurved and dark brown. Legs pale brow Juvenile similar to adult but upperparts spotted; almost indistinguishable from short-toed treecreeper.

Short-toed Treecreeper
Certhia brachydactyla

Status: Resident; widespread; **Voice:** Call shrill 'zeet', and 'srriih'; song comprises short, loud phrase; **Length:** 12.5cm **Wingspan:** 17–20.5cm; **Habitat:** Parks, avenues, orchards forest edge; **Behaviour:** As treecreeper

Very similar to treecreeper; often best distinguished by voice. Sexes similar. Adult brown above and whit below. Compared to treecreeper sustained observation reveals these differences: (a) upperparts and wings dulle browner and less obviously spotted; (b) dull-brown rump; (c) shorter, duller supercilium often not showing in front eye; (d) breast and rest of underparts washed grey or brov most noticeably on flanks; (e) bill longer and more slende bent at tip rather than gently decurved. Hind toe shorter t treecreeper's but this feature useless for field identificatic Juvenile similar to adult but upperparts more spotted.

Wallcreeper

Treecreeper

Short-toed treecreeper

Penduline Tit
Remiz pendulinus

Status: Resident; local; **Voice:** Call soft drawn-out 'tseeoo' tit-like 'tsi-tsi-tsi'; song finch-like trill; **Length:** 11cm; **Wingspan:** 16–17.5cm; **Habitat:** Luxuriant vegetation by fresh or brackish water; **Behaviour:** Gregarious, active and confiding; builds amazing cup-like nest

Smaller than blue tit, with relatively longer tail. Sex similar; female duller than male. Adult has pale-grey head with black mask. Mantle, scapulars and wing coverts chestnut. Flight feathers black, fringed with buff. Back and rump greyish, contrasting with nearly black tail, which has off-white feather margins. Underparts off-white with chest smudges on breast and flanks. Bill black; legs bluish-black. Juvenile lacks black face mask and has cinnamon back.

Golden Oriole
Oriolus oriolus

Status: Summer visitor; local; **Voice:** Call cat-like; alarm rattle; song a melodious, flute-like whistle; **Length:** 24cm; **Wingspan:** 44–47cm; **Habitat:** Tree-loving, favouring parks large gardens, copses, open woods; **Behaviour:** Secretive, male has distinctive far-carrying song

Adult male has bright yellow head and body, black wings and tail. Head marked by black lores. Black-centred tail has yellow corners. Wings black with short yellow bar across tips of primary coverts. Eye crimson; bill dark p legs dark grey. Female has yellowish-green body, greenish-brown wings and brownish-black tail with yellow corners. Underparts palest on chin to upper breast; all underparts streaked dull brown. First-year male is streaked and dull olive-yellow. Some mature females almost as yellow as ma but lores always grey. Juvenile as female but has dark-brown eye and slate-grey bill; attains adult plumage after two yea

Red-backed Shrike
Lanius collurio

Status: Summer visitor; local; scarce passage migrant; **Voice:** Call harsh 'chack, chack'; song subdued, lengthy, with mimicry; **Length:** 17cm; **Wingspan:** 24–27cm; **Habitat:** Su open terrain, with bushes; **Behaviour:** Hunts insects from perch; impales spare food on thorns and barbed wire

Adult male has blue-grey crown and nape, chestnut back, blue-grey rump and black tail with white outer feathers. Underparts pinkish-white. Shows narrow black b across forehead extending into broad black mask through and across ear coverts. Flight feathers, tertials and greater coverts brown-black with chestnut margins. Bill black with hooked tip; legs grey-black. Female rufous-brown above, w reddish tail, pale-buff supercilium and cream underparts w brown crescent. Juvenile similar to female but upperparts barred with black crescents.

Penduline tit

♂

♀

Golden oriole

♂

♂

♀

Red-backed shrike

JUVENILE

Lesser Grey Shrike
Lanius minor

Status: Summer visitor; local; rare passage migrant; **Voice** Calls variable; song a soft, musical, chattering ramble with mimicry; **Length:** 20cm; **Wingspan:** 32–34.5cm; **Habitat:** Warm, open country with scattered bushes; **Behaviour:** Chases insects; glides well; hovers and pounces like kestre Male has broad black band across forehead, over eye and ear coverts. Rest of upperparts blue-grey. Under parts white, with breast and flanks washed pink. Wings bla with broad white bar across base of primaries. Tail black w wide white outer edges. Bill black, short and stubby. Legs brown. Female as male but shows grey speckles on forehea less pink below and not so blue-toned above. Juvenile has black and white patterns of adult on wings and tail but underparts creamy white, upperparts brownish-grey with darker bars. Face mask reduced to broad eyestripe. Bill gr

Great Grey Shrike
Lanius excubitor

Status: Resident; widespread; **Voice:** Call harsh 'sheck, sheck'; song a quiet, rambling warble with mimicry; **Length** 24–25cm; **Wingspan:** 30–34cm; **Habitat:** Open country wit bushes; **Behaviour:** Often perches on trees or wires Northern European adult has black face mask, wing and tail, grey upperparts and white underparts. Pat broken a little by white supercilium, white patch on scapulars, white-edged tail and white, narrow bar across b of primaries. Bill long, hooked, black; legs black. Sexes similar, but female has faint brown barring on breast in winter. Juvenile has brownish-grey upperparts and browni white underparts with faint brown wavy bars from throat t breast and flanks. Birds from south, including Iberia, may separate species: southern grey shrike, *Lanius meridiona* adult similar to northern bird but with pink wash to under parts. Juvenile as juveniles of other races of great grey shr

Woodchat Shrike
Lanius senator

Status: Summer visitor; local; rare passage migrant; **Voice** Call 'kiwick, kiwick'; song a rich warble with mimicry; **Leng** 18cm; **Wingspan:** 26–28cm; **Habitat:** Woodland margins, o orchards, maquis; **Behaviour:** Favours perches in cover Adult has chestnut rear crown, nape and upper mar Male has black forehead, continuing as broad black patch through eye and ear coverts, and black wings and tail. Shows white outertail feathers, rump, scapulars and underparts. Bill short, hook-tipped, black; legs black. Fem as male but duller. Base of bill white. Juvenile grey or buff above; pale whitish-buff scapulars, all barred with dark brown. Rump rufous and barred underparts dull white. Wi brownish-black with paler edges. Tail dark with white edg

ADULT

Lesser grey shrike

JUVENILE

SOUTHERN BIRD

Great grey shrike

NORTHERN BIRD

NORTHERN BIRD

Woodchat shrike

JUVENILE

Masked Shrike
Lanius nubicus

Status: Summer visitor; local; **Voice:** Calls hard 'tsr' and re
'keer'; song a vigorous warble; **Length:** 17–18cm; **Wingspan**
24–26.5cm; **Habitat:** Wooded country, including citrus and
olive groves; **Behaviour:** Agile on the wing; hunts from low
tree branches

Small shrike, more slightly built than woodchat, and
with proportionately the longest tail of the region's
shrikes. Male distinctively pied: generally black above and
white below with reddish-orange flanks. Has white forehea
and supercilium, white outertail feathers, white scapulars
and broad white bar across base of primaries. Bill slight,
black. Legs black. Female similarly patterned to male but
greyer head, browner wings, less rusty underparts. Juvenil
has scaly grey-brown plumage; hard to separate from youn
woodchat shrike but has longer tail and greyer upperparts

Isabelline Shrike
Lanius isabellinus

Status: Vagrant from central Asia; rare; **Length:** 17–18cm;
Wingspan: 26–27cm; **Habitat:** Open grassy areas with scru
Behaviour: As red-backed shrike

Distinctly pale shrike. In most plumages contrast
between grey-brown back and reddish-brown lower
rump and tail is distinctive. Male has mainly grey-buff
upperparts, warmest brown on crown; lower rump and tail
reddish-brown. Underparts whitish but with buff wash to
breast and flanks. Head has black mask through eye. Wing
have striking pale patch at base of primaries. Female simi
to male but has more subdued plumage colours, pale patc
base of primaries usually absent and eye mask brown not
black; shows faint scaly markings on underparts. First-win
bird (plumage most likely to be encountered in Europe)
similar to female but scaly markings more extensive and
present on face. All birds have dark bill and dark-grey legs

Jay
Garrulus glandarius

Status: Resident; common; **Voice:** Loud, harsh, raucous ca
including 'skaaak skaaak' – far carrying; **Length:** 34–35cm
Wingspan: 52–58cm; **Habitat:** Broad-leaved woodland; als
conifers; **Behaviour:** Depends on acorns in winter; these a
cached in autumn

A small crow, the most colourful in Europe. Sexes
alike. Adult body pinkish-brown with white rump an
undertail coverts, white forehead and crown streaked blac
and broad black moustachial stripe. Wings black with whi
at base of outermost secondaries forming short bar on clos
wings; outer greater coverts, primary coverts and bastard
wing have shiny blue bars. Bill dark; legs pale brown. Juve
similar to adult, but plumage redder and crown less streak

Masked shrike ♂

FIRST WINTER

Isabelline shrike

JUVENILE

Jay

ADULT

Siberian Jay
Perisoreus infaustus

Status: Resident; local; **Voice:** Calls 'tchair', 'kook kook' an 'kij kij'; mewing like buzzard; **Length:** 30–31cm; **Wingspan** 40–46cm; **Habitat:** Natural, dense, coniferous forest; **Behaviour:** Secretive but unafraid; becomes tame if offere food regularly

Smallest member of crow family in Europe, with proportionally longer tail than jay and shorter, pointed bill. Sexes similar. Adult has sooty-brown crown, n, and upper face. Has dense pale-buff bristles at base of bill. Back and underparts brown-grey, becoming foxy red on run upper and lowertail coverts and belly. Wings sooty brown w foxy-red coverts and bases to flight feathers. Bill and legs black. Juvenile similar to adult.

Azure-winged Magpie
Cyanopica cyanus

Status: Resident; local; **Voice:** Main call a husky whistling 'zhreee', rising at end; **Length:** 34–35cm (nearly half is tail **Wingspan:** 38–40cm; **Habitat:** Groups of trees, cork oak ar olive groves, pine and eucalyptus plantations; **Behaviour:** Secretive in breeding season, otherwise noisy and bold; gregarious throughout year

Small, elegant, long-tailed crow. Sexes alike. Adult h forehead, crown and nape velvet black to a line belo the eye. Back, rump and uppertail coverts grey-brown. Underparts off-white, with pale tinge of ashy colours on flanks and undertail coverts. Wings azure blue, with inner webs of tertials, greater coverts and primaries black. Tail noticeably graduated, blue above, dark grey below. Bill and legs black. Juvenile similar to adult but plumage duller.

Magpie
Pica pica

Status: Resident; common; **Voice:** Commonest call a stacc: chatter 'chacker chacker chacker chacker'; **Length:** 44–46 **Wingspan:** 52–60cm; **Habitat:** Mainly a lowland bird in lig wooded country; also urban; **Behaviour:** Gregarious, especially in spring; roosts communally

An unmistakable pied bird with a long, graduated ta Sexes similar. Adult has scapulars, belly and flanks white. Rest of plumage black with beautiful iridescence wl seen closely in sunlight: purple on most of head and body, green on crown and scapulars, blue-green on wings, and brilliant bronze-green on tail with bands of several shades purple near tip. Bill and legs black. Juvenile similar to adu but has shorter tail, duller plumage and less iridescence.

Siberian Jay

Azure-winged Magpie

Magpie

Nutcracker
Nucifraga caryocatactes

Status: Resident; local; **Voice:** Utters far-carrying 'kraak'; spring call 'kerr-kerr'; alarm call 'churr'; **Length:** 22–23cm; **Wingspan:** 52–58cm; **Habitat:** Cool forests of spruce or pin in northern lowland and southern mountains; **Behaviour:** Secretive in breeding season, but favours conspicuous perches on treetops; irruptive migrants are tame

Size of a jay. Sexes similar. Adult body chocolate-bro with teardrop-shaped white spot at tip of most feathers. Forehead and crown very dark brown, nasal bristl and lores creamy white. Wings brown-black, glossed bluish-green, with white spots on lesser and median coverts. Tail brownish-black with blue-green gloss above and feathers tipped white, becoming progressively wider from centre outwards; tail appears mostly dark from above but mostly white from below. White undertail coverts contrast black b of tail and brown body. Bill long and black; legs black. Juvenile paler than adult, with less well-defined white spot

Chough
Pyrrhocorax pyrrhocorax

Status: Resident; local; **Voice:** Common call a yelping 'cheeow' or 'kiaa'; **Length:** 39–40cm; **Wingspan:** 73–90cm; **Habitat:** Inland crags or coastal cliffs (for nesting); nearby grassy swards (for feeding); **Behaviour:** Masterful flier; oft flips wings and tail conspicuously when perched

Sexes similar. Adult plumage all black, with most pa having a blue gloss, although tail, tail coverts and fli feathers have a greener iridescence. Has long, decurved bil and bright red legs. Juvenile duller than adult, with shorter yellowish-pink bill. Adult chough separable from adult Alpi chough by longer, decurved bill, shorter tail, about as long as primary tips when bird is standing, 5–6 primary 'fingers' (in flight) and distinct call.

Alpine Chough
Pyrrhocorax graculus

Status: Resident; local; **Voice:** Calls include a frequent 'chirrish'; in chorus often utters a piercing 'treee'; **Length:** 38cm; **Wingspan:** 75–85cm; **Habitat:** Strictly montane, ranging from tree-line to snow-line; **Behaviour:** Flies fast a skilfully; often becomes tame in winter at ski resorts

Sexes alike. Adult has all-black plumage with a shee blue-green gloss, particularly on wings. Bill pale yello Legs orange. May be distinguished from chough by its yello shorter bill, duller plumage, longer tail, only four separated primaries in flight and straight leading edge to the wings. Juvenile similar to adult.

Nutcracker

Chough

Alpine chough

Jackdaw
Corvus monedula

Status: Resident; widespread; **Voice:** Short, loud 'kjack' is t[...] common contact note; many other short call-notes; **Length** 33–34cm; **Wingspan:** 67–74cm; **Habitat:** Groups of old tree[...] avenues in town or country; sea cliffs, mountain crags; **Behaviour:** Gregarious; nests in colonies and often associa[...] with rooks on feeding grounds

One of the smallest members of the crow family in Europe. Sexes alike. At a distance adult appears bla[...] with grey nape and ear coverts. Close views reveal black crown has purple gloss, some blue gloss on wings and back[...] greyish cast on underparts. Eyes of adult pale grey, very distinctive. Bill short and black. Legs black. Juvenile dulle[...] than adult, and grey patch less contrasting; eyes brown, taking a year to become grey.

Rook
Corvus frugilegus

Status: Resident; common; **Voice:** Commonest call is a prolonged 'kaah'; **Length:** 44–46cm; **Wingspan:** 81–99cm; **Habitat:** Wherever tall trees (for nesting) border agricultu[...] land (for feeding); **Behaviour:** Gregarious all year; winters[...] large concentrations

Sexes similar. Adult all black except for whitish-grey[...] skin around base of bill, from lower forehead, behind[...] the gape, and on upper throat. Black is beautifully iridesce[...] in sunlight with shades of greenish- and reddish-purple. Separable from carrion crow by whitish face, steep forehea[...] narrower bill, more fingered wingtips in flight, round tippe[...] tail, glossier plumage and loose thigh feathers, giving a 'baggy trousers' effect. Juvenile has black nasal bristles and no bare grey skin.

Jackdaw

Rook

Hooded/Carrion Crow

*Corvus corone cornix
(hooded)/Corvus corone
corone (carrion)*

Status: Resident; common; **Voice:** Call an abrupt 'kawr', of
three together; also a range of other short, hard calls; **Len**
45–47cm; **Wingspan:** 90–100cm; **Habitat:** Open country w
scattered trees, hedgerows; also in towns; **Behaviour:** Floc
gather in springtime displays and at winter roosts

Occurs as two clearly distinguishable subspecies. Se
alike in both races. Carrion crow has all-black
plumage, bill and legs. Hooded crow has back of neck,
mantle, back, rump, scapulars, lower breast, belly, flanks,
axillaries and undertail coverts ash-grey. Rest of plumage
black. Bill and legs black in both races. Juvenile carrion cr
similar to adult. Juvenile hooded crow similar to adult but
grey element of plumage has buffish tinge.

Raven

Corvus corax

Status: Resident; widespread; **Voice:** Typical call a deep,
resonant 'karronk'; also utters a deep 'pruk' and 'toc-toc-to
Length: 64cm; **Wingspan:** 130–150cm; **Habitat:** From coas
3,000m, but not dense forest, dense settlement or cultivati
Behaviour: Solitary in breeding season; gregarious at wint
roosts

The largest member of the crow family, one-third
bigger than rook and crow, and as big as a buzzard.
Sexes similar. All-black, iridescent plumage; purple-blue o
wings, reddish-purple on tail. Shaggy throat feathers and
wedge shape to tip of tail distinctive. Black bill is massive,
especially deep upper mandible, markedly curved towards
the tip. Legs black. Juvenile similar to adult.

Raven

HOODED CROWS MOBBING BUZZARD

Hooded/Carrion crow

Raven

Starling

Sturnus vulgaris

Status: Resident; common; **Voice:** Calls include characteris
'tsiew', 'tcherr'; song a lively medley of whistles, gurgles and
mimicry; **Length:** 21.5cm; **Wingspan:** 37–42cm; **Habitat:**
Almost anywhere; very ready to live with man; needs holes t
nest in, open ground to feed on; **Behaviour:** Feeding partie
on grass have bustling, jaunty walk and are often quarrelso
Male in winter has glossy black plumage, with buff ti
to feathers of upperparts, buff edges to wing feather
and white tips to feathers of underparts from throat to bell
Bill grey-brown with yellow base. Legs reddish-brown. Eyes
brown. Male in summer loses buff and white feather tips an
looks darker with green, bronze and blue iridescence. Bill
lemon yellow. Female has broader spots in winter than ma
keeps some spots all year and is less glossy. Bill has pinkish
base in breeding season. Juvenile looks like a different
species with mouse-brown plumage, darker above than bel
Shows whitish chin and grey-brown bill. First-winter pluma
similar to adult; bill black.

Spotless Starling

Sturnus unicolor

Status: Resident; local; **Voice:** Similar to starling, but song
louder, especially introductory whistles; **Length:** 21–23cm;
Wingspan: 38–42cm; **Habitat:** Open woodland, near short
grass; fields and marshes in winter; **Behaviour:** Wary but
more approachable in towns, especially in winter
Male in summer has all-black plumage, glossed purp
(not green as in starling and without pale edges to
wing feathers). Feathers of throat are long and bird looks
bearded (more so than starling). Bill pale yellow with bluis
black base. Legs pale pink. In early winter shows pale tips t
feathers on head, mantle and underparts; bill dark. Female
similar to male but less glossy, has small white spots on fre
undertail coverts and pale-yellow margins to larger wing
feathers. Juvenile similar to, but darker than, juvenile
starling. First-winter birds have whitish tips to body feathe

Rose-coloured Starling

Sturnus roseus

Status: Summer visitor to Balkans; rare; autumn vagrant t
northwest Europe; **Voice:** Calls include a thin 'kri'; song
varied and twittering; **Length:** 21cm; **Wingspan:** 38–40cm;
Habitat: Typically arid grassland and semi-desert;
Behaviour: Vagrants associate with starlings
Male has has contrastingly dark and pink plumage.
During winter months pink elements appear grubby
and black elements lack sheen. Bill and legs pink, brightes
during summer months. Female similar to male but duller
all times. Juvenile pale sandy-brown, darkest on wings and
tail; bill yellow and legs dull red.

Starling

WINTER ADULT

JUVENILES

BREEDING ADULT

Spotless starling

WINTER ADULT

BREEDING ADULT

Rose-coloured starling

ADULT ♂

JUVENILE

House Sparrow
Passer domesticus

Status: Resident; common; **Voice:** Calls include familiar 'cheep' or 'chirrp'; song is a succession of chirps; **Length:** 14–15cm; **Wingspan:** 21–21.5cm; **Habitat:** Almost invariably associated with human habitation; **Behaviour:** Very tame; nests in loose colonies and feeds and roosts in flocks

Male warm brown above and greyish below, with grey crown, black eyestripe, black bib with boldly broken bottom edge, dull-white cheeks, grey rump, black-brown square-ended tail and white wingbar formed by tips to median coverts. Bill black in breeding season, grey at other times. Legs pink or brown. Female lacks strong plumage pattern. At a distance appears dull brown above and dingy white below. Close views show female has broad pale-buff supercilium and lighter brown or buff edges to wing feathers. Bill grey, legs pink. Juvenile similar to female.

Spanish Sparrow
Passer hispaniolensis

Status: Resident; locally common; **Voice:** Call distinct, contralto 'chup'; song similar to house sparrow's but richer; **Length:** 15cm; **Wingspan:** 23–26cm; **Habitat:** Cultivated land, settlements; but also arid regions, and woods and thickets; **Behaviour:** Huge flocks form in autumn to forage and roost

Slightly larger than house sparrow. Male has chestnut crown, nape and sides of neck. Short, white, broken supercilium. Extensive black bib extends to unique arrowhead streaks on breast and flanks. White cheeks very noticeable. Mantle and rump grey. Wings brown with two pale wingbars, and tail dark brown. Bill black in breeding season, paler at other times. Legs light brown. Female and juvenile dull brown and dingy white below; almost indistinguishable from equivalent plumages of house sparrow.

Tree Sparrow
Passer montanus

Status: Resident; widespread; **Voice:** Distinctive, repeated 'chet' or 'teck' is characteristic of birds taking flight; **Length:** 14cm; **Wingspan:** 20–22cm; **Habitat:** Small woods, roadside trees, ivy-covered cliffs, parks, wooded suburbs; **Behaviour:** Breeds in loose colonies; forages in flocks with finches and buntings in winter

Smaller and trimmer than house sparrow. Sexes alike. Adult has rich dark-chestnut crown and nape, and whiter cheeks, which almost form a white collar contrasting noticeably with crown and black bib (smaller than house sparrow's); cheeks show conspicuous black patches below and behind eyes. Back and rump yellowish-brown. Tail dark brown. Wings show two pale wingbars. Underparts whitish, palest on belly, and washed buff on flanks. Bill black; legs pale brown. Juvenile as adult but duller.

House sparrow

♂

♀

House sparrow

House sparrow

Spanish sparrow

House sparrow

Tree sparrow

ee sparrow

Rock Sparrow
Petronia petronia

Status: Resident; local; **Voice:** Characteristic call a nasal 'pey-ee'; song comprises a repetition of calls; **Length:** 14cm; **Wingspan:** 28–32cm; **Habitat:** Treeless terrain with sparse vegetation; sometimes vineyards, olive groves; **Behaviour:** Runs around on ground like a pipit; often nervous

Adult is superficially like female house sparrow, but has longer wings, shorter tail and heavier bill. Upperparts and wings dusty brown, heavily streaked with brown-black. Underparts buffish-white, streaked and spotted brown especially on flanks and undertail coverts. Tail dark brown with white terminal spots, which show clearly in flight. Striped head pattern distinctive: creamy-coloured central crown stripe, dark-brown lateral crown stripes, broad off-white supercilium and dusky ear coverts. Bill large, deep and greyish. Legs brownish-yellow. In spring male has bright yellow patch on the upper breast. Sexes otherwise similar. Juvenile similar to adult but without yellow on throat.

Snow Finch
Montifringilla nivalis

Status: Resident; local; **Voice:** Sparrow-like song includes chaffinch-like 'pink'; **Length:** 17cm; **Wingspan:** 34–38cm; **Habitat:** Bare, stony sites, above the tree-line in summer; **Behaviour:** Often near ski-lifts; shuffling and hopping gait

Finch-like member of the sparrow family with considerable amount of white in plumage. Adult has blue-grey head, white underparts and brown mantle. Wings white with black tips, extremely striking in flight. Tail white with black central bar. Male has black bib and dark bill in summer; bill yellow and loses bib in winter. Female similar to winter male. Juvenile similar to winter male but bill dull.

Chaffinch
Fringilla coelebs

Status: Resident; common; **Voice:** Call 'chink'; male's call in spring, 'wheet'; song an accelerating phrase ending in a flourish; **Length:** 14.5cm; **Wingspan:** 25–28cm; **Habitat:** Woodland, farmland, parks and gardens; **Behaviour:** Gregarious and often tame outside breeding season

Male very distinctive, with pink face, breast and belly, white undertail coverts and black forehead. Blue-grey crown, nape, upper mantle. Mantle chestnut-brown. Green rump. Tail black with white outer feathers. Wings black with pale fringes to flight feathers, broad white wingbar across tips of greater coverts, long, deep white blaze from shoulder to scapulars. Bill bright lead-blue in breeding season but dull pinkish-grey at other times. Legs grey or brown. Female and juvenile have same diagnostic tail and wing patterns as male. Plumage otherwise pale olive-brown above and greyish-white below. Bill pinkish-grey and legs reddish.

Rock sparrow

Snow finch

Chaffinch

♀

♂

Brambling
Fringilla montifringilla

Status: Resident; locally common; **Voice:** Call a wheezy 'tsweep'; song a monotonous, repeated 'dwee'; **Length:** 14cr **Wingspan:** 25–26cm; **Habitat:** Birch and mixed forest; woodland, and open ground in winter; **Behaviour:** Roosts i huge numbers in winter; lives mainly off beech-mast

Identified at all times by buffish-orange breast and shoulder, diagnostic long white rump and black, slightly forked tail. Breeding male has glossy black head an mantle, orange throat, breast and shoulders; rest of underparts white. Wings black with narrow white bar acros tips of greater coverts and white patch below orange shoulder. Bill blue-black. Legs brownish-flesh. In winter, male's head and mantle mottled with brown, bill yellowis with black tip. Female has underparts and wing pattern of male but in washed-out colours. Head has dark-brown crov greyish nape with brown lateral stripes, buff supercilium a ear coverts, whitish chin and throat. Bill grey in summer, blue-black in winter. Juvenile as female.

Serin
Serinus serinus

Status: Resident; common; **Voice:** Call a distinctive 'tirrilil song a rapid succession of chirps, jingles and twitters; **Length:** 11.5cm; **Wingspan:** 20–23cm; **Habitat:** Forest edge clearings, parkland, orchards, vineyards, gardens; **Behavio** Sings throughout year; very tolerant of humans

A tiny finch. Male streaky, greenish-brown above witl bright yellow head, breast and rump. Blackish-browr wings have pale fringes to wing coverts showing as pale wingbars. Tail deeply forked. Black eye looks beady on yell face. Stubby bill grey; legs brown. Female patterned as mal but browner above, and yellow parts duller. Juvenile like d female. Distinguished from female or juvenile siskin by sm bill, narrow wingbars and uniformly streaked underparts.

Citril Finch
Serinus citrinella

Status: Resident; locally common; **Voice:** Call a metallic 'chwick'; flight call 'dididadid'; song a fast tinkling twitter; **Length:** 12cm; **Wingspan:** 23–24cm; **Habitat:** Woodland, especially spruce bordering Alpine meadows between 700–3,300m; **Behaviour:** Forms flocks outside breeding season, pairs sticking together

Adult mainly yellow-green, with slate-grey nape and sides to neck, yellow rump and unstreaked underpar Tail and wings black, latter with yellowish-green lesser wingbars in flight. Bill greyish with dark tip; legs brownish. Female similar to male but duller. Juvenile buff-brown abo whitish-buff below, with dark-brown streaks on crown, mar and all underparts except belly.

Brambling

ADULT ♀

BREEDING ♂

WINTER ADULT ♂

Serin

♀

♂

Citril finch

Greenfinch
Carduelis chloris

Status: Resident; widespread; **Voice:** Call loud nasal 'tswee⬛ flight call rapid twitter; song strong, twittering trill; **Lengt⬛** 15 cm; **Wingspan:** 25–27cm; **Habitat:** Densely leafed trees⬛ woodland edge, orchards, parks, graveyards, gardens; **Behaviour:** In breeding season has erratic, circular song-flight on slow wingbeats

Male is olive-green and yellow, darker olive above an⬛ yellower below. Tail and flight feathers brown-black⬛ with brilliant yellow fringes to primaries (forming bold pat⬛ on folded wing), and brilliant yellow on bases of outer tail feathers. Underwing yellow, noticeable in flight. Tail short, distinctly forked. Bill stout, conical, pale flesh. Legs pale flesh. Female similar to male but duller overall, with indistinct streaks on crown and mantle. Juvenile even dull⬛ than female and more distinctly streaked.

Goldfinch
Carduelis carduelis

Status: Resident; widespread; **Voice:** Call a liquid 'tswitt-w⬛ witt'; song a cheerful tinkling; **Length:** 12cm; **Wingspan:** 21–25.5cm; **Habitat:** Parks, gardens, thickets, rough grassland; **Behaviour:** Takes seeds directly from plant; for⬛ nomadic flocks outside breeding season

Adult unmistakable with golden-yellow panel along centre of black wing and head patterned vertically i⬛ bands; red from bill to eye, white behind eye, black crown nape. Sexes similar. Mantle, back, breast band and flanks pale rufous, rump whitish. Tail black. White spots to tips o⬛ flight and tail feathers. Bill noticeably pointed, pinkish wit⬛ dark tip. Legs pale flesh. Juvenile reveals yellow on wings ⬛ flight but has head and body plumage greyish-brown, spott⬛ and streaked brown, until autumn moult.

Siskin
Carduelis spinus

Status: Resident; widespread; **Voice:** Calls include 'dluee' and 'tsüü', often in flight; song a twitter with wheezy endin⬛ **Length:** 12cm; **Wingspan:** 20–23cm; **Habitat:** Coniferous forest; birches by streams; gardens in winter; **Behaviour:** Feeds on seeds in trees, hanging on to cones and twigs

Small, elegant finch. Adult male strikingly green ab⬛ and yellow below, with diagnostic black forehead, crown and chin. Wings black with broad yellow wingbar across tips of greater coverts and inner primaries. Tail fork⬛ black, edged along basal two-thirds with yellow. Belly and undertail coverts white; latter streaked black. Pointed yellowish bill; legs dark brown. Female lacks black crown. Breast yellow, rest of underparts white, streaked black. Ye⬛ on wings and tail like male but less obvious. Juvenile simi⬛ to female but browner and more streaked.

Greenfinch

ADULT

JUVENILE

JUVENILE

Goldfinch

ADULTS

JUVENILE

iskin

ADULT ♂

Linnet
Carduelis cannabina

Status: Resident; widespread; **Voice:** Alarm call 'tsooeet'; flight call 'tihtihtihtit'; song a musical, soft warbling twitter **Length:** 13.5cm; **Wingspan:** 21–25cm; **Habitat:** Scrub, heath maquis, uncultivated fields; **Behaviour:** Breeds in neighbourhood groups; forms large feeding flocks in winter

Male has chestnut mantle, scapulars and wing covers. Wings and tail dark brown with white edges to some flight and tail feathers, showing as indistinct wingbar on perched bird and as greyish patches in flight. Bill greyish-brown and head grey except for crimson forehead. Crimson breast, white belly, buff flanks. Bill greyish. Legs dark brown Female lacks male's crimson breast and forehead. Brown back streaked darker than on male and underparts streaked buff-brown. Like male, shows distinctive whitish wing and patches. Juvenile like female but more heavily streaked.

Redpoll
Carduelis flammea

Status: Resident; common; **Voice:** Trilling, unmusical song delivered in flight; utters fast 'chuchuchuh-uh' call; **Length** 13–14cm; **Wingspan:** 20–25cm; **Habitat:** Birch and alder woodland; also conifer plantations and forests; **Behaviour:** Feeds on alder and birch seeds; associates with siskins

Generally has brown, streaked upperparts, pale underparts streaked on flanks, and streaked rump; shows two white wingbars. Bill short, triangular and yellow with curved culmen. Male has black chin, red forecrown and narrow band of white from base of forecrown above eye; shows pinkish flush to breast, most apparent in breeding season. Female similar to male but red on forecrown less extensive; lacks pink flush to breast. Juvenile similar to female but lacks red forecrown.

Arctic Redpoll
Carduelis hornemanni

Status: Resident; local; **Voice:** Flight call similar to redpoll but slower; **Length:** 13–14cm; **Wingspan:** 21–27cm; **Habitat:** Breeds on Arctic tundra; in winter, most remain in northern latitudes; **Behaviour:** Feeds on ground or in low scrub

Plumage generally much paler than redpoll, in some races almost white, rumps of adult birds always unstreaked. Bill triangular and yellowish with straight, not curved, culmen. Male has pale buffish-brown, streaked upperparts and pale, usually white, underparts with faint streaking on flanks; in breeding season may have pink flush on breast. Shows black bib and red forecrown, base of which is white and continues above eye; white on forecrown more extensive than on redpoll. Female similar to male but upper parts usually darker and lacks pink flush on breast. Juvenile similar to female but buffish and lacks red forecrown.

JUVENILE

Linnet

♂

♀

JUVENILE ♂

♂

Redpoll

♀

Arctic redpoll

Twite
Carduelis flavirostris

Status: Resident; local; **Voice:** Call nasal 'chweek'; constant twitter in flight; song hoarse and twanging; **Length:** 14cm; **Wingspan:** 22–24cm; **Habitat:** Almost treeless countryside cool and often rainy climate; often overwinters on saltmarshes or coastal grassland; **Behaviour:** Gregarious outside breeding season

Adult is liable to be confused with female or juvenile linnet but plumage is generally darker, more tawny above and more heavily streaked below; the ground colour warm buff. Shows white wing patches and tail sides but the features less noticeable than on linnet. Sexes similar but male has rose-pink rump, that of female being same colour mantle. Both sexes have bill yellow in winter but grey in summer. Juvenile similar to winter adult.

Two-barred Crossbill
Loxia leucoptera

Status: Resident; locally common; **Voice:** Rattling and buzz song; utters chattering call in flight; occasionally toy trumpet call heard; **Length:** 15cm; **Wingspan:** 26–29cm; **Habitat:** Conifer forests, especially larch; **Behaviour:** Feeds mainly larch seeds; will move en masse if conifer seed crop fails

Striking and colourful finch. Adults of both sexes distinguished by relatively long and slender bill with overlapping mandible tips and two striking, white wingbars conspicuous at rest and in flight. Male has pinkish-red plumage, while female is yellowish-green. Juvenile shows double wingbars but has grey-brown, streaked plumage and lacks adult's white tips to tertial feathers.

Parrot Crossbill
Loxia pytyopsittacus

Status: Resident; locally common; **Voice:** Utters 'chip chip' flight call, lower pitch than crossbill; song comprises greenfinch-like elements, lower pitch than crossbill; **Length:** 17.5cm; **Wingspan:** 32cm; **Habitat:** Conifer forests, mainly pine; **Behaviour:** Feeds on pine cones, in trees and on ground

Superficially very similar to crossbill and sometimes indistinguishable from large-billed individuals of that species. Generally shows larger and heavier bill, the mandible tips of which cross but cannot usually be seen projecting in silhouette. Head and neck also appear proportionately large. Male has red plumage with dark wings. Female has yellow-green plumage with dark wings. Juvenile has grey-brown, streaked plumage.

Twite

Two-barred crossbill

Parrot crossbill

Crossbill
Loxia curvirostra

Status: Resident; common; **Voice:** Loud, persistent 'chip c[ ]
flight call; song comprises trilling notes followed by
greenfinch-like calls; **Length:** 17cm; **Wingspan:** 27–30cm;
Habitat: Conifer forests, mainly pine and spruce; **Behavio[ ]**
Feeds actively in conifers, especially spruce

 Dumpy finch with robust bill, the mandibles of whic[ ]
cross at the tip. Male has mainly bright red plumage
except for the dark wings. Female is green except for the
dark wings. Juvenile has brown, heavily streaked plumage[ ]
sometimes shows faint wingbars but these much less
conspicuous than on juvenile two-barred crossbill.

Scottish Crossbill
Loxia scotica

Status: Resident; local; **Voice:** Loud 'chip chip' flight call;
song includes trilling and greenfinch-like notes; **Length:**
16cm; **Wingspan:** 28–30cm; **Habitat:** Conifer forests;
Behaviour: Bill shape has evolved specifically for Scots
pine; relatively easy to see in Caledonian pine forests of
Scottish highlands

Out of range, could easily be confused with small-bi[ ]
parrot crossbill or large-billed crossbill. Bill is heav[ ]
with tips of mandibles overlapping. Male has bright red
plumage except for darker wings. Female has green pluma[ ]
except for darker wings. Juvenile has grey-brown, heavily
streaked plumage with bill shape as adult.

Trumpeter Finch
Bucanetes githagineus

Status: Resident; local; **Voice:** Song recalls sound of a toy
trumpet; **Length:** 12.5cm; **Wingspan:** 25–28cm; **Habitat:** A
semi-desert; **Behaviour:** Easy to see when drinking at poo[ ]
or irrigation pipes; otherwise unobtrusive

Small, compact finch with proportionately large,
stubby bill; this is red in summer male but pinkish-b[ ]
in winter male and in female. Plumage is mainly uniform
buffish but that of male has pinkish flush to underparts an[ ]
wings. Legs pinkish in both sexes. Juvenile similar to fema[ ]

Crossbill

Crossbill

Scottish crossbill

Trumpeter finch

Scarlet Rosefinch
Carpodacus erythrinus

Status: Summer visitor; widespread; **Voice:** Male has distinctive, far-carrying, whistling song; **Length:** 14.5cm; **Wingspan:** 25cm; **Habitat:** Scrub and forest edge; **Behaviour** Spends most of its time feeding or resting in cover; appear ungainly when clambering about in the open

Medium-sized finch with proportionately large, stu bill; all ages and plumages show two pale wingbars. Mature adult male distinctive with red head, breast and rump; wings brown with wingbars tinged pink and underp white. Immature male and adult male in winter have less intense colour. Female and juvenile have undistinguished brown plumage with pale and streaked underparts.

Pine Grosbeak
Pinicola enucleator

Status: Resident; local; **Voice:** Loud, fluty and yodelling s **Length:** 18.5cm; **Wingspan:** 31–35cm; **Habitat:** Northern taiga forest; **Behaviour:** Unobtrusive but not shy; hops or walks along ground or clambers among branches

Comparatively large, dumpy finch with large head a stout bill. Both sexes show two conspicuous pale wingbars, those of male tinged pink. Wings of both sexes appear dark grey and show grey feathering on undertail a lower belly. In flight, tail looks relatively long. Adult male pinkish-red plumage, while that of adult female is mainly greenish-yellow. First-year male and female resemble dull version of adult female. Juvenile plumage is dull grey-brov

Hawfinch
Coccothraustes coccothraustes

Status: Resident; widespread; **Voice:** Loud, robin-like 'tic' call; **Length:** 18cm; **Wingspan:** 29–33cm; **Habitat:** Mixed woodlands, mainly deciduous; **Behaviour:** Small flocks ga in good feeding areas in winter; especially favours hornbe

Large and unmistakable finch with distinctive profi both when perched and in flight. Bill proportionate massive and triangular in outline. Bird looks top-heavy ar large-headed when perched; in flight, shows a considerab amount of white and looks short-tailed with proportionate large head and neck. Male has mainly orange-buff and pinkish-buff plumage. Shows black around base of bill anc bib. Mantle reddish-brown and wings dark but showing br white band on coverts. Undertail feathering and tip of tail white. Female similar but with duller colours. Juvenile ha brownish plumage and spotted underparts. Easily recogni by profile and white band on wings.

Scarlet rosefinch

♀

♂

Pine grosbeak

Hawfinch

Bullfinch

Pyrrhula pyrrhula

Status: Resident; widespread; **Voice:** Call a distinctive, low piping 'teu'; **Length:** 15cm; **Wingspan:** 25cm; **Habitat:** Undergrowth near woodland edge, hedgerows and gardens; **Behaviour:** Feeds on fruit tree buds in spring

Dumpy finch with a stubby black bill and conspicuous white rump, seen in flight. Male has black cap, blue-grey nape and mantle, and pinkish-red underparts, except for white undertail feathering; hue of red underparts distinctly different from other birds in same habitats. Wings black with broad white wingbar, and tail black. Female similar to male but colours more muted, appearing pinkish-buff. Juvenile similar to female but lacks black cap.

Lapland Bunting

Calcarius lapponicus

Status: Locally common in summer; local in winter; **Voice:** Calls include dry, quick rattle, 'tik-ik-ik-it' and liquid 'tew'; song a rapid trill, sung either from perch or in flight; **Length:** 15.5cm; **Wingspan:** 26–28cm; **Habitat:** Nests on Arctic tundra; on migration, seen on coasts; in winter, on cultivated land, often coastal; **Behaviour:** Crouches low and runs quickly and jerkily like clockwork toy

Male in breeding season unmistakable. Head has striking black, white and chestnut markings and black-tipped yellow bill. Underparts white and back brown with bold streaks. Female in breeding season similar to male but has black on face replaced by brown feathering. Non-breeding birds of both sexes lose bold markings on head but usually retain hint of chestnut on nape; chestnut wing coverts bordered by two white wingbars are good identifying features. Juvenile recalls winter female but lacks chestnut on nape.

Snow Bunting

Plectrophenax nivalis

Status: Locally common in summer; widespread in winter; **Voice:** Song a rapid trilling, sung from perch or in flight; tinkling calls; **Length:** 16cm; **Wingspan:** 32–38cm; **Habitat:** Breeds on Arctic tundra; in winter, on grassland, often coastal; **Behaviour:** Often confiding on migration; adopts horizontal stance on ground; runs like clockwork toy

Male in breeding plumage unmistakable, with striking black and white plumage and black bill. Breeding female has white plumage tinged with orange-buff wash and black element of male's plumage replaced by brown. Bill dark. In autumn and winter, plumage of adults and juveniles rather variable but back and nape usually appear orange-brown. Often shows buffish-orange on cap, cheeks and as breast band. Underparts always white and bill yellow. In flight, shows considerable amount of white on wings and tail in all plumages.

♂

Bullfinch

JUVENILE

♀

Lapland bunting

SUMMER
ADULT ♂

NTER ADULTS

NTER BIRDS

SUMMER ADULT ♂

Snow bunting

JUVENILE

FIRST AUTUMN

FIRST WINTER

SUMMER ADULT ♂

WINTER ADULT ♂

Yellowhammer
Emberiza citrinella

Status: Resident; common; **Voice:** Chirping song, often rendered in English as 'a little bit of bread and no cheese'; rasping call; **Length:** 16.5cm; **Wingspan:** 23–29cm; **Habitat** Farmland, heaths, scrub; **Behaviour:** Male sings from exposed perch in breeding season

Male in summer is attractive, with mostly lemon-yell plumage on head and underparts; often has suffusion of chestnut forming breast band and chestnut on wings, mantle and rump; bright, unstreaked rump striking in fligh In winter, male's plumage is duller, the feathers having greyish-green tips. Female much duller than male in all plumages and with more of a suggestion of facial stripes. Juvenile similar to female but with extensive streaking on head and breast in particular.

Cirl Bunting
Emberiza cirlus

Status: Resident; widespread; **Voice:** Male's song a metallic rattle on one note; **Length:** 16cm; **Wingspan:** 22–25cm; **Habitat:** At least partly wooded Mediterranean habitats, hedgerows, scrub and farmland; **Behaviour:** Breeding male sing from prominent perch; gathers in small flocks in winte

Superficially yellowhammer-like in size and shape. Male has striking head pattern with black throat and black through eye. Underparts mainly yellow but shows grey and chestnut breast band. Upperparts mostly chestnut but rump grey-brown. Female lacks male's bold head markings and rest of plumage is washed-out version of male's. Juveni similar to female but plumage generally buffish-brown.

Cretzschmar's Bunting
Emberiza caesia

Status: Summer visitor; local; **Voice:** Song a ringing 'tsee-tsee-tsee'; flight call a sharp 'chit'; **Length:** 16cm; **Wingspan** 23–26cm; **Habitat:** Dry, sunny slopes; **Behaviour:** Feeds unobtrusively on ground; retreats into cover if alarmed

A well-marked and colourful bunting, superficially rather similar to ortolan bunting, with reddish bill an legs. Male has blue-grey head with reddish-orange 'moustache' stripes and throat; eyering buffish. Underparts reddish-orange and back and wings reddish-brown. Female similar to male but with more subdued colours and some streaking on head. Juvenile very similar to juvenile ortolan but plumage has reddish, not sandy-olive tone.

Yellowhammer

♀

♂

JUVENILE

♂

♀

Cirl bunting

♂

♂

Cretzschmar's bunting

Rustic Bunting
Emberiza rustica

Status: Summer visitor; local within breeding range; rare autumn vagrant to northwest Europe; **Voice:** Song a ringing 'see-see-see-see'; call a sharp 'tik'; **Length:** 15cm; **Wingspan** 21–25cm; **Habitat:** Breeds in northern woodlands; **Behaviour:** Feeds mainly on ground but will perch in trees

Recalls reed bunting, but has proportionately longer bill with straight, not curved, culmen; in all plumages has pale white spots on otherwise dark ear coverts. Breeding male has bold black and white stripes on rather peaked head. Has rustic chestnut nape, back and breast band with chestnut streaks on flanks and white underparts. Breeding female similar to male but black on head replaced by brown. Non-breeding adults and juveniles less well marked and best identified by bill proportions and rustic chestnut tone to back, breast band and streaks on flanks.

Little Bunting
Emberiza pusilla

Status: Summer visitor; local within breeding range; rare autumn vagrant to northwest Europe; **Voice:** Song a series of sharp phrases; call a metallic 'tik'; **Length:** 13cm; **Wingspan** 20–22cm; **Habitat:** Breeds in swampy forests; **Behaviour:** Feeds unobtrusively on ground; moves like a pipit

Similar to non-breeding reed bunting but appreciably smaller and with proportionately longer, finer bill, with straight, not curved, culmen. Breeding male has rusty-brown head with white supercilium and black stripe above eye defining rusty crown stripe. Shows thin dark stripe running from behind eye and around ear coverts; shows small pale spot on otherwise rusty-brown ear coverts. Underparts white, streaked on breast and flanks; upperparts streaked brown. Female, non-breeding male and juvenile similar to breeding male but with subdued colours and markings.

Yellow-breasted Bunting
Emberiza aureola

Status: Summer visitor; local; **Voice:** Jingling song like ortolan bunting's; call sharp 'tsee'; **Length:** 14cm; **Wingspan** 22–24cm; **Habitat:** Flooded woodland and scrub; **Behaviour:** Feeding birds unobtrusive; males sing from exposed perches

Mature summer-plumage male unmistakable, with black face and chestnut cap, nape, back and breast band. Underparts and partial throat band yellow; shows white undertail feathering and two white wingbars – one broad, the other narrow. First-summer male has incomplete markings on head. Female has striped head with white throat and white stripe above and behind eye. Underparts pale yellow, and upperparts streaked brown; wingbars less conspicuous. Juvenile has warm buffish-brown plumage, broad pale supercilium and dark brown streaked rump.

Rustic bunting

JUVENILE

Little bunting

♂

ADULT ♂

Yellow-breasted bunting

♀

Rock Bunting
Emberiza cia

Status: Resident; local; **Voice:** Male has dunnock-like song; calls include a sharp 'tsee'; **Length:** 16cm; **Wingspan:** 22–27cm; **Habitat:** Sunny slopes with broken ground; **Behaviour:** Often found beside roads in southern Europe; occasionally mixes with other bunting species outside breeding season

Attractive bunting with triangular, silvery-grey bill in all plumages. Male is a distinctive and attractive bird with grey head boldly marked with black stripes. Underparts orange-brown and upperparts, including rump, reddish-brown. Female similar to male but plumage always washed-out and less distinct. Juvenile has brown, streaked plumage

Ortolan Bunting
Emberiza hortulana

Status: Summer visitor; local in breeding range; regular autumn passage migrant to northwest Europe; **Voice:** Male has ringing 'see-see-see-see' song; 'chip' flight call; **Length:** 16cm; **Wingspan:** 23–28cm; **Habitat:** Agricultural land and rocky slopes; **Behaviour:** Unobtrusive, ground-feeding bird

Attractive bunting with rather subdued colours and pinkish bill and legs. Male has greenish-grey head with pale yellowish eyering, 'moustache' markings and throat. Underparts orange-red and upperparts mostly reddish-brown. Female has less intense colours on head than male and streaking on breast, but otherwise similar. Juvenile has mostly sandy-brown plumage but shows pale 'moustache', throat markings and pinkish bill.

Reed Bunting
Emberiza schoeniclus

Status: Resident; common; **Voice:** Song a short series of chinking phrases; call a thin 'seep'; **Length:** 15–16cm; **Wingspan:** 21–27cm; **Habitat:** Favours wetland habitats, but sometimes found in drier terrain; **Behaviour:** Male sings prominently in breeding season; forms small flocks in winter often mixed with other species

In breeding season male is distinctive, with black bill and black head. White on underparts extends around nape as narrow collar and as moustachial stripes to base of bill. Back brown with dark streaking and rump greyish. In non-breeding male, pale feather tips on head make black elements of plumage appear brownish. Female has stripy-headed appearance with black 'moustache' being prominent plumage otherwise similar to that of male. Juvenile similar female but with even less distinct markings on head.

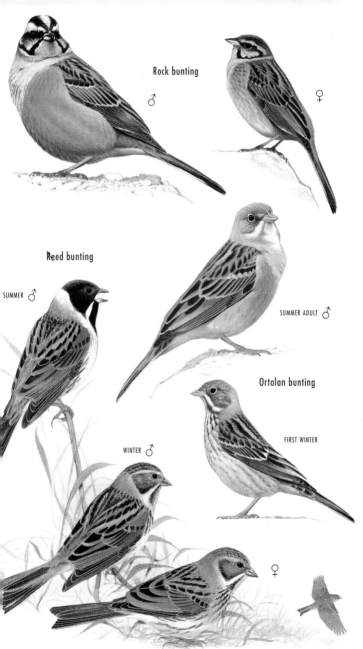

Rock bunting

♂

♀

Reed bunting

SUMMER ♂

SUMMER ADULT ♂

Ortolan bunting

FIRST WINTER

WINTER ♂

♀

Black-headed Bunting
*Emberiza
melanocephala*

Status: Summer visitor; locally common; **Voice:** Song comprises initial harsh phrases followed by series of notes with tinny ring; flight call a sharp 'tsit'; **Length:** 17cm; **Wingspan:** 26–29cm; **Habitat:** Olive groves, orchards and maquis; **Behaviour:** Male sings prominently at start of breeding season, but feeding birds unobtrusive on ground

Comparatively large bunting with robust, grey bill. Male unmistakable with black head, bright yellow underparts, yellow sides to neck and chestnut back; wings and tail dark. Female has much more subdued colours, head being greyish-brown. Underparts very pale dirty yellow and back shows hint of male's chestnut colour. Juvenile superficially resembles corn bunting; has rather plain, buffish-brown plumage with streaking on crown and back.

Corn Bunting
Miliaria calandra

Status: Resident; common; **Voice:** Song a unique, discorda jangling; flight call a low-pitched, loud 'kwit' or 'quilp kwit **Length:** 18cm; **Wingspan:** 26–32cm; **Habitat:** Farmland wi hedgerows; **Behaviour:** Sings distinctive song from wire fe or exposed branch all day; often flies on fluttering wings a. with legs dangling

A large, dumpy bunting with rather plain, nondescr plumage. Bill is large and pinkish and dark eye proportionately large. Upperparts are buffish-brown and heavily streaked. Underparts are whitish and also heavily streaked, particularly on breast. Sexes similar, and juvenil similar to adult.

Black-headed bunting

♂

♀

Corn bunting

COMPARING IMMATURE BUNTINGS

As with many other passerines, buntings are easiest to iden in the spring. The males of most species are colourful distinctive and all sing unique songs, which can be recogni with comparative ease. Even adult females are relatively e to identify, not least because of their association with male. the same species. In the autumn, however, problems identification do arise, with many immature buntings look confusingly similar and, in the case of migrant birds, of occurring outside their normal range in unexpected habita

SNOW BUNTING: Has characteristic orange-buff elements to plumage with whitish underparts and striking black and white wing pattern; bill yellowish

LAPLAND BUNTING: Plumage generally rather nondescript streaked brown with rather clean pale belly; always shows chestnut panels on wings (greater coverts) bordered by pale wingbars

YELLOW-BREASTED BUNTING: Plumage recalls female yellowhammer, with sandy-brown streaked upperparts and yellowish tinge to paler underparts; shows broad pale supercilium and streaked, rather rufous rump; bill dull pink

ORTOLAN BUNTING: Head and back olive-brown while underparts and wings suffused with pale rufous or sandy tints; has white eyering and pink bill; moustachial stripe and throat pale, sometimes appearing yellowish

CIRL BUNTING: Superficially similar to immature yellowhammer but lacking that species' yellow wash to head, throat and underparts; throat and supercilium appear particularly pale; rump greyish-brown and only faintly streaked; bill grey

ROCK BUNTING: Plumage overall pale rufous-brown; grey elements of adult plumage absent or much reduced in intensity; black facial markings less distinct than on adult and white wingbars rather indistinct

CRETZSCHMAR'S BUNTING: Warm sandy-brown plumage, including rump, moustachial stripe and throat; shows white eyering and pink bill

YELLOWHAMMER: Has yellowish-buff head, throat and underparts and dull rufous-brown back and wings; rump is rufous-brown and unstreaked; bill dull pinkish-grey

REED BUNTING: Plumage recalls adult female but facial markings less intense; ear coverts uniformly dark, lacking pale spot seen on rustic buntings of similar age; moustachial stripe and throat white and streaks on breast and flanks blackish

TLE BUNTING: Plumage similar hat of adult but chestnut on coverts and supercilium s intense; shows racteristic pale spot rear ear coverts

RUSTIC BUNTING: Well-marked plumage with chestnut-brown upperparts and chestnut streaks on breast and flanks of otherwise pale underparts; head markings distinctive with pale yellow-buff supercilium, moustachial stripe and throat, and pale spot on rear of ear coverts

RN BUNTING: Relatively large, plump nting; plumage essentially istinguishable from adult in the field — eaked sandy brown upperparts and er underparts; bill more ostantial and conical than er buntings'

BLACK-HEADED BUNTING: Plumage rather uniform sandy brown, palest on underparts, which have only faint streaking; shows pale lemon-yellow undertail coverts; bill dull pinkish-grey

**VAGRANT PASSERINES
FROM NORTH AMERICA**

Unlikely as it may seem, tiny American songbirds oc
regularly in Europe each autumn; all are classified as rarit
Not surprisingly, their appearance is often associated w
strong westerly airflows, and most records occur on the coa
and islands of western Europe. All birds are shown in fi
autumn plumage, that most likely to be seen in Europe. Fc
few species there are records of adult birds occurring in spr

RED-EYED VIREO
(*Vireo olivaceus*); Length:
12–14cm: All birds have red eye
and stout bill. Sexes similar. Adult
has greenish-brown upperparts, striking
head pattern and whitish underparts; first-
autumn bird has pale-yellowish wash to flanks

**YELLOW-RUMPED
WARBLER (*Dendroica
coronata*); Length: 13–15cm:** All
plumages show diagnostic yellow rump;
breeding male streaked blue-grey; female and first-
winter birds much duller with warm-brown upperparts

AMERICAN REDSTART
(*Setophaga ruticilla*); Length:
13–14cm: Adult male upperparts
slaty black with red patches on sides of
breast; female and juvenile grey-brown
with yellow patches

BLACKPOLL WARBLER (*Dendroica striata*); Length: 13–14cm:
In all plumages shows two conspicuous white wingbars
and white spots on outertail feathers; female
heavily streaked and washed buffish-yellow;
first-autumn bird similar to female but
less streaked

**COMMON YELLOWTHROAT
(*Geothlypis trichas*); Length:
12–14cm:** Adult male has striking
black mask, olive-brown upperparts and
bright yellow throat and upper breast;
female and juvenile lack black mask, having
greyish lores and ear coverts

**SCARLET TANAGER (*Piranga olivacea*); Length:
15–16cm:** Breeding male bright red with
black wings and tail; winter male olive-
brown; female and first-winter
male olive-yellow

**NORTHERN PARULA (*Parula
americana*); Length: 11.5cm:** Adult
male has blue-grey upperparts, yellow
throat and flush of orange on breast;
female and first-winter male similar but
breast markings less conspicuous and
flight feathers fringed green

**NORTHERN ORIOLE (*Icterus galbula*);
Length:** 18–20cm: Adult male has black head, breast and upperparts, and orange rump and underparts; female and juvenile brown instead of black and dull orange-buff rather than orange

**ROSE-BREASTED GROSBEAK
(*Pheucticus ludovicianus*); Length:** 19–21cm: Large-headed, large-billed bunting-like bird; female streaked brown with white wingbars and white supercilium and moustachial stripe; first-winter male similar to female but with faint pink flush to breast

SONG SPARROW (*Melospiz melodia*); Length: 15–16cm: Sexe similar; adults and juveniles hav streaked dark grey-brown upperparts an white underparts with brown or black streaks head markings grey and rufous-brow

**BLACK AND WHITE WARBLER (*Mniotilta varia*);
Length:** 12–13cm: Plumage entirely black and white; all plumages similar except that first-autumn males have buffish wash to sides of neck and flanks, and have greyish, not black, ear coverts

NORTHERN WATERTHRUSH
(*Seiurus noveboracensis*);
Length: 13–15cm: Superficially thrush-
like warbler; bobs up and down like a dipper
when feeding; sexes similar and juvenile
resembles adult; upperparts olive-brown and
underparts off-white marked with black spots

3OLINK (*Dolichonyx
zivorus); Length:
-19cm: Bunting-like but
 pointed-tipped, triangular bill and sharply
 ted tail feathers; breeding male black with buff
 e and white on scapulars and rump; female and
 -breeding male buffish-brown and streaked;
 nile similar to female but less streaked on underparts

DARK-EYED JUNCO (*Junco hyemalis*); Length: 14–15cm:
Adult male has slaty-black head, neck, breast, wings,
tail and back; outertail feathers white; underparts
white; female similar but grey-brown rather
than black; first-winter bird similar to
adult but shows brown fringes to
tertials and wing coverts

INDEX

INDEX TO SCIENTIFIC NAMES

ACKNOWLEDGEMENTS

The Automobile Association would like to thank the following illustrators for their assistance in the
preparation of this book.

All illustrations are held in the Association's own library (AA PHOTO LIBRARY)

R Allen 58/9; **N Arlott** B/cover e, 10, 15, 16, 25c, 27b, 29b, 29d, 43c, 67c, 69c, 71b, 71c, 77a, 79b, 79d, 83c,
87a, 87c, 89a, 89c, 91a, 91c, 125b, 127b, 127c, 129c, 131c, 133a, 135a, 149a, 161, 163a, 163b, 163c, 165a, 16
167c, 171b, 173c, 175–181c, 185a, 187b, 189, 219b, 231b, 245, 249c, 251b–255c, 257c, 259a, 261b, 265–26
275, 277c, 279–281b, 283–287, 299a, 319c, 321c, 323c, 329c, 339c, 341a, 341c, 343a, 344/5, 351c, 359d, 363
365b, 373b, 377a, 395d, 395g, 406–409; **T Boyer** 17b, 67a, 67b, 69b, 71a, 73, 75a, 75b, 77b, 77c, 79a, 79c, 8
83a, 83d, 87b, 87d, 89b, 89e, 91b, 91d, 91e, 93b, 221a, 221c, 223a, 223b, 223c, 233a, 233d, 237c, 239a, 241
241b, 291b, 293b, 293c, 295a, 295b, 297b, 309c–313, 367c, 369d, 371b, 373a, 373c, 375, 377b;
H Burn B/Cover f, 17a, 18, 55–57, 61a, 63–65, 69a, 75c, 85, 89d, 93a, 145c, 147a, 147b, 147c, 151a, 151b, 15
153c, 155b, 155c, 157a, 159c; **J Cox** B/cover c, 39c, 80/1, 129a, 129b, 131a, 143a, 145a, 145b, 225, 231a, 25
257c, 259b, 259c, 261a, 261c, 262/3, 359a, 359c, 359e, 361, 363b, 365a, 365c, 367a, 377c; **D Daly** 149c, 15
153b, 155a, 157b, 157c, 159a, 159b, 163d, 165b, 165c, 167b, 169, 171a, 171c, 173a, 173b, 181d–183c, 185b
185c, 187a, 187c, 190/1; **J Gale** 27c, 31a, 33b, 37a, 37c, 41b, 41c, 43a, 43d–47b, 49–51, 83b, 133c, 137a, 13
139a, 141a, 141c, 143b, 149b; **R Gillmor** 13, 31c, 39, 41a, 43b, 47c, 53a, 53b, 53c, 53e; **P Hayman** B/cover d, 3
33a, 35b, 53c, 53d, 125a, 125c, 127a, 131b, 133b, 347b–349b, 351a, 351b, 351d, 351e, 353–355a, 357, 379–39
395e, 395h, 397a, 397b, 401b, 403b; **I Lewington** 247b, 249a, 249b, 289a, 289c, 291a, 291c, 297a, 299b, 299
300a, 303–309b, 395c, 395f, 397c–401a; **D Quinn** 9b, 12, 14, 193a, 193b, 193d, 195c, 197a, 197d, 199a, 199
201a, 201b, 201d–205c, 206/7, 207b, 209a, 209c, 210/1, 213a, 213b, 215a, 217c, 219a, 219c, 219d, 221b, 35
404/5; **D Rees** 315b, 315c, 317b, 317c, 319a, 321b, 323b, 325, 327b–329b, 331a–333a, 337, 339a, 369a, 369
369c, 371a, 371c; **C Rose** F/cover a, b, c, B/cover a, b, 1, 19–25b, 25d, 27a, 29a, 29c, 29e, 33c, 35a, 35c, 37
61b, 61c, 95–122/3, 137b, 137c, 139b, 139c, 141b, 193c, 195a, 195b, 197b, 197c, 199b, 201c, 207a, 209b, 209
209e, 213c, 215b, 215c, 217a, 217b, 227–229, 233b, 233c, 235–237b, 239b, 239c, 241c, 242/3, 247a, 251a,
271–273, 289b, 315a, 317a, 319b, 321a, 323a, 327a, 333b–335b, 337c, 339b, 341b, 343b, 343c, 347a, 349c, 35
C Schmidt 231c, 277a, 277b, 281c, 289d, 293a, 295c, 300b, 301, 367b, 377d